HISTORY AND IDEALISM

HISTORY AND IDEALISM
Essays, Addresses and Letters

ROBERT BIRLEY

Edited by Brian Rees

JOHN MURRAY

TO
CLIVE AND IRENE MENELL

Frontispiece: Photograph by Jane Bown
© *The Observer*

British Library Cataloguing in Publication Data
Birley, Sir Robert, *1903–1982*
History and idealism.
I. Title   II. Rees, Brian
824.912

ISBN 0-7195-4837-3

Photoset by Rowland Phototypesetting Ltd,
Bury St Edmunds, Suffolk
Printed and bound in Great Britain by
Butler and Tanner Ltd, Frome and London

CONTENTS

SIR ROBERT BIRLEY

A Biographical Table

Born Midnapore (Bengal), 14 July 1903.

Rugby School, 1917–22.

Balliol College Oxford (Brackenbury Scholar), 1922–25.

Gladstone Memorial Prize, 1924.

Assistant Master, Eton College, 1926–35.

Married Elinor Margaret Frere, 1930.

Headmaster, Charterhouse, 1935–47.

Educational Adviser to the Military Governor in Germany, 1947–49.

Head Master of Eton College, 1949–63.

Visiting Professor of Education, University of Witwatersrand, South Africa, 1964–67.

Head of the Department of Social Science and Humanities, The City University, London, 1967–71.

Gresham Professor of Rhetoric in The City of London, 1968–82.

He served on the Fleming Committee on Public Schools 1944. He gave the Bruge Memorial Lecture 1948, the Reith Lectures 1949, the Clark Lectures 1961, the Chancellor's Lecture (Witwatersrand) 1965, the Chichele Lectures (All Souls College, Oxford) 1967. He was Chairman of the Headmasters' Conference, 1951–52, 1957–58; and President of the Bibliographical Society, 1979–80. CMG 1950. KCMG 1967. He received Honorary Doctorates from a number of British and foreign universities, including an Honorary D. Litt. from The City University.

Died Somerton 22 July 1982.

FOREWORD AND
ACKNOWLEDGEMENTS

This book is the portrait of a teacher rather than a work of instruction, though there is much information and observation to be found in it. As a shot in the battle over the importance of History in the educational curriculum I hope it is timely. The contents range from papers delivered to small school societies in drawing-rooms to speeches delivered to large audiences in huge university lecture halls. The description of lessons given in the townships of Africa is a relatively rare example of the teacher talking of his dialogues with the pupils. The memoirs of public school masters tend to cover every aspect save their own performances in the school-room. What gives Robert's teaching its individuality is, besides his talent for the apt reminiscence, that he sees History not just as a matter of set periods and movements, but as a thing of twists and turns and unexpected outcomes. The range of allusion is wide. To have traced every reference to its source would have piled Pelion on Ossa. It could be said of him, as it was of William Temple, that he elevated the quality of his audience. By assuming our familiarity with St Augustine and Kant, Fox and Dundas, Macaulay and Acton, he polishes up the lamps of our ambition as part of his teaching technique. The exception is the speech on German Education, where he was addressing an audience familiar with the events and individuals of which he spoke, and to this I have added fuller notes.

I owe a debt of gratitude to the Provost and Fellows of Eton College who have welcomed this volume as part of the 550th Anniversary Celebrations and supported it generously. The Vice-Provost, Mr T. S. B. Card, has been a persuasive advocate of publication from the start. I must thank also Professor Raoul Franklin, Vice-Chancellor of The City University, who first conceived the idea that the Birley Papers should be explored. It was possible to implement this project thanks to the generosity of the Council of Gresham College. The grant which they have made would have touched Robert particularly. He valued highly his connection with the College and his final appointment as Gresham Professor of Rhetoric, which gave him the opportunity to speak on a wide range of subjects. I am grateful for the help given by the Librarian and Staff of the City University Library, and the London Library, and by the Archivist of Eton College Library, Mr P. R. Quarrie. In pursuing particular points, valuable assistance has been given by Keith MacLennan and Hywel Williams of Rugby School; Ernst Zillekens of Charterhouse; the Reverend J. C. Polkinghorne, President of Queens' College, Cambridge; Dr Anthony Kenny, Warden of Rhodes House, Oxford; the Reverend John Latham, Marjorie Spence, Arthur Hearnden, and Robin Macnaghten. Herr E. Dornberg, KultusMinister of North-Rhine Westphalia, found time in the busy weeks before retirement to write at length on post-war German education. Archbishop Trevor Huddleston and Dame Lilo Milchsack have most kindly helped to put me in touch with other sources of information.

My Essay, 'Robert Birley as a Teacher', is included by permission of the Hon David Astor, Mary Benson and the Oxford University Press, reprinted from *Robert Birley 1903–1982* published in 1983. The Maurice Bowra Lecture, 'The Most Dangerous Subject in the Curriculum', is included by permission of the President and Council of Cheltenham College; the Clayesmore Lecture, 'Nationalism Today', by permission of the Council and Headmaster of Clayesmore School. The Essay, 'Robert Boyle at Eton', is reproduced by permission of the President and Council of the Royal Society. The University of the Witwatersrand has given permission to reprint 'The State and Education'. I should like to express my thanks to all these bodies and also to Mr Edward Cazalet, Fellow of Eton College, for providing the copy of Robert's letter to P. G. Wodehouse.

In the introductory passages I have referred to the author as 'Robert'. To call one's father-in-law by his surname seemed unduly arch, and 'Sir Robert Birley' ponderous. I should like to conclude by saying that the intensive reading and the interest in public affairs represented in these selected pieces – and they are but the tip of the iceberg – would never have been possible without the constant support of Elinor, who not only took from Robert's shoulders a multitude of domestic and business matters, but remained serenely undismayed as each new crusade or enthusiasm became superimposed upon others. Idealism may take a public or a private form and in this partnership one was able to discern a fruitful mixture of both.

The rapid approach of the Eton Celebrations has made the task of Roger Hudson, who has edited the book for John Murray, an urgent one. I am most grateful for his experience and tolerance in the preparation of what follows. Miss Beverley Smith has given much appreciated secretarial help.

Brian Rees

ROBERT BIRLEY AS A TEACHER*
by Brian Rees

I NEVER HAD the experience enjoyed by Robert's Carthusian and Eton pupils of a whole term of consecutive lessons on some large-scale topic – Medieval Europe, the French Revolution, or Nationalism – but I remember over the years some occasional lectures to larger audiences, or his own descriptions of the preparation of new courses. He never ceased to produce new ideas for lessons from his earliest days of teaching to the final plans for the Gresham Lectures on 'Lesser-known Racial Minorities in Europe'.

The presentation of the theme in his major lectures bore a resemblance to the structure of the Finale of Brahms's First Symphony (incidentally, a work by his favourite composer). The start, after he somewhat hesitantly had mounted the platform, seemed disconnected and groping, and a school audience, especially, might have thought that rambling and unarresting thoughts were about to be wafted over their heads for an hour or so: 'Great pleasure to have this opportunity . . . previous headmaster a particular friend . . . absolutely invaluable on a committee with me . . . subject no longer an issue but really *vital* at the time', etc. Then, suddenly, as Brahms (out of a confusion of hinted themes) sounds the great horn call, there would come some arresting phrase: 'In the centre of their city the Spartans erected a Temple to Fear' – 'King Charles I died of what we would now call influenza in the winter of 1633'. In the early 1950s he lectured all the History Specialists at Eton on 'Paolo Sarpi', the Venetian historian, with whom even those of us fresh from university had little or no acquaintance. As we filed into the Music Room, a gaunt place of instruction long since refurbished, shepherding lines of boys who piped up 'Sir, Sir, who's Paolo Sarpi, Sir?' members of the History Department looked anxiously at one another for any information

* From *Robert Birley, 1903–1982*, edited by David Astor and Mary Benson, Oxford University Press, 1983.

beyond a hazy recollection of the name. Robert, after threading a perilous course through music stands and timpani, reached the front of the stage, towering over the front rows, alternately swinging his spectacles in one hand or bunching up his gown behind him in both hands, and started on the surprising and not immediately meaningful story of Mr Gladstone's Secretary missing his Sunday breakfast and being sent on an empty stomach to some church a long distance from Downing Street to listen to a preacher of whom the Prime Minister had heard good reports. Later, famished and weary, he ventured to interrupt Gladstone's monologue by admitting he had never heard of Paolo Sarpi. Robert's rendering of Gladstone's amazement lacked nothing in rhetorical skill: 'Never heard of Paolo Sarpi? *Never heard of Paolo Sarpi??*' At that moment the audience was ready for the equivalent of Brahms's march-like movement to begin, and there followed an unfolding of the history of relations between Church and State, and between Venice and Rome during the Counter-Reformation. A few days later the junior members of the History Department sent to Robert the present of a book in which was inscribed 'From five masters who had never heard of Paolo Sarpi!'

One knew that the exposition sections would be masterly, as he was possessed of great ability to endue any subject with momentous importance. The style was not unlike the manner which Dr Arnold used in his first professorial lectures at Oxford, when his description of Massena's siege of Genoa is said to have moved the then Master of Balliol to tears. Strange but perfectly valid combinations of ideas would make their startling entry into the narrative: 'You see the real reason for Napoleon's defeat was that he just simply hadn't realised the potentialities of balloons.' He had a particular delight in taking some theme that was notoriously complicated and somehow finding a path through it under clear skies, however quickly the clouds rolled over once again after he had departed. If one passed through his schoolroom on the way to Chambers, the Eton Masters' morning break, the blackboard was more often than not covered with information such as the family tree of the Hohenstaufen, or the royal families of the Crusading States.

The development of any theme allowed for the interweaving of several different techniques. Sometimes he would use the occasion to make a point relevant to modern society and to the pupils listening. The name of Herman von Weid, a sixteenth-century Archbishop of Cologne, does not spring immediately to English lips. His part in the Reformation, however, was referred to by Robert with a sudden change of voice and manner, a deep glance which swept around the hall, and the words: 'It is to him we owe that *tremendous line* in the Marriage Service – "Whom God hath joined together, let no man put asunder".' He claimed quite often that one of his main purposes in teaching Dante so frequently was to enunciate moral principles which would have sounded sententious in the content of a sermon, or to use Dante's imaginative roll-call of human frailties that are not always obviously covered by the Ten Commandments: 'I mean to say – take the case of the young Venetian who threw away gold pieces into the lagoon. It is such a marvellous way of making young Etonians think about extravagance.' Sometimes his imagination would allow a kind of high-table wit to play over a theme. His lecture on the (mythical) death of Charles I in 1633 was masterly, as it was delivered with total seriousness. He explained how the King had been carried off by sudden illness, how a wise regency for the young Charles II had avoided the explosion of political and religious issues into civil war, and how country gentlemen such as Cromwell, without the opportunities of war, played minor roles in the development of Parliament. I forget how the succession passed to the Hanoverians earlier than true history relates (after all, this lecture was only given once, over thirty years ago, and no written version exists) but I recall 'Good Queen Sophie', renowned for her bonhomie and broad humour, was long remembered by her subjects with affection. Then he would begin to develop sly allusions. Henrietta Maria, the Queen Mother, had been the centre of sinister intrigues – later transformed by Rubens into a series of tableaux greater, some art critics say, than those devoted to the 'Triumphs of Marie de Medici' now in the Louvre. A minor poet called Milton had shown some talent for romantic poetry so that experts had gone so far as to say that, if he had lived in times which were more stirring and heroic, he might have left a greater epic to posterity. As it was, his major work was a pale narrative poem 'Lancelot and Guinevere' and there were some who detected a feeling that Lancelot and not Arthur himself was the truly heroic figure in the story!

This was on a high plane for many History Specialists recently through O Level, who took notes rather despairingly which they later found unable to fit into any context. No doubt a number of Old Etonians still believe that Charles I died in 1633. Yet he derived equal pleasure from a project which involved taking a class of some of the least able academic pupils for A level. English had never at that time been taken as a subject at Eton for external examinations, but when AS levels began to supplement the 'Grand July' as a leaving examination, a third subject had to be found for some boys who had already difficulty in coping with two. Robert volunteered to enter a group of the least able pupils for English and teach them himself, not a light task for someone administering a huge and complicated school and absorbed in the Headmasters' Conference and numerous obligations outside. For several months, the English set books and ways of expounding them occupied a major place in his thoughts. As Pope's 'Rape of the Lock' was one of these, and as eighteenth-century card games are referred to, he mastered the rules of ombre, and visitors to the Headmaster's drawing-room found him, to their surprise, sitting playing card-games with the boys. It is fair to say that not all the candidates passed with flying colours, but all, I am certain, will have a vivid if somewhat confused notion throughout their lives that the world, without 'The Rape of the Lock', Milton's *Comus*, and half a dozen other works, would have been a cultural desert!

Hannibal (a hero of Dr Arnold also) and his Alpine crossing with elephants fascinated Robert throughout his life and he built several talks about the theme of 'Elephants in History'. It was one of his sublimest moments when, one morning, sitting deep in thought by the moat of his favourite Wells Cathedral, he saw before his blinking gaze a real live elephant sauntering along the path, having escaped from some nearby circus and, I have no doubt, been guided by some Dantean angel. *Macbeth* was another favourite subject, and he planned at various times to complete a book on the historical background. He also planned a 'History of the Papacy' for schools. (Ecstatic praise for the labours of Pastor on his *History of the Popes* was one of the finest of his perorations.) Shakespeare provided another example of his per-cipience as a teacher, for when in South Africa he volunteered to give lessons in African schools to groups of students, he found himself on one occasion teaching *Richard II*. The relevance of what may seem a very minor episode in the play to the atmosphere in the Republic is described on p. 167.

He had devices which were employed, sometimes unsparingly, of which the phrase 'the second most' was one. 'I think that was the second most important moment in the whole of the Middle Ages' he would aver, so that the listeners hung on to discover the first. Like the Olympic Committee, he loved to hand out Gold, Silver, and Bronze medals for achievement to statesmen, soldiers, artists, and writers. (Gibbon was awarded the Gold for Footnotes, Carlyle failed to gain a place.) I recall a discussion on the 'greatest' work of art from each century. When I ventured to discuss entries for the nineteenth century he was surprised that *War and Peace* should even be challenged. His choice for the twentieth century was *Ariadne auf Naxos*. He had – and relished – a light chagrin for the fact that he had nearly met Richard Strauss, but failed. As a young man he was walking down a street in Salzburg when Strauss was seen approaching on the opposite pavement. 'There's Strauss,' said his hostess, 'I'll take you over and introduce you.' Then, as they came closer, 'Oh no! Sorry, not with that woman.' The occasion passed, never to return.

A very definite coda ended each lecture, drawing the strands together, but adding some new, possibly contemporary dimensions. His lecture on Charles I had been devised to show that, despite the great movements in history, the slightest accidents of birth and death could cause it to be rewritten. His historical explanation of the situation in South Africa ended in a dark and portentous look into the future. These final moments were often Beethovenian rather than Brahmsian. The final chords struck and came again in several guises before they reached their conclusion. Yet few, I think, came out of the lesson, lecture, discussion paper, or sermon, without an ardent wish to read more, remember more, reflect more, and seek a deeper understanding of things about them. They had also had experience of sheer oratorical entertainment that has almost disappeared from our computer-stocked and mechanically aided classrooms.

ETON

VOSTRE ROYAL COLLEGE
ET DEVOTE PLACE DE ETON

This paper, first given to the Ascham Society and then printed in
Etoniana *(November 27, 1965 and June 4, 1966), was a response to*
those sermons which fell often upon young Etonian ears, especially from
one devout housemaster, which emphasised the responsibility of the
modern generation to follow the high ideals which the Royal Founder
would expect of them. Of course, the disparity between King Henry's
intentions and the results would not in Robert's eyes detract in any way
from the civic and moral duties of present generations. His whole
conception of History was based upon the diverse and unexpected results
that derive from often remotely linked human actions. The 'symphonic'
style of his composition is very evident here. Everything moves towards
the description of the Wallfahrskirchen and the drunk who falls into the
Thames, though there are many digressions en route. From much
exploring in documents and speculation the tempo quickens into vivid
eyewitness recollections and, finally, imaginative reconstruction.

I DO NOT think that it is generally realised that Eton College Chapel is
referred to by Shakespeare. As the reference is a disreputable one, that
may be just as well. But as it is also one of very great significance, I
hope I may be forgiven if I bring it to your attention.

The play is *The Merry Wives of Windsor*. Anne Page, you may
remember, is in love with Master Fenton. Her father wishes her to
marry Slender; her mother has decided that her husband should be
Doctor Caius, a French physician. Mistress Page arranges that Anne
shall go to the Deanery in Windsor Castle and there marry the Doctor,
unknown to her father. Page arranges that she shall marry Slender at
Eton, unknown to her mother. Anne agrees to both plans, but has
other intentions for her future. The play moves on to its absurd

denouement in Windsor Great Park. Falstaff, 'with a buck's head upon him,' is at the trysting place to meet Mistress Ford. The Fairies surround him, pinch him and sing about him. During the scene Caius comes one way, and steals away with a Boy in green; Slender another, and takes off a Boy in white; and Fenton steals Anne Page.

Falstaff is made aware that he has been gulled by all, when suddenly Slender rushes in with his own tale of deception and woe.

– I came yonder at Eton to marry Mistress Anne Page, and she's a great lubberly boy. If it had not been i' the church, I should have swinged him, or he should have swinged me. If I did not think it had been Anne Page, would I might never stir! and 'tis a postmaster's boy.

– Why (says Page), this is your own folly. Did I not tell how you should know my daughter by her garments?

– I went to her in white and cried 'mum' and she cried 'budget', as Anne and I had appointed; and yet it was not Anne, but a post-master's boy.

Doctor Caius now rushes in.

– Vere is Mistress Page? By gar, I am cozen'd: I ha' married un garçon, a boy; un paysan, by gar, a boy; it is not Anne Page; by gar, I am cozen'd.

'My heart misgives me,' murmurs Page. 'Here comes Master Fenton.'

And there I think we may leave it. The only comment I have to make on this deplorable incident is that Slender's mock marriage must have taken place in College Chapel. Shakespeare in this play was writing about his own time; it is full of contemporary allusions. There was no other Church then in Eton. College Chapel was the parish church and, until about a hundred years ago, all the marriages of the townspeople of Eton were solemnised in it. Incidentally, the earliest reference to the building as 'Chapel' was in 1622, the name becoming established during the Commonwealth. Before that, it was known as the Church, though under the influence of a humanist Vice-Provost, who had done much to revolutionise the teaching of Classics at Eton, William Horman, it was often referred to during the sixteenth century as *Templum*. It is the purpose of this paper to show that it was the Eton Parish Church which caused Eton College to be founded, that Henry VI's decision to build the new Parish Church, which we now call College Chapel, had nothing to do with the school, and that, if it had not been for its connection with the parish, Eton College before long would have ceased to exist.

By 1440 the town of Eton was about as large as it is now, excluding that part which contains the buildings of the College and the school.

There were a few houses and shops north of Barnes Pool Bridge. Its Church is first mentioned in 1198. It stood near or probably partly on the site of the graveyard, now to the south of College Chapel. Nothing else is known of it before the founding of the College, except that in 1425 it had a chantry chapel dedicated to St Nicholas, that the Church itself was dedicated to the Assumption of the Virgin and that it was known as the Church of St Mary of Eton.

On 11 October, 1440, Henry VI issued the Charter by which he founded Eton College, a College 'in the parochial Church of Eton beside Windsor, not far from our birthplace'. Two days later, seated in the Parish Church, the Commissioners of the Bishop of Lincoln declared that 'we have raised, transformed and converted the parish church of Eton into a Collegiate Church,★ and this church, so raised, translated and converted shall henceforth and for all future time be styled the Collegiate Church of the Blessed Mary of Eton next to Windsor.'

In April, 1920, Provost James published in *Etoniana* a charter which he had found shortly before. This was after the latest edition of Maxwell-Lyte's *History of Eton College* and the account of Eton by A. F. Leach in the *Victoria County History of Buckinghamshire*. Though it was displayed in the Eton Quincentenary Exhibition of 1947 it has remained entirely disregarded, but it seems to be a critical document for the early history of the College. It is dated 17th July, 1446, and is addressed to the parishioners of Eton. Its purpose is to relieve them from the burden of repairing the nave of their parish church, the enclosure of its churchyard and of supplying its chalices, books, and vestments, because it had been made a Collegiate Church. In the preamble Henry refers to his original intention to honour in some special way the Blessed Virgin and to establish some church to the glorious festival of the Assumption. He had, he said, at last turned his eyes upon the Church of Eton because, although it was very poor and humble, it was dedicated 'under the name of the Assumption of the Most Blessed Virgin, to which feast we are very much attached.'

In 1441, the year after King Henry had decided to found his College, Thomas Bekynton, then Archdeacon of Buckinghamshire and the King's secretary, went on a voyage to Bordeaux. On 11th July he was, somewhat incongruously, becalmed in the Bay of Biscay. He then vowed an offering to the Blessed Virgin of Eton and persuaded those with him to sing an antiphon in her honour. The result was a

★ A church in which a corporate body replaces the parish priest, and therefore has the right to hold lands and collect revenues.

favourable wind. It is true that by that time the King had decided to build a new Collegiate Church, but no more had been done than to lay its foundation stone. I think that this is additional evidence that the Virgin of Eton – and that meant of Eton Parish Church – was already held in reverence.

King Henry, in fact, did not institute the special reverence paid to the Virgin of Eton; he recognised something that already existed. He did so by making the parish church collegiate.

Henry VI also said in this Charter of July, 1446, that, on account of the dedication of Eton Parish Church to the Assumption, he had for some time maintained there certain boys to be taught singing and the elements of grammar. Tenses in mediaeval documents are always rather a problem. The Charter certainly reads as though King Henry was claiming that he had been maintaining the boys there before he had decided in 1440 to make the Church collegiate. A. F. Leach, writing before Provost James published the Charter, pointed out that it was quite likely that the priest of St Nicholas chanting in the parish church had taught grammar to the boys of the town. I doubt whether King Henry, writing in 1446, by which time he had linked his school with King's College, Cambridge and had said that it should surpass all other grammar schools in excellence of foundation and richness of endowments, would have referred to its scholars simply as 'quidam pueri'. It is true that Henry VI was only eighteen when he founded the College, but maintaining the boys to be taught would have meant no more than paying the chantry priest. It is, at least, quite possible that the origins, not only of the College, but also of the School, of Eton are to be found in the parish church of the town.

We may find here a clue to the solution of a very puzzling problem. When was the School of Eton started? There is absolutely no evidence of its existence before December, 1443, when Waynflete was installed as Provost and the oath was tendered to eleven scholars – except that there certainly seem to have been Etonians before then. Two scholars are named in the original Charter of 1440, Richard Cokkes, who is never heard of again, and William Stokke, who was one of the eleven who took the oath in 1443, went up to King's in 1445, and lived to hold the remarkable office of Serjeant of the Porter's transport in the royal household and to be Keeper of Rockingham Park under Henry VII. Moreover, John Pagett was elected a scholar at Winchester in 1441, contingently on his not receiving a nomination to Eton. He is never heard of at Winchester and does not seem to have been admitted there, but nor is he heard of anywhere else. If the School as we know it was a direct continuation of a local chantry school, there would be no difficulty in accounting for the existence of Etonians from the moment the College came into being.

At any rate it is quite certain that the first school-room of Eton was not Lower School; it was connected with the Parish Church. In 1444 a house and two rooms, where the scholars were to be taught grammar, were erected at one end of that building; they are referred to as 'nova constructio'. (No doubt they were pulled down when the old Church was eventually demolished.)

When in 1440 King Henry decided to found a College *in* the parochial Church of Eton, he can have had no intention of building a new church. If he had already decided to do so it would certainly have been mentioned in his first Charter, and the Commissioners of the Bishop would not have said that the Parish Church would be for ever styled the Collegiate Church. There would certainly have been some reference to it in the immensely long Bull of Pope Eugenius IV, dated January 28th, 1441, which gives the whole history of the new foundation and quotes liberally from all its earliest charters and documents. Instead the Pope repeatedly speaks of the Parish Church itself being made collegiate. But very soon after Henry decided to build a new church. The date often given for the laying of the Foundation Stone is shortly before Passion Sunday, 2nd April, 1441. This date, however, depends entirely on the evidence of a little poem in Latin with a contemporary English translation of unknown authorship, preserved at King's. I think June 5th in the same year is a more likely date. From 1442 this is always referred to as 'Dedicacion day' and the workmen had a holiday with full pay on it 'by the Kinges command'. The Chapel cannot have been dedicated in the ordinary sense of the term in June, 1441, and there is nothing except the laying of the Foundation Stone which can have been commemorated then.

To determine why King Henry made this decision to build a new Church is crucial to any study of the history of Eton College.

The College fits naturally into an important religious and social movement of the time, the founding of Collegiate Churches. These were sometimes new foundations, but more often an existing Parish Church was created a Collegiate Church. Quite often the Parish Church was subsequently abandoned and a new one built. In either case the Collegiate Church continued to be the Parish Church, fulfilling henceforth two functions. Out of many examples I take one, that of Wye in Kent. It was founded by John Kempe, then Archbishop of York, at his birthplace in 1432. Kempe first secured the advowson of the parish church, as Henry VI was to do at Eton. Again like Henry VI, he eventually decided to build a new Collegiate Church in place of the original parish church. The College consisted of a master, six priests, two clerks, two choristers and a master of grammar, who was to teach both rich and poor gratis. A grammar school – at Wye it was a purely local one – was attached to the College and it survived the dissolution of the College in 1545 down to 1892, when it became an Agricultural College. Other Collegiate Churches show other characteristics which are to be found at Eton. At Glasney in Cornwall and Wingham in Kent, for instance, the head of the College was given the title of Provost; at Tong in Shropshire the College included thirteen poor persons, at Higham Ferrers in Northamptonshire twelve poor bedesmen to pray for the good estate of King Henry V, Queen Katherine and the founder, Henry Chichele, during their lives and for their souls after their death; choristers are found as members of nearly every Collegiate Church. The main purpose of these Colleges was, no doubt, to maintain masses and prayers for the souls of the founders and others named by them, but very often they also provided almshouses for old men and women and education in grammar for boys.

In July, 1441, Henry VI visited Winchester. Maxwell-Lyte said that he did so to see how a school was administered. More probably he wanted to find how a large College, which included a Grammar School, was organised. He did not find there a Church built for the boys of the School to worship in. William of Wykeham, indeed, had laid it down that the scholars of Winchester should only attend the services on Sundays and feast-days. This was not one of the Wykehamist statutes copied by our Founder, for at Eton the scholars were to be present at the morning service every day, though the Commensals★ were to attend only at the great festivals and then only those selected by the Provost. However, Winchester College Chapel had to be large enough for the whole College, including the scholars, to worship together on Sundays, and it can give us, therefore, as it must have given King Henry, some idea of the size of a building needed for the type of community Eton was intended to become. Winchester, like Eton, was founded to include seventy scholars and the addition of a few commensals would not have increased the number by many. Winchester College Chapel is 93 feet long. King Henry's first plan for Eton College Chapel would have made it more than twice as long; his eventual design more than three times. A building appreciably larger than the Chapel at Winchester was quite unnecessary for Eton College. It should be realised, however, that the

★ The Commensals or Commons were boys who were not Scholars but were allowed to dine in Hall and live in the buildings. They paid for everything but tuition.

Choir of the Church according to Henry's first plan would not have been much larger than the Chapel at Winchester. It was the addition of the nave, doubling the size of the building, which made it so much larger. But in his final design, known as 'the King's own avyse', both Choir and Nave were to be half as large again.

One result of Henry's visit to Winchester in July, 1441, may well have been his decision to link Eton with King's College, Cambridge, though he did not make it immediately after. There is no reference to any such link before July, 1443, two years later, but he said then that he had had this intention for some time. He certainly did not originally found King's with any idea of its being supplied with scholars from Eton. In fact, his first intention seems to have been to create a link between Eton and Oxford. In February, 1442, he made a grant of a manor in Hampshire, one of the properties of the Alien Priory of Ogbourne St George, to John Carpenter, Warden of St Anthony's Hospital in London and at that time Chancellor of Oxford University, to defray the cost of sending five scholars to Oxford, who had been taught grammar at Eton.

Much the most puzzling fact in the early history of Eton is that in its first hundred years its connections with Oxford were much closer than those with Cambridge, even with King's College. It was not until 1504 that the first Cambridge Provost was elected, Roger Lupton; not until 1536 the first Etonian and Kingsman, Robert Aldrich. There was only one other Provost from Eton and King's before 1724. The names are known of 52 Fellows of Eton elected before 1500 and we know the University of all but four; not one was from Cambridge. We know the Universities of all but two of the 35 Fellows elected between 1500 and 1540, and only five came from Cambridge, one of these by way of Cardinal College, Oxford. No Kingsman was elected a Fellow of Eton before William Smythe in 1521 and before him only one Etonian, William Wither of Merton in 1477. There were only three Cambridge Head Masters out of eleven in the fifteenth century; Lower Masters came a little more frequently. The first Etonian and Kingsman to return to Eton was John Peynton who was appointed Head Master in 1458 and perhaps none could have been expected before, although Head Masters in those days were usually appointed when about twenty-five years old. In the next hundred years after 1458 we know the names of 144 Provosts, Fellows, Head Masters and Lower Masters; only 27 came from Eton and King's, thirteen of them being Lower Masters, usually holding office for a year or two only. It took a long time for the traffic between Eton and King's to flow in both directions.

But the centre of the College – of any College at that time – was not the School, but the Church, and during Henry VI's reign this was the old Parish Church or, as it was now called, the Collegiate Church. It was there that Thomas Bekynton was consecrated Bishop of Bath and Wells on 3rd October, 1443. After the service he went across to the spot where the foundation stone of the new church had been laid two years before and there, under an awning, he celebrated his first episcopal mass. It was in the Parish Church that William Waynflete was installed as Provost in December, 1443, by the Earl of Suffolk and Bishop Bekynton and then took his seat on the south side of the Choir and tendered the oath to five fellows, two clerks, eleven scholars and two 'choiristers'; that John Carpenter was consecrated Bishop of Worcester in 1444; that Waynflete was consecrated Bishop of Winchester on 30th July, 1447, and that he held his first ordination five months later by special permission of his brother of Lincoln.

The Parish Church of Eton, although in 1446 it may have been called 'poor and humble' compared with the 'nova ecclesia', which Henry had decided to build by then, was large enough for episcopal consecrations. Willis and Clark by calculations which were ingenious, but rather hazardous, concluded that the Chancel of the original Parish Church measured about 70 feet long by 30 feet broad. This was smaller than the Chapel of Winchester College but, as we shall see, the King was quite ready to enlarge it. In any case, when Henry decided to build a new church, he still had in mind a grammar school a good deal smaller than the one at Winchester and, therefore, a smaller community for the services. Why then did he decide to build a new church?

It was in the very earliest days of the College that Henry made a decision which was of critical importance in its history. Even in this he was not wholly original. Indulgences★ for those who visited Collegiate Churches already existed. In 1291, for instance, Pope Nicholas IV had granted indulgences to penitents visiting Wingham at certain times in the year and there are frequent references in the fourteenth and fifteenth centuries to indulgences granted at the Collegiate Church of Cobham in Kent. But Henry went much further than any other founder of a Collegiate Church in England before him. There is no reference to indulgences in the first Bull of Pope Eugenius IV, dated 28th January, 1441, but four months later, on 28th May, the King obtained a Bull granting to all penitents who visited the Collegiate

---

★ An ordinary indulgence shortened the time that a soul spent in Purgatory. A plenary indulgence secured immediate entry into Heaven after death.

Church of the Blessed Mary of Eton at the Feast of the Assumption indulgences equal to those which might be obtained on the Feast of St Peter ad Vincula at the church in Rome dedicated under that name. This, however, was only a beginning. Next year the Pope made these indulgences plenary, though the licence for them was limited to the life-time of the Founder and three-quarters of the offerings of the pilgrims were to go to the defence of Christendom against the Turks. Henry published the Bulls throughout England and in May, 1443, despatched Dr Vincent Clement to Rome to ask for more. In particular, he was instructed to ask that the privileges should be made perpetual and not limited to his life-time. In fact Henry was ready for the indulgences to be smaller in order to secure this. This is important as the purpose of the indulgences up to this point had been, besides the defence of Christendom against the Turks, the building and maintenance of the College. A time-limit was, therefore, reasonable, but Henry now had in mind a permanent centre for pilgrimages. We are told that he used to ask daily, 'When shall we hear news of Master Vincent?' Clement had to work hard and disburse a good deal of money, but in the end he was successful. All limitations on the duration of the privilege and all stipulations on the use of the payments were removed; the confessors at Eton were empowered on the Feast of the Assumption to absolve all penitents from their vows to make other pilgrimages, except to Rome or Santiago de Compostella; and indulgences for seven years were granted to all visitors to the Church on any of the festivals of the Virgin, on the feast of of St Nicholas and on that of the Translation of St Edward the Confessor.

The result was to raise the Collegiate Church of Eton to quite another plane from that of any other Church in England. Henry, in fact, claimed that the indulgences were greater and more remarkable than those granted before to any church in any kingdom of Christendom. Pilgrimages began quickly. The regular staff of Chaplains (apart from the Fellows) soon rose to ten. At the feast of the Assumption in 1445 the College was finding it necessary to hire thirty beds for additional Chaplains and their servants on the great day of the pilgrimage. In 1448 a papal bull refers to the concourse of penitents who visited the College.

One immediate result of all this was the acquisition of the fields to the north of the College, not for the games of the scholars, but for the great fair to be held on the six days following the Feast of the Assumption. Another was the building of College Chapel.

What made the new church necessary was the decision that Eton was to be the most important centre of pilgrimages in England. For a pilgrimage church needed many altars and space for great processions. And, as it rose in the scale of pilgrimage churches, it needed to become larger and larger, until eventually King Henry planned a church longer than any other in England. Nothing shows more clearly his devotion to his Collegiate Church than the lists of its relics, ornaments and church-plate, compiled in April 1445 and in 1465, astonishing catalogues including the skulls of two of the Eleven Thousand Virgins who had accompanied St Ursula to Cologne, fragments of the True Cross and of the Crown of Thorns, the nails, the scourge and the spear of the Passion, 'an ampull closid in silver and gilt full of the blode of oure Lorde', a piece of the 'tumbe of oure lady', some of the blood and brains of St Thomas Becket, relics of St Anne, St Thomas the Apostle, St Andrew, St Bartholomew, St Paul, St Stephen, St George, St Wulfstan, St Edwin, St John of Beverley and many others. There was also a large number of ornaments and vessels. Not one has survived. Of all of them I think I regret most an image of the Virgin sitting in a vineyard, entirely of gold with 80 clusters of white pearls. These relics were not needed for the School. King's College, liberally provided with plate and ornaments for its Chapel, had no relics.

But the relics at Eton were not placed by the Founder in College Chapel. It was not built yet and King Henry knew that for some time he would have to make do with the Parish Church. 'Tax not the royal saint with vain expense.'* A 'Croceile' or Transept was added to the Church in 1445; the Chancel was probably completely rebuilt. A new roof, a rood loft and new stalls were provided, the last in time for the Feast of the Assumption in 1446. The chancel and the nave were paved with tiles; over a thousand feet of glass, some of it painted, was placed in the windows, the west window being greatly enlarged. Very necessarily, a treasury for the relics, ornaments, plate and vestments was constructed beyond the chancel. It was not until 1447 that a temporary tiled roof was put up to protect the High Altar of the new church, and not until the spring of 1448 that heavy timber was being procured for its scaffolding. But in the same year yet more painted glass was being placed in the windows of the parish church and next year a great image of the Virgin was brought from London for its High Altar.

Disaster did not overtake Eton until 1461, when Henry was deposed and Edward of York became King. But from August, 1453, when Henry first became insane – he recovered more than a year later – England was in a very disturbed state. There was an outbreak of civil

---

* Wordsworth: Ecclesiastical Sonnet No 43

war in 1455 and the Wars of the Roses began in 1459. The College
continued on its way; its revenues reached their highest point in 1458,
though they showed some decline during the next three years. There
was no falling off in the number of scholars. In November, 1459, Pope
Pius II reimposed the stipulation that three-fourths of the offerings of
the penitents should be devoted to the defence of Christendom against
the Turks. But this is not surprising: he was at that moment en-
deavouring at the Congress of Mantua to persuade the Powers to
undertake a Crusade. The building accounts, however, tell a different
story. Some 75 masons had been employed at one time in 1442; the
number dropped from 40 in 1452 to only 14 in 1460. But work
continued slowly and by May, 1459, it was beginning on the great east
window of the Choir and in February, 1460, on its 'upper history'. A
bill has survived for some iron to be used somewhere in the building of
the College, not necessarily of the Church, dated January, 1461. Then
all work stopped for eight years. In 1468 Provost Westbury was
conferring with Bishop Waynflete 'in order to begin the works of the
Church' and how to find the money for it. The ante-chapel was added
and the building became the one we know today. The East Window
did not receive its glass until 1476. When the wooden roof was taken
down ten years ago, it was found that beams from the original roof
had been used in the reconstruction at the end of the seventeenth
century. Some of them were decorated with Edward IV's emblem, the
Sun of York. These beams must have been later than 1461. The
Church cannot have been roofed, and therefore cannot have been used
in Henry VI's reign. In 1476 the stallwork was removed from the old
Parish Church and re-erected in the new. In 1480 the Audit Book
refers to a latrine, built 'ex opposito antique ecclesie'. The old church
is never mentioned again. At about this time it must have been
demolished.

In the interval after the deposition of King Henry, Eton College had
legally ceased to exist. At Edward IV's request, Pope Pius II on
November 13, 1463, issued a Bull uniting it with St George's,
Windsor. In 1467, however, Edward changed his mind and petitioned
the new Pope, Paul II, to revoke his predecessor's Bull, though it was
not until 1470 that the Pope gave the Archbishop of Canterbury power
to cancel it, if the circumstances seemed to warrant the decision, and
not until August 30, 1476, that the Archbishop finally gave judgement
in Eton's favour. Edward, however, had not waited for this. He
clearly regarded Eton as legally existing from 1467, when he returned
to it some of its original estates. Little can be discovered about this
calamitous period. The only Audit Roll between 1461 and 1468 is that

of 1466–7. This, however, along with Westbury's two statements in July, 1465, that he remained Provost and would never consent to the suppression of the College, show that the amalgamation never took place. Wasey-Sterry thought that the School may have ceased to exist altogether. I am not quite convinced, but in 1466 the number of scholars had fallen to 21.

In September, 1465, Edward IV had forced the College to hand over to St George's all its relics, ornaments, vestments, plate and books. The list with the signed receipt of the Dean of Windsor has survived. In 1470 they were ordered to be restored. Later lists of Church ornaments show that a good many were recovered. We regained, for instance, 'the tabernacull of oure lady of silver of gylde sotelly anamyled in every part weyying 64 lbs' and the 'grete Reliquar of silver and gilt stondyng uppon a fote with vi antelopis and having ii leves conteyning a bon of Saint Andrew in the myddes with many dyvers other holy reliques', and the ampulla with the blood of our Lord, and 'a part of the nayle that our lorde was nayled withall closid in silver all white', and the two skulls of St Ursula's virgins, the brains of Thomas Becket and the finger joint of St John of Bridlington. But we never recovered the Virgin in the vineyard. A present made by the College to the Dean of Windsor a few months after the restoration of the property of one trout and one pike, which is noted in the Audit Roll, must have been, I feel, a gift without much love behind it.

I believe that the solution of the problem how Eton managed to continue to exist after it had been legally brought to an end is to be found in the terms of the Bull of 1463 itself. For in a sense it was not destroyed by this. The vested rights of the existing Fellows were to be preserved by transferring the Fellows to St George's and the actual site and buildings of the College, having been consecrated, were not to be put to secular uses. I imagine that for this period Eton still existed in the sense that the Fellows remained technically members of a joint corporation and that they were allowed to stay where they were because there was no other use to which the buildings could be put.

The annihilation of an established corporation in the Middle Ages was an exceedingly difficult thing to achieve. But Eton did not survive because it was a school. Grammar Schools had little security. In 1439 William Bingham, the founder of God's House at Cambridge, had said that to his knowledge seventy grammar schools had disappeared during the last fifty years. Eton survived because it was a College and the Collegiate Church was then still the old Parish Church of Eton.

What did come to an end was Eton as a centre of pilgrimages. It is true that in 1479 Pope Sixtus IV renewed some of the indulgences at

Eton, but that is the only reference to them after the restoration of the College. There is no evidence of any kind to lead one to suppose that penitents came any longer to Eton. With the end of the pilgrimages the 'nova ecclesia' which Henry VI had planned became quite unnecessary. Fortunately the chancel was near enough to completion to make it reasonable to finish it, though it lacked until seven years ago the culminating glory of the stone roof, which, it must surely be accepted now, the Founder had intended for it. But it was large enough for its double purpose, to be the Church of a College which included a Grammar School, now of about a hundred boys, and to be the parish church of the town. It was, in fact, larger than was necessary. When the Church was refurnished at the end of the seventeenth century, the organ screen was placed more than one bay to the east of the arch of the ante-Chapel, crossing the building between the second windows from the west end. In the Appeal for Subscriptions issued by the Provost and Fellows in November, 1699, they speak of the necessity of 'enlarging the Choir . . . so that the children of the Schole [there were now about 350 of them] may appear under one view, and likewise that they, and all the people of the Parish, may be so conveniently seated, as to hear with ease all the publick Offices of the Church, which at present by reason of their number, and the ill disposition of the place, they cannot possibly do.' It is surely clear that College Chapel before that must have been divided to make a choir and a nave, and that the division must have been even further to the east. As the school had grown it had become necessary for some of the boys to sit in the nave and so they were no longer 'all under one view,' and for some of the parishioners to sit there also so that not all of them could hear the services with ease.

We may speculate what would have happened if the Founder had not decided to make his collegiate church a great centre of pilgrimages and had been satisfied with the old church, which was quite adequate for a college. No doubt he would have carried out even more work on it. But would the extraordinary growth of Eton in the nineteenth century have been possible without a College Chapel as large as the one we have, even though it is only the chancel of the church King Henry had planned? Would Eton have developed more in the way that Winchester has done? At any rate, it would seem possible that College Chapel would now be a large nineteenth century building and Lower Chapel the original church of the foundation.

But let us look back for a moment at Eton as it was in the reign of the Founder. Can we imagine it as it was then? I felt that I was helped to do so one day during a summer holiday. The closest parallel, I believe, to

the Eton of its first twenty years is found in the great baroque
pilgrimage churches, the Wallfahrskirchen*, of South Germany and
Austria. I was at one, Maria Taferl, which stands high above the
Danube, on a hot, brilliant morning last August, ten days after the
Feast of the Assumption. There were charabancs, cars and motor-
bicycles parked all over the Platz in front of the great church. But I
realised that I was probably the only tourist there. The crowds in the
church and outside it were pilgrims. No doubt there was much of the
tourist in many of them, just as there was in the Wife of Bath. But I do
not think that any of them entered the church without saying a prayer
and without realising that the church was there because a statue of the
Virgin had drawn pilgrims to the place for centuries. Outside the
Church it all seemed very vulgar. There were rows of stalls selling
candles, postcards, objects of piety, badges to stick on the back
windows of your car or to tie on the handle of your motor-bicycle,
ices, soft drinks, Coca-Cola. But, then, I have no doubt that Eton in its
first twenty years would have seemed vulgar too. As soon as the
College was founded the inhabitants petitioned the King and obtained
from him the privilege of a weekly market. I imagine that the market
and the great fair in August were very like what I saw at Maria Taferl.
The only reference we have to the Fair is not edifying. One of the early
Court Rolls of the College tells us that twelve jurors (their names are
given, the first being that of Thomas Jourdelay, a name still remembered here†) 'came charged upon the view of the body of one Roger
Hancok found dead in the Thames within the liberty of the College on
Wednesday 21 August 1448 to inquire concerning the death of the said
Roger, who say upon oath that upon their scrutiny they were not able
to find other than that the said Roger on the night of the Assumption
of the Blessed Virgin last, not being hurt by anyone, or wounded, or
coerced, but overcome with too much drink about the middle of the
night strayed into a place between the land of the Royal College of the
Blessed Mary of Eton and the land of Richard Spraket being on
the west side of Windsor bridge, and fell accidentally over the root of a
willow there into the water of the Thames and was drowned.'

    I do not think there is a school at Maria Taferl, but if there were, I
know from other great baroque foundations in Austria where it would
be found, hidden away among the conventual buildings behind the
Church. We may forget that, if Henry VI's church had been completed, one would have entered it not through School Yard, but by a

---

* Pilgrimage churches.
† Jourdelay's is still the name given to one of the Boys' Houses.

great west door about where Evans'* now stands. I doubt whether the crowds of pilgrims, who in the earliest days of the College thronged to Eton on the Feast of the Assumption, thought much, if anything, about the school.

But were there these crowds? By an astonishing piece of good fortune there has survived one convincing piece of evidence for them, a letter written by a French sculptor, Jean Goherol, to Henry VI. He wrote that he had almost finished the image of the Virgin of the Assumption which the King had ordered, but he needed £15 for 2000 leaves of fine gold, a pound of fine azure and some other colours to paint it. The King, he knew, was expecting its delivery by the next Feast of the Assumption, so there was not much time. On that day crowds of people would be coming from London and other parts of the country. He hoped it would be ready. It would be a great honour and profit for 'vostre Royal college et devote place de eton.'

* A Boys' House some sixty or seventy yards from the present West Front of the Chapel.

THE EVER-MEMORABLE
JOHN HALES

A Lecture on John Hales was certainly given to the Eton History Specialists in the 1950s. Some additions in the MS used here suggest that it was also read at a literary or historical association meeting outside the School.

THE ORIGINAL INTENTION of our Founder, to quote the words of Sir Henry Maxwell-Lyte's *History of Eton College*, 'united the characteristics of a college of secular priests, a school for boys and an almshouse for poor men'. The almshouse was abandoned during King Henry's lifetime. The school grew into something which he could never have contemplated. The College of Secular Priests or Fellows, as they were later called, lasted until 1869, when the new constitution of Eton was established under the terms of the Public Schools Act. These Fellows existed, then, as a resident corporate body for over four hundred years. No one can suggest that they were, taken as a whole, a remarkable line of men. I am afraid that they contributed but little to scholarship. They lived quiet and obscure lives and it is only occasionally that they come out into the limelight of English History or Literature, as when Boswell dined at the Fellows' Table in College Hall on bringing his eldest son to the school. 'I made', he said, 'a creditable figure. I certainly have the art of making the most of what I have. How should one who has had only a Scottish education be quite at home at Eton? I had my classical quotations very ready.' I have no doubt that conversation at the Fellows' Table through the centuries was often suitably adorned with classical quotations, but that was about as far as their learning usually went. Peace be to them, however. Under their Provosts – and the Provosts, of course, were often men of renown – they maintained the affairs of the College, not always very well but adequately for it to become what it is. They need no other memorial.★

Among them, however, is to be found one figure who is worth a more individual study, John Hales, Fellow of Eton from 1623 to 1649. He is, I should say, quite one of the most attractive among the minor personalities of English History. It was only a strange misfortune, as I shall show you, that prevented him from becoming someone well-known to us today. He was a more learned man, a better writer, a more interesting person, and a nobler Christian than many whose names have not been, like his, forgotten.

John Hales was born at Bath on April 19, 1584, the son of a prosperous Somerset landowner. After receiving his 'grammar learning', as it would have been called in those days, at Bath Grammar School, he went up at the age of thirteen to Corpus Christi College, Oxford. There he had the good fortune to attract the attention of the great Sir Henry Savile, Warden of Merton and, since 1596, Provost of Eton, one of the greatest classical scholars, known as the 'lay-bishop' because of his theological knowledge, and a famous mathematician and astronomer. Through Savile's influence Hales, after he had been ordained a priest, became a Fellow of Merton College, and his extraordinary learning caused him while still a young man to be chosen as Professor of Greek in the University. In 1613, and again we may see the hand of Savile, he was appointed a Fellow of Eton. According to Anthony Wood, the historian of Oxford, Hales assisted the Provost in the preparation of his great edition of the works of St John Chrysostom. This tremendous work in eight huge folio volumes was the one notable English contribution to classical scholarship during the Renaissance and is one of the finest examples at any time of English printing. It was printed at Savile House, in Weston's Yard at Eton, unhappily destroyed by a bomb during the War. Its splendid title-page contains the earliest known picture of Eton, if we except a drawing of the temporary chapel of the College against the background of Windsor Castle, executed on a page of a book belonging to Henry VI's Confessor in 1443, which is now in College Library.

I hope Hales did in fact have a share in the production of this book, but there is no other evidence of it. It is, I think, likely enough that Savile would have called on the assistance of his learned young friend, but if so it was before he became a Fellow of Eton as the Chrysostom was completed in the year of Hales' appointment.

★ Robert is kinder here than in private when he remarked that the achievements of the pre-Reform Fellows, 'constituted a record in the history of human idleness'.

Three years later he left England, though without giving up his Fellowship, to be Chaplain to Sir Dudley Carleton, the English Ambassador at The Hague. In 1618 was held in the Netherlands the famous Synod, or Council, of Dort, and I must say a word about this, as it was to prove a turning point in Hales' life. The Synod was ostensibly called to settle a great theological dispute in Holland, though actually it amounted to something very like a planned demonstration against one of the parties in the controversy. This was between the followers of Calvin and those of a Dutch theologian, Jacob Harmensz, whose name was latinised as Arminius, and the main point at issue was the Calvinist doctrine of Predestination. It was a great deal more than a merely local squabble. The Synod was attended by representatives of several German states and of England and Scotland. 'It was', it has been said, 'the nearest approach that was ever made to a universal meeting of the Calvinistic Churches.' The authorities of the Netherlands took good care to see to it that the followers of Calvinist orthodoxy won the day. The Synod proved to be an example of the wranglings of theologians at their worst.

The position of the Church of England at that time was in many ways unusual. Much in its traditions, above all its Book of Common Prayer and its retention of the order of Bishops, linked it with the Church of the Middle Ages and was shocking to the Calvinists, whether they were Presbyterians in Scotland or the zealous Burghers of Holland. But its doctrine was at the time very nearly Calvinist, James I was a violent opponent of Arminius, and so on matters of doctrine the English representatives upheld at Dort the majority Calvinist view.

John Hales was sent to the Synod by Carleton to act as observer and he sent the Ambassador a series of letters from Dort which are of great historical interest. But what mattered there to Hales was that the proceedings of the Synod brought about a complete revolution in his own outlook. Like most young scholars of his time he had been brought up to accept the theological views of Calvinism. At the Synod the statements of the followers of Arminius so impressed him that, as he said himself, it forced him 'to bid John Calvin good-night'. But his experience there did more than that. It turned him into a life-long opponent of religious dogmatism. His influence, henceforth, was to be on the side of toleration. This influence, which was largely a personal one, was more considerable than is generally recognised. He was a very learned man, but his point of view may be summed up in his own words, 'It was never the intent of the Holy Ghost to make it a matter of Wit and Subtlety to be saved'. He believed most earnestly that men of different persuasions in the Church of Christ might and should worship together the Master whom they all professed to serve. By the Church, he said, he understood, 'all factions in Christianity; all that entitle themselves to Christ, wheresoever dispersed all the world over'. The descent of his ideas can be traced through the Arminian leaders whom he had met in Holland, especially Simon Episcopius, one of the noblest and most attractive figures in the history of the Reformation, back to Erasmus. There were others in England at the time who felt much the same. Their point of view may be defined as a toleration based on charity rather than on indifference. Donne had written in 1609, 'You know I never fettered nor imprisoned the word religion, not straightening it . . . nor immuring it in a Rome, or a Wittenberg, or a Geneva; they are all virtual beams of one sun . . . They are not so contrary as the North and South Poles, and they are co-natural pieces of one circle.' One of the leaders of this school of thought was Sir Henry Wotton and his epitaph which you can see inscribed on a slab in the floor of the Ante-Chapel, sums up their views on the religious disputes of the time,

Hic jacet hujus Sententiae primus
Author
Disputandi pruritus Ecclesiarum Scabres
Nomen alias quaere

'Which', Isaak Walton wrote, 'may be Englished thus, "Here lies the first Author of this sentence: the Itch of Disputation will prove the Scab of the Church. Inquire his name elsewhere".'

It is not to be wondered at that Wotton was one of Hales' dearest friends. But it was through his association with Lord Falkland and his membership of the company which used to gather at Falkland's house at Great Tew, near Chipping Norton, that his influence on English thought proved strongest. The importance of this circle, among whom Falkland himself, Chillingworth and Hales were the foremost, has recently been emphasised by Mr Wormald in his work on Clarendon.* 'The Tew theologians', he says, 'wished to divert energies from the present channels of doctrinal disputation into those of practical and moral improvement. They did not identify Christianity with ethics, but they indicated that it should be concerned more with

---

* B. G. H. Wormald: *Clarendon: History, Politics and Religion*. Clarendon, Minister of Charles II whose name was associated with the intolerance of the High Church Clarendon Code, had in his younger days, as Edward Hyde, been a member of the Tew Circle. It is very probable that one of the Colleger sons of Mr Wormald was in the audience.

correct action than with correct thought . . . They preferred the
Gospel narratives to the theology of St Paul.' Hales particularly
distrusted the tendency of the time constantly to refer to the *obiter dicta*
of the early Fathers, which were used merely as missiles in the
theological warfare. His experience at Dort made him highly sceptical
about the early Councils of the Church, on which the Laudian High
Anglican party took their stand. He had no illusions about these
solemn gatherings of ecclesiastics. The greatest part of Church
History, he declared, 'consists in the factionating and tumultuating of
great and potent bishops'.

It was Hales' fate in the end to be caught up in the violence of
religious strife and to be all but crushed by it, and he died at a time
when England seemed far from attaining the ideals for which he stood.
But if he believed in toleration and grew to suspect dogma this does
not mean that he was a pliable or weak character. He used to say that he
could never be a martyr, but I feel he came as near it as almost any
other Englishman of his day.

Soon after the Synod was over, Hales returned to England and for
the next twenty years or more, until the Civil War broke out, he lived
a quiet life as a resident Fellow of Eton. Though his books and
sermons circulated freely in manuscript, he published nothing because
he was afraid that his own hostility to dogma might undermine the
faith of others. This caution led, perhaps naturally, to his being
suspected of the authorship of certain anonymous pamphlets which
caused considerable disquiet, for they seemed to advocate a doctrine
which put every orthodox theologian on the alert, that of Socinianism, which denied or at least minimised the divinity of Christ. It bears
a resemblance to the views of the Unitarians of today. But it was an
actual work of his, 'A Tract Concerning Schism and Schismatics',
which nearly led him into serious trouble. For a manuscript copy
came, in 1638, to the notice of the redoubtable Archbishop Laud and
he scented in it both Socinianism and a dangerously critical attitude
towards Bishops. What happened then is a remarkably obscure story.
Hales wrote a firm letter to Laud in answer to his charges, which was
not published till after his death, and it has been suggested that he
could never actually have sent it or the fat would have been properly in
the fire. At any rate, Laud summoned him to Lambeth. Of what
happened there we only know from an account by Peter Heylyn,
Laud's chaplain, who met Hales on his way out and was told by him
what had occurred. Hales and the Archbishop had spent nearly the
whole day strolling in the gardens of the Palace and, so Hales told
Heylyn, 'he had been ferreted by the Archbishop from one hole to

another till there was none left to afford him any shelter; that he was resolved to be orthodox and declare himself a true son of the Church of England, both for doctrine and discipline.' A surrender like this does not sound at all like John Hales. Further, a few months later, the Archbishop made him a Canon of Windsor and in many ways showed that he held him in high esteem, and that does not sound at all like Laud.

I have no doubt that Mr Trevor-Roper [now Lord Dacre], the latest biographer of Laud, was right when he said that Hales was pulling Heylyn's leg. A French Huguenot refugee who wrote a Life of Hales in 1719, of which more later, gave the same explanation. It would have been very like him to do so. What really happened we do not know; probably Hales convinced Laud, who was not by any means as intolerant a man as he is sometimes supposed to have been, that he was an honest writer, that he had no wish at all to stir up trouble and that he was something of a saint.

I have given you so far a picture of a man who was an eminent scholar and theologian, but one who hid his light under a bushel and may seem to have been little different from other undistinguished Fellows of Eton. Perhaps it will not be so very surprising if I add that he was a man who was consulted at Eton by scholars from all over Europe on points of difficulty in classical learning or theology. He received and answered countless letters from them. Wearily, he said once that they used to buy tops and expect him to whip them. Among them, for instance, was Grotius, the founder of modern International Law. Hales had come to know him in Holland and his portrait hung in his study. Sir Henry Wotton, diplomat and poet, perhaps the greatest of all the Provosts of Eton, used to call Hales 'the walking library' and everyone was always wanting to refer to it.

But what is really surprising will appear if I mention some of his other friends. With the great Ben Jonson he would have immense debates on English poetry. Courtiers of Charles I used to insist on meeting him whenever the King came down to Windsor. Young poets like Thomas Carew and John Suckling sought his company and wrote him poems begging that they might see him. John Milton, living at Horton and studiously preparing to become a great poet, used to walk across the fields to see him. But he was not just a kindly old man whom the young sparks of the time liked to have with them. There is another side of Hales to be seen in a story told of the poet Carew. He was probably the most dissolute of all the poets of the time. Falling dangerously ill, he sent for Hales to receive his confession and give him absolution. But on recovering from his sickness, he went

back to London and lived even more scandalously than before. Falling
ill again, he once more summoned his friend, asking for his prayers
and absolution. This time Hales was not so compliant. He told the
young cavalier that he would certainly have his prayers but not his
absolution or the sacrament.

'He was,' wrote Clarendon, 'of a very pleasant and open conversation and therefore was well pleased with the resort of his friends to
him, who were such as he had chosen and in whose company he
delighted, and for whose sake he would sometimes, once in a year,
resort to London, only to enjoy their cheerful conversation.' And, we
may be sure, go to the theatre. This we may infer, I feel, from an
incident which was certainly one of the most memorable in the life of
John Hales, and in the history of Eton. We hear of it from someone
who could not have known him personally, but who knew many who
had been his friends, the poet Dryden.

One day – it must I think have been between 1630 and 1640 – Hales
advanced what then seemed to be the preposterous view that
Shakespeare was the greatest of all poets, greater even than the poets of
antiquity, and that 'there was no subject any poet ever writ, but he
could produce it much better done in Shakespeare'. The suggestion
was warmly contested and it was finally decided to bring the matter to
a regular debate which was held in his house in the Cloisters. Great
preparations were made. The opponents of Shakespeare sent down a
great many books from London to sustain their cause; Falkland and
Suckling and – as Dryden puts it – 'all the persons of quality that had
wit and learning and interested themselves in the quarrel met there'; a
jury was chosen to decide the issue and in due course, we are told, 'the
judges chosen by agreement out of this learned and ingenious assembly unanimously gave the preference to Shakespeare'. At Eton
then was the preeminence of Shakespeare among the world's writers
first maintained. It is no small claim to honour.

Nicholas Rowe, the first of the eighteenth-century editors of
Shakespeare, refers to an incident which may be the same one, rather
altered in the telling, though there is nothing in his account of the
debate at Eton. Rowe tells how Suckling, D'Avenant, Endymion
Porter, Ben Jonson and Hales were once together when Suckling
engaged in the defence of Shakespeare against Jonson, who re-
proached him (Shakespeare) with want of learning and ignorance of
the Ancients. Hales punctured the author of Sejanus and Catiline rather
neatly by commenting that, if Shakespeare had not read the Ancients,
he had also not stolen anything from them.

I have no wish to consider now the rights and wrongs of the Civil

War which broke out in 1642, shattering the peace of England, the happy gatherings of poets and philosophers in London or at Great Tew, and Hales' own quiet life at Eton. Some thought that a man of his unorthodox views, who had been known to criticise bishops, would be found on the side of the Parliament and the Puritans. But he never wavered for a moment. From the beginning of the struggle he proved himself to be a staunch supporter of the King and the Church of England. We shall in fact find all those in the Church of England whose views were similar to Hales' on the Royalist side. They knew quite well that the Puritans stood for a new outburst of intolerance. The tolerance which has generally been found in the attitude of the Independents seemed to them quite illusory. Hales, like others, felt that an essential test of Tolerance was a readiness to tolerate the Roman Catholics. He and his friends knew that Cromwell and his party set strict limits to the bounds of their Toleration and that the Roman Catholics were a long way on the far side of it. Hales did not search for trouble, but he was living in one of those times when trouble itself will find out a man of principle who is not prepared to compromise.

Windsor was in that part of England controlled by the Parliament and he lost his stall at St George's soon after the war began. The Puritans took over Eton College, the Provost was dismissed and John Hales disappeared. I only wish we knew more of this extraordinary episode. Apparently he had with him certain documents and keys which had been entrusted to him by the other Fellows. For nine weeks he could not be found. We do not know where he had been, why he appeared again or what happened then, except that, rather surprisingly, he was not ejected from his Fellowship. All we do know is that he was hidden by an 'old Woman', who charged him sixpence a week for the 'brown bread and beer' which is all that he lived on – he characteristically insisted on paying her a shilling – and that his concealment was 'so near the College and highway that', he said after pleasantly, 'those that searched for him might have smelt him if he had eaten garlic'.

I cannot forbear a reference here to an incident of the time which shows one of the Fellows of Eton in a pleasant light and the close connection between Eton and St George's. In 1644 the use of the Book of Common Prayer was made illegal, the Directory was substituted for it, and, of course, the church music, which was then as now gloriously rendered in the two Chapels of Eton College and St George's Windsor, had to be abandoned. One of the oldest of the Fellows at Eton was Thomas Weaver. Years before in 1625 he had done much to beautify the Chapel, giving incidentally, 'four strong forms to stand in the aisles of the Church for the Townsmen to sit on', as is found recorded at length, strangely enough, in the fly-leaf of Bomberg's Pentateuch in College Library. Two of the benches are still in the Ante-Chapel at Eton. He was rather a scandalous old man. At Archbishop Laud's Visitation of Eton in 1634 it was reported that he was irregular in his appearances at the Chapel Services, that he sometimes omitted the Prayer for the King, that he had made for himself a sawpit in the Churchyard and that on one occasion he had deliberately shortened morning prayer on a Saint's Day so as to have more time 'to pull down a tree'. But he was certainly no Puritan or Parliamentarian. When the Choirs of the two Chapels were disbanded, he used to assemble the members every day for an hour to perform the sacred music as of old against the day when they might once more sing it at the services. Colonel Venn the Parliamentarian Governor of Windsor got to hear of it and, we are told, 'asked him why he could not be as well satisfied with the Psalms as they were sung in the Church as with this Popish music'. To which, the story continues, 'the good old gentleman warily replied that he humbly conceived that God was as well pleased with being served in tune as out of tune.'

King Charles I was executed on 30th January 1649 and Parliament decided at once on a list of persons who were to be forced to take an oath that they would be true and faithful to the new Constitution. Included in the list were the Master (at Eton the Provost), the Fellows, headmaster and scholars of Eton, Winchester and Westminster, evidence, incidentally, of the position of these three schools at the time. John Hales absolutely refused to do so and was expelled. The person nominated in his place offered him half the income but he declined to accept it. Hales was now 63 years old and he had lost the position which he might have expected would last him till he died. He went to live with a Mrs Salter, the owner of Richings House near Iver. There he acted as her Chaplain and as tutor to her son, who we are told was a blockhead (another writer of the time says 'blockish') but Hales like a good tutor does not seem to have allowed this to prevent him from liking his pupil. Richings House became, it was said, 'a sort of college', that is a college of priests, and among those who found refuge there was Henry King, Bishop of Chichester, a saint, a divine and a poet. (Hales always seems to have attracted poets to his company.) But this was a dangerous game for the services of the Church of England were now illegal. The passing of an Order against harbouring malignants made him feel he was placing his friend,

Mrs Salter, in danger and in spite of her entreaties, he insisted on leaving.

He returned to Eton and took rooms with a lady called Mrs Hannah Dickenson, the widow of his butler in the old days. She subsequently re-married and became a Mrs Powney, by which name she is called in most of the stories about Hales. She lived in a house adjoining the Christopher Inn to the south, opposite the Churchyard. This was certainly on the site of the House called Jourdelays, which was built between 1714 and 1720. The college records show that it was first leased to John Dickenson in 1636, perhaps when he retired from being Hales's butler. We have a description of it from the famous antiquarian, John Aubrey, who visited him there in 1655. It was, he says, 'a handsome dark, old-fashioned house. The hall, after the old fashion, above the wainscot, painted cloth, with godly sentences out of the psalms etc. according to the pious custom of old times; a convenient garden and orchard.'

We have from several sources a charming picture of him in his last years. He had always been very generous. He had been called the common godfather of the neighbourhood and people told how he had used to walk into Windsor with his pocket full of groats, giving them away to the children as he passed until by the time he reached Windsor he had not a groat left. Now, in his poverty, he received much kindness from the poor whom he had befriended, more, Mrs Powney pointed out, than from those who were well off. He sold his library which had been one of the finest in England for only about a quarter of what it was worth – I suppose those were not good days for disposing of learned books. He kept only a few works of devotion. Mrs Powney tried to dissuade him from the sale, because as she told Aubrey, 'She knew it was his life and joy'. She was, you will see, the best type of landlady. But he gave away the money he received to poor scholars and clergy who had been ejected from their livings by the Parliamentarians.

'I saw him,' Aubrey tells us, 'a pretty little man, sanguine, of a cheerful countenance, very gentle and courteous. I was received by him with much humanity: he was in a kind of violet-coloured gown with buttons and loops, (he wore not a black gown) and was reading Thomas à Kempis; it was within a year before he deceased. He loved Canary; but moderately to refresh his spirits.' It is pleasant to think that he was to become the friend of yet one more poet. In 1653 Andrew Marvell became tutor to a ward of Oliver Cromwell, who was sent to Eton. As was not uncommon in those days, the private tutor accompanied his pupil to his school and at Eton Marvell came to know John

Hales. As he wrote later, 'I account it no small honour to have grown up into some part of his acquaintance and conversed a while with the living remains of one of the clearest heads and best prepared breasts in Christendom.'

Among those whom he had helped with money from the sale of his books was a Mr Anthony Faringdon, who had been Divinity lecturer of St George's Windsor and Vicar of Bray, but not, I may say, the jovial turn-coat about whom the famous song was written. Some time later Faringdon was invited by the parishioners of St Magdalene's, Milk Street, in London, to be their pastor, but he was soon turned out of this living also. His parishioners made two collections for him at the church door on successive Sundays, enabling them to present him with the remarkable sum of four hundred pounds. Soon after, Faringdon came to see John Hales at Eton and I think I might give you the account of the visit as it is given by John Walker in his well-known book, *The Sufferings of the Clergy*, from a note in Faringdon's own hand. I know of no episode in the history of Eton which I treasure more.

Mr Faringdon found Mr Hales at his mean lodgings at Mrs Powney's house but in a temper gravely cheerful, and well becoming an excellent Christian under such circumstances. After a slight and homely dinner, suitable to the lodgings, some discourse passed between them concerning their old friends and the black and dismal aspects of the times; and at last Mr Hales asked Mr Faringdon to walk out with him into the Churchyard, where this great man's necessities pressed him to tell his friend that he had been forced to sell his whole library, and that for money he had no more than what he then showed him which was about seven or eight shillings, and besides, said he, 'I doubt I am indebted for my lodging.' Mr Faringdon, it seems, did not imagine that it had been so very mean with him as this came to, and therefore was very much surprised to hear it, and withal said, 'I have at present no money to command, and tomorrow will pay you fifty pounds, in part of the many sums I and my poor wife have received of you in our greatest necessities, and will pay you more suddenly as you shall want it'. To which he answered, 'No, you don't owe me a penny; I know you and yours will have occasion for much more than what you have lately gotten; but if you know of any other friend that hath too full a purse and will spare some of it to me, I will not refuse that.' To which he added, 'When I die (Which I hope is not far off, for I am weary of this uncharitable world) I desire you to see me buried in that place of the church-yard' (pointing to the place). 'But why not in the Church,' saith Mr Faringdon, 'with the Provost Sir Henry Wotton and the rest of your friends and predecessors?' 'Because,' saith he, 'I am neither the Founder of it nor have I been a benefactor to it, nor shall I ever now be able to be so, I am satisfied.'

And a few days later on 19th May 1656, John Hales died and was buried in the churchyard of Eton College. In his Will he said that he wished his grave to lie near that of little John Dickinson who had been his godson. A former pupil of his, Peter Curwen, placed over his grave a monument with a Latin inscription which you can see there now. His funeral, he said in his Will, was 'to be done in plain and simple manner, without any sermon or ringing the bell or calling the people together; without any unseasonable compensation or com- putation, or other solemnity on such occasions usual.' But we may be sure the people of Eton sorrowed for their friend and as they walked up the road past the great church, would think of one who had been the greatest scholar in England, and whose company had been sought by lords and divines and poets, but whose pockets used to be filled with groats for his 'godchildren' as he walked to Windsor Bridge.

The 'Ever-memorable John Hales' he was called, but the title proved false. Among those whom he had known at Eton was Isaak Walton, who used to come down to stay with the Provost Sir Henry Wotton, as keen a fisherman as he was himself. Walton wrote a beautiful life of Wotton and he meant to write one of Hales also, but alas, only a few notes are left of the projected work. If he had completed it we may be sure that John Hales' name would now be well-known to all students of English Literature. Anthony Faringdon also intended to write the life of his friend, but all he did too was to collect notes for it, and these were left to a Mr Fulman. He in his turn meant to write a life as a preface to a collection of Hales' works, but he too died without ever carrying out his intention and when the book was published in 1659, *The Golden Remains of the Ever-Memorable John Hales*, the Preface by Bishop Pearson was merely a short panegyric giving us little information about him. This book, however, contains a not unfitting memorial to his genius, one of the most splendid title pages of any English book. It was engraved by Wenceslas Hollar. On either side of the Title are two figures in niches, one representing Reason, holding a pair of dividers, the other Revelation holding a Bible. Below this figure is a reference to 'page 15'. Let us look up this passage. It will serve as no bad example of his prose style, clear, fluent, and humorous, decrying epigrams and purple passages.

There can therefore be but two certain and infallible interpreters of Scripture: either itself; or the holy Ghost the Author of it. Itself doth then expound itself, when the words and circumstances do sound unto us the prime, and natural, and principle sense. But when the place is obscure, involved and intricate, or when there is contained some secret and hidden mystery, beyond the prime sense; infallibly to show us this, there can be no Interpreter but the holy Ghost that gave it. Besides these two, all other Interpretation is private. Wherefore as the Lords of the Philistines some-times said of the kine that drew the Ark unto Bethshemesh; If they go of themselves, then this is from God; but if they go another way, then is it not from God, it is some chance that hath happened unto us: so may it be said of all pretended sense of Scripture★. If Scripture come unto it of itself, then is it of God: but if it go another way, or if it be violently urged and goaded on, then is it but a matter of chance, of man's wit and invention. As for those marvellous discourses of some, framed upon presumption of the Spirit's help in private, in judging or Interpreting of difficult places of Scripture, I must needs confess I have often wondered at the boldness of them. The Spirit is a thing of dark and secret operation, the manner of it none can descry. As underminers are never seen till they have wrought their purpose: so the spirit is never perceived but by its effects.

'As underminers are never seen until they have wrought their purpose'. Perhaps this phrase inspired Hollar to design the rest of his engraving, a strange scene in which little gnomes or cobbolds are working underground in the shaft of a mine. Above it are the words, 'Controversers of the Times like Spirits in the Mineralls, with all their labour nothing is don. Pag 37.' The gnomes represent all the theo-logical busybodies, the scholars who dug up texts from the Fathers to prove their points in their violent, uncharitable disputes.

Opposite the title page is a splendid engraving. Before a far-stretching landscape stands a dignified classical table-tomb and on this, lying like a monumental figure, is the form of John Hales in the sleep of death. Above is the simple word, in a scroll, 'Resurgam'.

Sixty years later a life of Hales at last appeared, and a most unusual production it is. It was written by one Pierre Desmaiseaux, as a kind of advertisement, a Specimen of an Historical and Critical English Dictionary which he intended to publish. The author was a Huguenot refugee, who flitted on the outskirts of the political literature of England in the early eighteenth century. He was, wrote Leslie Stephen, a careful and industrious literary drudge, but by no means a lively writer. It tells us little new about Hales and is chiefly interesting for its extraordinary form. The life consists of 90 pages of altogether

★ 1 Samuel 6. The Philistines had captured the Ark of the Lord, but subsequently suffered many misfortunes. In order to verify the Hand of God in these they yoked kine to the Ark, but left them free to choose their way. The kine without human guidance delivered the Ark back to Israel. Unfortunately their bovine intuition failed to appreciate that they would be immediately offered up as a burnt sacrifice by the joyful Beth-shemites.

3000 lines. Of these only some 500 are given up to the life of Hales: all the rest, about 2500, are footnotes. This very slender volume ends with an Index of no fewer than 6 pages.

In 1765 Sir David Dalrymple, Lord Hailes, a Scottish Judge and a friend of Dr Johnson, published an edition in three volumes of 'The Works of the Ever Memorable Mr John Hales of Eton'. In this he modernized the language. Dr Johnson did not at all approve. 'An Author's Language, Sir,' he said, 'is a characteristic part of his composition, and is also characteristical of the age in which he writes. Besides, Sir, when the language is changed we are not sure the sense is the same. No, Sir, I am sorry Lord Hailes had done this.'

We are left in the end with little but glimpses of John Hales from the writings of his friends, and those few of his own works that have been preserved. From these, however, we gain a strangely vivid picture of one of the greatest scholars and one of the kindliest, most humorous, most modest and generous of men, Canon of St George's, Fellow of the College and common Godfather to the town of Eton.

THE JOHN PIPER WINDOWS

This is an extract from one of the very last lectures which Robert gave, 'The Christian Religion when the world comes of age', at Ammerdown House, Radstock, Bath. It begins in the little village of Haselbury Plucknett, twenty miles or so from Radstock, and finishes at the Nuremberg Trials. The theme emerges from the almost comical legends of St Wulfric and primitive superstition, through Elizabethan Tragedy and the rejection of God's use of the supernatural in Tourneur's The Atheist's Tragedy, *through the Eighteenth-Century Enlightenment, to modern African fundamentalism and finally to the teachings of Dietrich Bonhoeffer and the faith of the victims of Nazism in the eventual triumph of goodness.*

I CAN GIVE an incident from my own experience, which may show you how I came to feel that somehow through Bonhoeffer one might be able to get to the answer of how, in this entirely different world, we have now come of age. For we have passed, as it were, from St Wulfric through Cyril Tourneur and Newton and Kant to what we are now.

At Eton when I was there, we had the most wonderful piece of work to do. By the most extraordinary piece of good fortune almost all the stained glass in the College Chapel was destroyed by bombing. It was probably the best thing that Hitler ever did. I remember once the dear old Provost of Eton, Montague James, taking me to look at one of the windows. All the glass was nineteenth century and, although some nineteenth century glass is certainly good, these windows were not. In this glass there was a portrayal of Belshazzar's Feast and the old Provost said to me, 'My dear Birley, you may learn something from this glass. You will see two things which you will not find recorded in Holy Writ. One is that the only food they had to eat at Belshazzar's Feast was roast toad and the only drink they had was bath tubs of lemonade.' But this was all destroyed, so we had to put in some new windows. Besides a magnificent east window, by an Irish lady, we decided on eight windows of coloured glass, and we got John Piper to do them.

This was a great experience for me because I was constantly at his house and workshop discussing what they were to be. He had first the idea of some immense angelic figures looking down on the Chapel at either side. I remember that I told him about a Mozarabic Liturgy about angels which he stuck up in his study so that he could be looking at it. Then one day he said, 'Look here, tell me honestly, do you really believe in angels?' So I said, 'Well, if you ask me, no I don't.' 'Nor do I,' he said, 'we can't have angels.' And you know Bonhoeffer, in one of his letters to the lady who would have been his wife, said, 'Who is Jesus Christ today in a world of adults who no longer believe in angels?' What Piper did instead was to produce eight windows and, if you do not know them, I beg of you, if ever you get the chance, to go and see them.

These windows have a very hard transom line across so that the top and bottom have to be separate. If you know Piper's work you will appreciate that they are obviously not pictorial. (Kenneth Clark once told me that John Piper was the worst person at doing head, body and legs that he had ever known. Still, that is neither here nor there.) It was decided that four of the windows on one side should represent miracles and four on the other parables. In these windows the lower half was to depict the evil, the upper half the good. For example, the first one was the raising of Lazarus. In the lower half you see nothing but a shut tomb. Then above it you see a form coming out, and the hand of God is there. He said that this was going to show, of course, evil as barren, futile; the good is when life returns. The next window, the stilling of the storm, where the lower half is a raging storm and the top half is 'Peace be still', he said, was the other side of the picture; evil can be anarchic, violent, cruel; good can be serene. But the one which really means the most to me – it means more to me than any other modern work of art – is the one of the story of the loaves and the fishes. I remember that he said to me: 'I am defeated by this. I've got absolutely nothing to play with except five barley loaves and two small fishes.' And then he had the idea. If you look at this window you will see there are five barley loaves and the two small fishes in the bottom half and round them are hands, horrible, grasping, cruel hands trying to get at them. What this shows is that shortage is not a good thing; it leads to violence, acquisitiveness, aggressiveness. And the top (and really you know, in a very large window to make a great work of art out of this is remarkable), the top is simply those baskets with the bread slopping over the edges. The answer, you see, is a generosity which does not just think that, 'I must give the right amount', but rather that, 'I shall give so much that very likely there will be too much'. It seemed to me that this was seeing these things in a way that would have meaning for a generation of boys who would have 'come of age'. You could explain this to them: and it needs explanation. These were things that really they could understand, whereas angels would not have meant anything to them!

ROBERT BOYLE AT ETON

Two essays by Robert Birley on Robert Boyle at Eton appeared in the Royal Society's Notes and Records *in 1958 and 1959. This second short one is a light-hearted postscript to the first. In the first, when quoting from the great scientist's autobiographical sketch of his early life (which was published in 1744 as part of the Preface to his Complete Works), he observed, 'There is no other boy about whom we know half as much as about Robert Boyle, until we come to Thomas Gray and Horace Walpole, a hundred years later'. The essay listed the scientific books in the collection of John Harrison, Head Master at the time of Boyle's arrival in 1635. Harrison appears to have encouraged him in such a love of study that, in his own words, 'his master would sometimes be necessitated to force him out to play'. In 1636, Harrison ceased to be Head Master and was elected a Fellow, but it seems likely that Boyle had lodgings with him and received individual tuition, for many Commensals, sons of noblemen or particular friends of the College, often enjoyed a 'tutorial' system of this sort. Harrison shared with the Provost, Sir Henry Wotton, a deep interest in the scientific questions that were stirring in the seventeenth century. Boyle, who left Eton after three years, at the age of eleven, cannot have mastered any great mass of scientific knowledge, but could well have had his curiosity kindled by the extensive library which Harrison amassed.*

IN *Notes and Records* Vol. 13, No. 2, I referred to a copy of Cicero's *Epistolae Familiares* (1550), which belonged to Robert Boyle when he was a boy at Eton and in which he had scribbled his name. Since then I have discovered two more books in Eton College Library written in by him. One is a copy of two works of Aristotle bound together, both in the Greek text: the *Ethica* (Frankfurt, 1584) and the *Politica* and *Oeconomica* (Frankfurt, 1587). On a fly leaf is written in a childish hand: 'I, Robert Boyle, do say Albert Morton is a brave boy'. The other is a

copy of two works by Joannis Treminius, a Spanish theologian, also
bound together: *In Ionae Prophetiam Commentarii* and *Commentarii in
quatuor priores Davidis Regis & Prophetae celerrimi Psalmos*, both
published at Oriola in 1623. This has written on a fly leaf in the same
hand: 'Albertus Morton is a most brave and rare boy, 1638'.

Albert Morton was at Eton from 1634 to 1639, first, like Boyle, a
Commensal of the second table, and then a Colleger. He was the son
of Sir Robert Morton, a captain in the Dutch service, and nephew of
Albert Morton, who was Sir Henry Wotton's secretary in Venice
from 1604 to 1615, and was appointed Secretary of State in 1625. He
died a few months later, his wife following him very shortly to the
grave. On her Wotton wrote what is, perhaps, the most perfect
English epitaph:

> He first deceased; she for a little tried
> To live without him: lik'd it not, and died.

The Morton brothers were Wotton's nephews and the younger Albert
Morton was, therefore, his great-nephew. He received the singular
honour of being appointed one of the Provost's executors under his
Will, while still a boy at Eton. He was admitted a scholar of King's
College, Cambridge, in 1639, but went down in 1640 and joined the
army in Ireland. That is all that is known of him, except that he was
still alive in 1660.

It can hardly be supposed that Robert Boyle, when only eleven
years old, owned copies of Aristotle in Greek and of an obscure
Spanish Divine. The Treminius volume is in the same binding as
many of John Harrison's scientific books. It looks as though Boyle
minor had been scribbling in his Head Master's books.

It is pleasant to think that this little schoolboy joke has at last been
washed up on the Shores of Time.

P. G. WODEHOUSE:
AN EXCHANGE OF LETTERS

*In 1970 Robert compiled a pamphlet entitled 'One Hundred Books',
which was a personal selection of 'the hundred most interesting books' in
Eton College Library. (A certain melancholy pervades the Preface,
listing the books which he had been obliged to exclude.) Referring to the
Library in which he frequently worked until the early hours he wrote: 'I
cannot express what it has meant to me since I was introduced to it by
Provost James. Later in my life I lived within a few yards of it and when,
at midnight, I had decided that some problem was insoluble – let us say
what to do about the kitchen in some Boys' House or how to arrange the
Mathematical divisions in Remove – I would go along to the Library,
take a shelf and see what I could find. As there was no catalogue of the
Library there was always the chance of a discovery. Following the
example of St Augustine I used to pray. "O Lord, let this Library be
catalogued – but not yet".'*

ITEM No. 17, the Library's greatest possession is listed as follows:-

17. THE GUTENBERG BIBLE – OR 42 LINE BIBLE. Fo Mainz. c.1455
The first printed book, of which forty-eight copies (some seriously
imperfect examples are counted) have survived; twelve of them
printed on vellum. This copy on paper, lacks only one blank leaf and is
in perfect condition. It is one of the earlier copies in which the opening
pages have 40 or 41 not 42 lines.

It has the original binding and is the only one with the name-stamp
of Johannes Fogel of Erfurt. Three other copies (at Princeton, Fulda
and Leipzig) have bindings with some of the tools which Fogel used,
but they were probably bound by some follower or followers of his. A
copy at Pelplin in Poland has a contemporary binding with the
binder's name-stamp of Henrieus Coster.

To the recorded copies of the Gutenberg Bible should be added one in the library of Blandings Castle in Shropshire.

The gift of John Fuller of Rosehill, Member of Parliament for West Sussex, the last member to be imprisoned by the House of Commons for defying the Speaker, who died in 1831. At the end of each volume is written '267 Feuillets' and '367 Feuillets'. Perhaps it belonged to some French monastery and was sold at the Revolution. Fuller bought it from the London booksellers, Payne and Foss.

(I have to thank Mr H. M. Nixon for his help over this note, and the note on No. 49.)

A copy of 'One Hundred Books' was sent to P. G. Wodehouse with the following letter:

Dear Mr Wodehouse,

I hope you will accept from me a copy of a small book I wrote recently on some books in Eton College Library. If you refer to No. 17 in the list you will see that the note on that book owes an important piece of information to you. (I may say that the help from Mr H. M. Nixon mentioned in the note refers only to some information on the binding. However Mr Nixon, who is the bindings expert in the British Museum Library, is a keen admirer of your books.) I had in mind, of course *Something Fresh*, Chapter III.

I am very hopeful that some German professor will write to me asking what he should do to inspect the book. I shall, of course, suggest to him that he catches the 11.18 or the 2.33 p.m. train from Paddington Station for Market Blandings, having secured a room at the Emsworth Arms' Hotel and making use of the services of Mr Jno. Robinson and his station taxi cab.

May I take this opportunity to thank you for the immense amount of enjoyment you have provided for me during the last fifty years. Your books have been a delight from the days when I was a boy at Rugby. I met you once for a very brief moment when you visited Eton one day with Mr S. G. Lubbock (generally known as Jimbo). I was then a very young master there. If I remember right, he had just taken you to see the Provost, Doctor M. R. James, the most learned scholar I have ever known. One day when I was in his study he referred to a house where Queen Elizabeth had stayed. I said, under my breath, 'One of those houses, no doubt, at which Queen Elizabeth had spent a night in her snipe-like movement about the country'. 'What, my dear

Birley', he said, 'do you read him too?' It became a great bond between us.

After the War I was for two-and-a-half years in charge of the German Education in the British Zone of Germany and Berlin. One day in Berlin I went to see one of the leading German artists of the time, Frau Renee Sinteunes. (Later I got to know her very well.) She told me that she had been reading a story of yours about Blandings Castle in which Lord Emsworth's grandson shot a secretary. It was appearing as a serial in the *Saturday Evening Post* (I may well be wrong about this as it was published in England in 1937, but it was some journal) and she had not been able to get later copies – I think because of the outbreak of war between Germany and the USA – and ever since then she had been wondering what happened. 'But, Frau Sinteunes,' I said, 'you mean "The Crime Wave at Blandings" in *Lord Emsworth and Others*, I have a copy in my mess in Berlin. I must lend it you at once.'

I might add, perhaps, that I think I have copies of all your books published since 1910 in my Library, except four, *The Man with Two Left Feet, Bill the Conqueror, Doctor Sally* and *Plum Pie*. (The last is sheer carelessness. It came out while I was in South Africa for three years, and I have only just realised that it is not there.)

Thanking you again and with my very best wishes,

Your sincerely,
Robert Birley

P. G. Wodehouse replied charmingly (though he failed to spot Robert's Professorship and Knighthood which was printed on the stationery!).

Remsenburg   Long Island NY 11960
                                                         July 3rd 1970

Dear Mr Birley,

I was so glad to get your letter and the book, which I shall cherish. What a sweat collecting all the stuff but it must have been a labour of love. I wonder if the Gutenberg Bible is still at Blandings. Surely one of the many Blandings imposters must have pinched it by now and Lord Emsworth would never notice.

I am so glad you have enjoyed my books so much. As soon as I can make it up into a parcel, I shall be sending you the American Edition of *Plum Pie* and I hope it will reach you safely. Postal conditions in this hamlet are always a bit uncertain. Last week I had a plaintive letter from Texaco (I think it was) in which I hold a few shares asking me if I wouldn't please pay into my bank the dividend they sent me in 1965.

How well I remember those visits to Eton. Victor Cazalet used to take me down. One time we were both booked for lunch, but Victor got hold of Randolph Churchill and tried to work him in too and was given one of Jeeves's nolle prosequi's. I remember thinking what a nice modest boy Randolph was. He certainly changed!

How awfully nice M. R. James was. I have always wished I could have seen more of him. My grandson Edward Cazalet now has two sons who will both be going to Eton eventually. I wonder if you have ever met him. He married Lord Gage's daughter, Camilla, who is a darling.

I have a new book coming out in the Autumn. None of my old characters this time. I am now trying to work out the plot of a Jeeves and Bertie novel and have got some good stuff, but as they say in the theatre 'It needs work'.

Talking of the theatre, my old collaborator, Guy Bolton and I have written a Jeeves musical. We have had a maddening experience with it. Tom Arnold took it and gave it up. Then Harold Fielding took it and the contracts were on the point of being signed when he gave it up too, this time because of difficulties of casting. These managers are always so keen on stars and it is difficult to find a recognised star who can play Jeeves and sing. Richardson very nearly signed up but got cold feet at the idea of singing. I think we shall eventually sell the thing but I shall be 89 in October, so there isn't all the time in the world.

All the best as they say over here

Yours Ever
P. G. Wodehouse

German Professors did not rise to the bait, but a letter came from The Library of Congress.

The Library of Congress
Washington, DC 20540   September 9th 1970

Reference Department
Rare Book Division

Dear Mr Birley,

I have just finished reading pleasant reviews in the TLS of your two recent writings devoted to your library. My interest was heightened through a reference to an unrecorded copy of the 42-line Bible. Can you furnish any more details concerning the copy located at Landings (sic) Castle.

Sincerely yours
Frederick R. Goff
Chief–Rare Book Division

Whether an emissary of the Library of Congress ever tried to purchase a ticket to Market Blandings at Paddington is not recorded.

WODEHOUSE IN ARCADY

It may safely be said that the one book Robert never opened was Debrett. His relations with the aristocratic and squirearchical Eton families were, with a few notable exceptions, distant. This essay, undated, but almost certainly given to the Essay Society at Eton, not only illustrates the admiration for the author displayed in the earlier letter, but divines unexpected virtues in a world which he often found extremely tiresome in practice. He knew virtually every Wodehouse book, including the rarities, and the essay was probably written from memory.

GREAT WRITERS – and for that matter, those not so great – can be divided into two categories. There are those who rarely, if ever, produce bad work; their technical skill, perhaps, or some strong critical faculty, or the support of a very strong literary tradition, enables them to avoid any serious fall from grace. They may be boring, in fact some of them quite often are, for inspiration cannot always be on the wing, but they are never simply bad. I am thinking of such writers as Sophocles, Horace, Milton, Jane Austen. In the other class are those writers – and among them are found some of the greatest – who can be very bad indeed; Dickens, for instance, or Keats. Pre-eminent among them stands Shakespeare. Mr P. G. Wodehouse is in this second category.

I am not, then, one of those who hold that Mr Wodehouse is a flawless writer or that all his books should be read, or are even readable. For instance, I find one of his characters, Ukridge, a bore, and an irritating bore at that. His juvenilia, the school stories, excite me not at all, with a few exceptions such as, in particular, *The Small Bachelor.* I think he is less happy when dealing with life in the United States. I cannot say that I feel certain, when one of his books comes out, that I shall much enjoy reading it, but then, did not Shakespeare write *All's Well that Ends Well?* And do we not find in *King Henry VI*

Part I the worst lines in all reputable literature, when the Maid of Orleans says to the Dauphin.

> I am prepared; here is my keen-edged sword
> Decked with five flower-de-luces on each side
> The which at Touraine, in Saint Katherine's churchyard,
> Out of a great deal of old iron I chose forth.

Of course these lines may have been written by Thomas Nashe, according to Professor Dover Wilson, or by Robert Greene, according to Mr Hart, or by George Peele, according to Professor E. K. Chambers. But Shakespeare revised the play; he might have altered the lines or left them out. He must accept responsibility for them. Still, Shakespeare is justly accounted a great writer, and so I think is Mr P. G. Wodehouse.

I believe that perhaps the most important characteristic of his writings is this – that he has created his own world. The charge is sometimes levelled against him that he is artificial, that his novels have no contact with reality. That is perfectly true, of course; it is the source of his greatest strength. For Mr Wodehouse has created the Modern Arcadia and it is as a writer of Arcadian romances that we should first consider him. Perhaps a word on this type of literature should come first.

Pastoral poetry is first found in Alexandria in the third century before Christ and perhaps it actually originated with Theocritus. It was from the first the product of an urban civilisation. It represents an escape from the city. We should not think of it, however, as being only on a par with the week-end country cottage, a momentary refuge from the bustle and strain of the town, although it always has an element of this. For it calls up the picture not only of a simpler, but also of a better world, one that is not only less sophisticated, but also more honest and more loyal.

It was Virgil who invented Arcadia – I say invented, because the real Arcadia was simply a very backward district of Greece with particularly barbaric and primitive customs. And since his time Arcadia has remained a land of literature, peaceful, remote, ageless yet very living. The immense prestige of Virgil has tended to prevent the development of Arcadian literature; too many poets and writers have felt that all that was necessary was to use his setting, but occasionally some writer has been more creative, such as Sir Philip Sidney, or Shakespeare in *As You Like It* or *The Winter's Tale*. Mr Wodehouse is one of these. In due course I shall draw attention to some characteristics of his Arcadia which are, I think, original.

If you have read his works you may have noticed that no breath of the disturbances of the outside world of our day, one of the most revolutionary periods of History, is allowed to disturb the placid serenity of his country houses, such as Blandings Castle. There it is always summer; the mornings break cloudless; the dewy meadows and parkland stretch out beyond the formal gardens; in the afternoons a slumberous heat broods over the scene, the only sound, the murmur of the insects, which so often have a way of interfering with the young people who are just energetic enough to walk down to the rose-garden or row on the lake. The evenings are luminous and heavy-scented, the silence broken only by voices of young men and women, in as elaborate a movement of intrigue as the last Act of *The Marriage of Figaro*, and by the rhythmic chomping of Lord Emsworth's prize pig, the Empress of Blandings, moon-like in her sty, reflecting the silver moon above. The only disturbances caused by the weather are not the depressing rain or the cold winds which we know to be the usual accompaniment of the English Summer, but an occasional violent thunder-storm, a deliberate echo of the passing storms of the lovers, serving to emphasise the happiness and gaiety which follow it. And it would all be thoroughly sentimental if the author were not quite conscious of what he was doing, if the artifice were not deliberate, if he were not inoffensively mocking all the time at himself and his readers.

It certainly must not be thought that there are no storms in Arcady.* There are quarrels and embarrassments and young men and women are love-lorn, though not for long. What is more original in the novels is that Arcady is the actual English countryside and the characters not nymphs and shepherds, but lords and ladies, young men about town, young ladies whom you can see at Lord's, butlers and gentlemen's gentlemen. What is more original still is that his world actually extends into the city itself; there are enclaves of Arcadia in the depths of London; in Bertie Wooster's flat, young men come to seek the help of Jeeves in their troubles. But these troubles are not due to Fascism or Communism or to the rise in the cost of living. It is characteristic that when a communist does enter one of these stories, Comrade Butt, the

---

* 'Et in Arcadia Ego': the words form the inscription on a tomb in a painting by Guercino. Two Arcadian shepherds come upon the tomb, surmounted by a rat-gnawed skull. But Death, the 'Ego' in 'Arcadia', would destroy this world or the author's creation and it may be noted that in all Mr Wodehouse's books no one ever dies. [Robert's own footnote. Guercino was a nickname, 'Squinter', which has a nice Wodehousian ring.]

suitor of Charlotte Corday Robotham, with whom Bingo Little gets himself entangled, he is really a completely démodé nineteenth-century anarchist; you cannot possibly imagine him as a shop steward. Another such enclave is the Drones Club, that home of the most charming vacuity and inanity. Mr Wodehouse in fact can describe storms of considerable violence. I have never read a more dreadful study of embarrassment than the story which tells how the Earl of Ickenham takes his nephew into a suburban villa, The Cedars, Mitching Hill, to seek shelter from the rain and then pretends, to the young man's consternation, to have come from the bird-shop to clip the parrot's claws with the help of his nephew, whom he introduces as 'My assistant, Mr Walkinshaw, who applies the anaesthetic'.

Mr Wodehouse, then, has created a world; he has created a style. Mr Wodehouse is one of the few baroque writers in English Literature. To paint his Arcadia he has to write in an artificial style. I could not say that it is a flawless style. Dare I say that I think his use of slang can become rather wearisome. But it is an excellent style; like the baroque, surprising. Think, for instance, of three similes used to describe Honoria Glossop's laugh (you may remember that she was the hefty and very handsome young blue-stocking whom his Aunt Agatha wished Bertie Wooster to marry). It is likened once to a noise like the Scottish Express going under a bridge, once to the thunder of waves on a rock-bound coast, and again to the sound of a squadron of cavalry crossing a tin bridge.

Or let me take two examples which are not often quoted, 'a swan moving moodily up and down a lake like a man looking for his lost collar stud', and – this comes from *The Indiscretions of Archie* – 'the head waiter began to drift up like a bank of fog'.

A world and a style in which to describe it – and new characters to people it. It is sometimes complained that Mr Wodehouse's characters do not vary. Up to a point of course, that is true. One would not expect the characters in Arcady to be too strongly individual; if you are going to people your landscape with figures, they must up to a point remain figures. But this does not mean they cannot have life or that within the limits of the pattern they must be all alike, 'aunt bellowing to aunt', as he puts it once, 'like mastodons across a swamp'. But they differ from one another in glory. There is a tremendous power, a devastating, uncompromising forthrightness in Aunt Agatha, the greatest of the herd, which you will not find, for instance, in Lady Constance Keeble. All the butlers are alike, but there is in Beach, the butler at Blandings Castle, a hierophantic dignity which places him above all the rest; he is, I think, one of the great characters of modern English Literature. The members of the Drones Club such as Barmy Fotheringay-Phipps and Freddie Widgeon may seem interchangeable, although even here there are characters of distinct individuality, like Oofie Prosser, whom everyone is always wanting to 'touch' but is, in fact, quite untouchable. If Bingo Little is different it is because his circumstances often introduce him into another world; he is married to a woman author of dreadful sentimentality, who was before marriage Miss Rosie M. Banks, and it must be allowed that there is a similarity in many of the situations into which his married life leads him and from which he is rescued by Jeeves. On the whole, I think Bingo Little is the least successful of Mr Wodehouse's main characters. Of his young heroines, I can only say that they really are all immensely alike. You could shuffle Joan Valentine, Stephanie Byng, Jane Abbot, Penelope Donaldson, Sally Painter and Angela Hunt and deal again and no-one would be any the wiser.

Four of his characters are to my mind the greatest: Aunt Agatha; Lord Emsworth, the wonderfully vague and indeterminate owner of Blandings Castle and of its most important occupant, the Empress of Blandings; Bertie Wooster and his valet, or as he styles himself, his gentleman's gentleman, Jeeves. Lord Emsworth is a difficult character to describe. He is in a sense a study of negation, as he wanders in and out of the stories, absent-minded and apparently purposeless, unless he is thinking of his prize pumpkin or his prize pig, occasionally in a state of feeble revolt against one of his sisters or his secretary, the efficient Baxter, or his domineering Scottish gardener, Angus McAllistir. (It was of him that Mr Wodehouse wrote, 'A curious expression came unto Angus McAllistir's face – always excepting the occupied territories', referring to the unshaven parts of his face, a phrase which is said to have gained its author his honorary MA at Oxford University.) In time, however, one comes to realise that Lord Emsworth always wins. His triumphs are the victories of Arcady over an apparently stronger Castle world. And with the help of this aimless and rather doddering old man, generosity, kindness and romantic love win their victories over caution, meanness and worldliness. In 'Lord Emsworth and the Girl Friend', an account of his partnership in revolt with a small girl from the London slums at a Garden Fete, we see Arcady in league with the poor and weak against the forces of conventionality and privilege. It is a surprising story and a very successful one, which might very easily have been sentimental.

It has been said that Jeeves is one of the only two characters in modern English Literature which have become familiar figures, such as Robinson Crusoe or Sam Weller, the other being Sherlock Holmes. I think one can fairly say that he is a brilliant creation. He still is extraordinary and reading of him one realises how successful Mr Wodehouse is at the management of a plot of intrigue, a type of literature in which I believe the Italians excel.

I think Jeeves's most remarkable achievements are to be seen in two short stories, 'The Purity of the Turf' and 'Jeeves and the Old School Chum'. The former succeeds immediately one of Mr Wodehouse's masterpieces, 'The Great Sermon Handicap'. Bertie Wooster and his friends, staying in the country, try to retrieve their fortunes after the drastic losses of the Sermon Handicap by betting on races in the village sports organised by the Vicar. In race after race the tricks of Steggles, their oily and unscrupulous opponent who is making the book, are successful in causing the defeat of their candidates. At last, only one race is to be run, the girls' egg-and-spoon race. Bertie and his syndicate are appalled to hear that Jeeves has laid £30 at ten to one on a complete outsider, Prudence Baxter. The race proceeds as they had feared; class will tell and Prudence is easily defeated, finishing fifth. And then the Vicar at the prize-giving, announces in serious tones that he has to tell them that the evil of financial corruption has entered the village; one of the manservants at the Hall has confessed to him that he had bribed several of the runners in the egg-and-spoon race on condition that they finished the course.

'It is no time for half-measures', continued the Vicar. 'I must be firm, I rule that Sarah Mills, Jane Parker, Bessie Clay and Rosie Jukes, the first four to pass the winning post, have forfeited their amateur status and are disqualified, and this handsome work-bag presented by Lord Wickhammersley, goes in consequence to Prudence Baxter. Prudence, step forward!'

In 'Jeeves and the Old School Chum', Bertie with Jeeves is on a visit to Bingo Little and his wife. An old school friend of hers comes to stay who turns out to be a food crank; her pointed references to Bingo's enjoyment of his meals are accepted by Mrs Little as an inescapable condemnation of her husband and their happy married life is in the direst peril. Jeeves succeeds in so arranging matters that when they attend a local point-to-point they find that their lunch has been left behind. On the return journey they run out of petrol – again Jeeves has seen to this. Mrs Little, robbed of her lunch and now, an even more serious matter, of her tea, awakens to the foolishness of her friend's views on food and turns upon her; the security of the marriage is restored. But, how pointless it is simply to tell the story without the zest of Mr Wodehouse's style, without being able to show, as he does, how Jeeves does more than solve a problem, rather how he dominates it.

At first sight Bertie Wooster seems to be merely a foil to Jeeves. Gradually, however, the reader realises that he is more than this. For one thing, the Jeeves stories are, with two exceptions, all told by Bertie himself. You see Jeeves through his eyes. In the one story which is told by Jeeves, Jeeves does not seem nearly so engaging a character. He is seen to be calculating and ruthless; it is Bertie with his charming modesty who has made him appear attractive. The more recent Jeeves book, *Ring for Jeeves*, in which the servant is separated from his master, is, in my view, a failure. Bertie Wooster is out of the story; he is attending a school to learn how to look after himself, if it becomes necessary in a new world where young men can no longer hope to live happily on a large unearned income. Why did Mr Wodehouse allow this shiver to pass through Arcady? It is with relief that one learns at the end that Bertie has been expelled from the school for cheating in an examination on darning socks and that Jeeves is going to enter his service once more.

I should claim myself that Bertie Wooster is really Mr Wodehouse's supreme creation. In the eyes of his Aunt Agatha, a ne'er do well; in the eyes of Jeeves, 'mentally negligible'; in his own eyes, a repeated failure; he is, in fact, the very spirit of goodness, unselfishness and modesty. 'Pastoral life', writes Professor Gilbert Highet in his book on *The Classical Tradition: Greek and Roman Influences on Western Literature*, 'Pastoral life in pastoral poetry and drama is characterised by purity of morals and simplicity of manners.' Bertie Wooster, like Lord Emsworth, is a typical figure of Arcadia. I do not see how one can help becoming fond of him. Have I made him out as an impossibly priggish young man? Anyone who has read the stories about him will know that there was never anyone less of a prig. Never was virtue less self-conscious than his. And above all, 'Le style est l'homme même', as Buffon said. It is in the style of his stories that Bertie shows the man he is, his appreciation of others, his understanding of them, his courtesy. He turns Jeeves into a man we can like; he even turns into something of a hero his friend, Gussie Fink-Nottle, a student of the life-history of the newt and the amazingly incompetent suitor of Madeline Bassett, a dreadful girl who believes that the stars are God's daisy-chain, and who thinks that Bertie is in love with her. Bertie's impeccable sense of honour leads more than once to his finding himself engaged to marry her and it needs all Jeeves's skill each time to save him from this terrible fate.

Finally, no writer, I feel, can claim to be a great comic author unless he produces what one may call a great scene, something which attains epic proportions, which remains fixed in the memory by a certain comic grandeur. One may think of Dicaiopolis* buying the Megarians' pigs, of Falstaff acting the part of King Henry IV, of Bardell v Pickwick. There is at least one such great scene in Mr Wodehouse's works, the prize-giving at Market Snodsbury Grammar School in *Right Ho, Jeeves*. This is one of the great comic scenes in English Literature. Nothing is more difficult than to write about a comic writer. If you have read the book the atmosphere of the crowded hall, the immense gusto of the speech of the inebriated Gussie Fink-Nottle, the pity and terror of the denouement, as he turns to say what he thinks of Mr Tom Travers, will come rushing back into your memory. If you have not – well, I can only advise you to read it.

* The leading character in Aristophanes' *Acharnians* who attempts to introduce his daughters into blockaded Athens disguised as pigs. The all-pervading presence of the Empress of Blandings must somehow have suggested this unexpected illustration.

CHARTERHOUSE

– Sermons in the
Shadow of War

The publication of sermons about fifty years old must seem like the activity of a grave-yard resurrectionist. Yet these four, given in Charterhouse Memorial Chapel during and immediately after the War, have a particular quality which makes one keen that they should be re-read. The mixture of History and Idealism, and the interplay of past and present, is focused sharply by the background of momentous events which seemed at times to evade human grasp or control. The materials employed are drawn from Biblical imagery and Church History but they are developed to emphasise the uniqueness of the individual, the unforeseeable results which grow from the smallest actions, the conviction that freedom brings as many problems as it solves.

A SERMON DELIVERED
ON 26TH JULY 1942

Robert states in this sermon that he is not just thinking of the War when reflecting on times when the individual scarcely seems to matter. Nevertheless July 1942 must have been a moment in History when the tides in human affairs seemed to have broken their banks. In Russia, after the clash of immense armies in the Don Basin, the Germans were advancing on Stalingrad. In the Western Desert, Rommel was being held back by desperate counter-attacks. The Nazis had unveiled plans to move three million Dutch to Eastern Europe. In Robert's beloved Czechoslovakia the village of Lidice had been razed to the ground and the male population murdered as a reprisal for the assassination of Heydrich.

'Then went Boaz up to the gate, and sat him down there: and, behold, the kinsman of whom Boaz spake came by; unto whom he said, Ho, such a one! turn aside, sit down here.' *Ruth IV 1*

'A woman when she is in travail hath sorrow, because her hour is come: but as soon as she is delivered of the child, she remembereth no more the anguish, for joy that a man is born into the world.' *St John XVI 21*

THE BIBLE IS a wonderful gallery of portraits. I can think of only one other book which we may compare with it, the Plays of Shakespeare. If you read the plays you will find that there are three kinds of characters that remain in your mind. First are the great characters, fully drawn portraits with their whole complexity exposed: Hamlet, Iago, Cleopatra, Falstaff and the rest. Then there are those characters whom you cannot know quite so completely, although they would appear real enough in the works of most great dramatists, like Roderigo in *Othello*, the perfect picture of the brainless but almost likeable young man about town; or Horatio, the true type of friend; or Bardolph the eternal clown, Falstaff's butt and companion. They cannot be complete portraits; they serve in part as foils to the great, almost epic, creations of the poet. Then there is a third class, characters who pass across the stage but for an instant and yet in that moment are astonishingly, vividly alive, real persons to remain with us for ever. I am thinking of characters like Barnadine, the condemned prisoner in *Measure for Measure*, who refused to be executed because he wanted to finish his sleep – for a moment we have a glimpse of that almost animal underworld which the most civilised society produces and forgets, until some time of upheaval gives it a chance dreadfully to assert itself; like Osric in *Hamlet*, the froth on a selfish aristocracy; like Francis, the Drawer at the Boar's Head Tavern in *Henry IV*, eternal example of all the ill-paid, harassed under-waiters who have served us in London restaurants or country hotels and whom we have scarcely even noticed.

I think we can look on the Bible, too, as a mine of characters, immortal because they are vividly true to life. There are the great figures of world history, like Moses, David or Elijah in the Old Testament, Saint Peter or Saint Paul in the New. There are characters full of interest, even if they are not dominating personalities, like Eli, the High Priest, not quite great enough a man for his position, or the honest simple-minded Barnabas. And finally there is that host of men and women who pass though its pages for a brief moment, but who will make such an astonishingly sharp impression on us, if we read the Bible carefully: like Eliab, David's elder brother, type of all superior elder brothers, counterpart to the one immortalised in the parable of the Prodigal Son, who took it for granted, when David came to the army that was paralysed by fear of Goliath, that he was there out of idle curiosity and had left his sheep unguarded; or like Gehazi with his lie and request for money so cunning in its moderation.* What an amazing throng pass before our eyes, the very world itself, 'a fair field full of folk' as the poet said, 'of all manner of man, the mean and the rich, working and wandering as the world asketh'.

It is of one of these last characters that I wish first to say something to you this evening. May I remind you of that little story in the Bible, the Book of Ruth. Ruth, a Moabitish woman and a widow, followed her mother-in-law, Naomi, an Israelite, back to her native town of

---

* II Kings, 5. Gehazi, the servant of Elisha, asked for a reward from Naaman, captain of the host of the King of Syria (whom Elisha had miraculously cured of leprosy), without the knowledge of his master. He was struck down with leprosy himself by that unforgiving prophet.

Bethlehem. There they lived, two widows in extreme poverty, and Ruth went out to glean corn in the harvest fields. By the custom in Israel it was the duty of the nearest male relative of a childless widow to marry her and bring up children to perpetuate the family name, and it was in the fields of a near relative, though not the nearest, that Ruth chanced to go behind the reapers. This man Boaz, a fine figure of a prosperous farmer, noticed her and determined himself to marry her. But first there was the nearest relative to be considered. Naomi had a small piece of land which was her own and which she decided to sell. Boaz took steps to make it known to this 'nearest relative' that the land was for sale and he as 'Kinsman' had the right to buy it before other desiring purchasers. He was at first very ready to seize his chance, but Boaz was then able to point out to him that to claim this kinsman's right entailed also accepting the duty to marry Ruth. This was quite another matter. The kinsman thought out a hasty excuse and surrendered his right to Boaz.

That was all we know of the Kinsman. Just for one moment he passes before our eyes, a pleasantly comic figure, ready to do himself a bit of good by acquiring the land, only too anxious to escape from the bargain when he realised all that it entailed. We do not even know his name. Perhaps the author of this little idyll did not know it. Boaz, when he called him at the gate, addressed him summarily, 'Ho, such a one! turn aside, sit down here'.

You and I and 'all manner of men', nearly all of us, at the very best, are fated in our lives to be no more than one of these minor characters, we are 'Such a ones' passing by the gate. Perhaps we feel that more clearly than ever at this moment, when great historic events are taking place around us. After all, we may think, as we watch the rise and fall of great figures in world history, the lives of most men are colourless indeed. Most men are necessary, because it takes two thousand million men to make a world, but individually they do not seem to count for very much. There are times in the history of this earth when that feeling of insignificance seems stronger among mankind than at others and I think that, for a variety of reasons, we are passing through such a time now. Modern inventions, we are sometimes told, have made the world much smaller. Of course, they have not. They have done the exact opposite. When a man's horizon was limited by the next range of downs he had to be someone. He was part of a small universe. But now he is not one of a thousand; he is one of many millions. His world has become unimaginably vast. And being a world of machines, he feels himself rather like part of a machine, small, possibly useful, but not at all distinctive.

Yet there is a moment in the lives of all men when they are very important, when in the eyes of someone at least they matter greatly, as no one else in the world does. By a turn of phrase, which is, to my mind most moving, Christ referred to that moment at the darkest hour of his own life. Round the table in the Upper Room sat his mournful, disconsolate disciples, knowing that they would soon lose him. Christ, sharing their sorrow, tried to persuade them that it would be turned to joy, they would be like a woman who 'when she is in travail hath sorrow, because her hour is come; but as soon as she is delivered of the child, she remembereth no more the anguish, for joy that a man is born into the world'.

'For joy that a man is born into the world'. Not that one two-thousand-millionth part of the world's population is born. Is it just an illusion, that joy, that clear realisation of the supreme value of one person? We know it to be right if we are Christians, for it is what Christ taught. It is the view God takes of each one of us. 'From the hands of Him who loves her before she is,' wrote Dante, 'there issues like a little child that plays, with weeping and laughter, the simple soul.' How much of Christ's teaching was to show that God was a loving father and that this did not mean a vaguely beneficent presiding genius surveying the vast world of man, but a God concerned with each one of his creation individually, personally, like the father running out to meet the prodigal son, or the shepherd searching among the rocks for the one lost sheep, or the careful housewife sweeping the floor to find the one lost coin.

It is impossible to exaggerate the importance of this vital message. At one stroke each single human soul is invested with a tremendous dignity, every such a one becomes a prince. Not only at the moment of his birth in the eyes of the mother who bore him, but throughout eternity, each individual man is seen to be of supreme importance and God, who gave him birth, loves him throughout the life he is to live.

Never in human History had that message been of greater importance than today. You will have been told often enough that you are going out into an immensely difficult world. I am not thinking of the War. The War is only a symptom of our inability to cope with the problems facing us. The world has become so difficult, because it is so complicated. Man has gone far to conquer Nature and somehow as a result he has produced a chaos of disorder. He grows mountains of wheat and cannot sell it; he digs up from the earth its riches and cannot distribute them; he builds huge cities and finds he has cut himself off from the most enduring and simplest pleasures of life. The only way he can deal with all the complications of his civilisation is to concentrate on their organisation, to 'plan'. Now to the organiser, the 'planner', variety and difference must be a difficulty. Inevitably he feels he must think of men as all alike. Otherwise he finds himself like someone in a hideous nightmare, trying to work out a jig-saw puzzle in which all the pieces get up and move about of their own accord. And the temptation is almost irresistible to force men to act as he would wish, to deprive them of their individuality, to make them as far as possible all alike.

I feel little doubt that this is going to be the supreme spiritual problem of your generation. If it cannot be solved, our civilisation is doomed and we can tell from the study of History what will happen. Man, in the end, will refuse to play his part. He will solve his problems in another way, by limiting the size of his world, by giving up the idea of a world-wide society and forming smaller, more manageable self-contained communities, even if they are more primitive and even more savage.

All this has happened once before in History, at the end of the Roman Empire. Men eventually rejected the effort to fit them into prearranged places on an enormous and complicated board. They preferred the squalor and ignorance of the Dark Ages, the little village community, the manorial estate.★

Perhaps this may seem to you like a History Lecture rather than a sermon. But then all History is really the story of the clash of spiritual forces. The new world is not going to be made by new inventions or a new technique of organisation, although these will play their part. It will only become a world in which men will be content to live, if it is one that recognises the essential nature of Man, and the Christian belief is that above all else Man is an individual soul, infinitely precious in the sight of God. It may be too much to hope that England, let alone the world, will in our time become a Christian community. But it is the duty of Christians to keep alive in the world today a great idea, the idea of the supreme value of the individual soul in the eyes of God and, therefore, in our eyes too. To go back, if I may, to the illustration with which I started: those minor characters in Shakespeare's plays: Barnadine, the prisoner, Osric the courtier, Francis the harassed ostler and all the others live for us because to Shakespeare they were real men, unlike all other men. Christianity sees, too, the reality of men. The Christian knows that the joy that is felt at a birth, because a man is born into the world, is a joy which follows him through life,

★ The resurgence of nationalities in the Eastern European countries today provides an example of the same process.

the great character in History and 'such a one' alike, for to every man is given the highest and grandest imaginable destiny: to be the beloved child of God.

A SERMON DELIVERED
ON 25th JUNE 1944

This sermon was given during the Battle of Normandy, three weeks after D-Day. Many of the boys listening must have had fathers and brothers involved in the fighting. The peroration harks back to one of Robert's persistent themes of the importance of individual reactions as against a mechanistic or materialistic interpretation of History. Behind even the most spectacular human events, greater movements might be germinating from a chance encounter or a personal impulse.

'God hath spoken once; twice have I heard this; that power belongeth unto God'. *Psalm 62.11*

AT A TIME like this the thoughts of all of us are turned towards Normandy. Many have noticed the obvious contrast between the invasion nearly nine hundred years ago, and that which took place across the Channel this month, certainly among the most important invasions in the history of the Continent. It is with the Norman Invasion of England, or with one aspect of it, that I wish to deal.

From many points of view the Norman Conquest of England was a victory for barbarians over a more civilised people. You have only to compare the sculpture of England in the years just before, calm, dignified, and often very skilful, with the crude figures to be found in the earliest Norman Churches in this country to realise that. Or to take an example from political history: William the Conqueror was responsible for a devastation of the North of England so brutally complete that for years afterwards whole districts were simply described as 'Waste'. From York to Durham not a single isolated village was left.

Yet it is quite clear that the Norman Conquest did in the end make of England a more civilised country. This was not only the result of the strange Norman genius for organisation. It was largely due to the fact that William, for all his barbarism and cruelty, was a man with a very deep respect for the one great civilising influence of his time, the Church. He regarded it to be his duty as a king, to support the mission of the Christian Church to bring new ideals of justice and humanity into a world where armed might was usually the only law and where men were still very like their pagan forefathers. William, himself, here followed the example of his own immediate predecessors as Dukes of Normandy, and their care for the Church may be seen especially in the number of monasteries founded in the Duchy during the seventy years, and especially the last thirty years, before the Conquest. There were thirty of them in a land a good deal smaller than England south of the Thames. Many of the places about which we are now reading were the sites of these early monasteries, such as Cérisy, which the Americans have just taken between Bayeux and St Lo; St Sauveur le Vicomte, which they took after a hard fight in their drive across the peninsula of Cherbourg; Montebourg, for some days on the right flank of our beachhead; Troarn which still marks the left flank; and above all Caen with its two great abbeys founded by the Conqueror and his wife, among the finest monuments of medieval architecture and now, we must fear, only too probably being destroyed in the battle.

But of all these, none was so important as the famous Abbey of Bec, standing about half-way between Caen and the River Seine. The influence of Bec on England was profound and lasting. From it came Lanfranc, William's Archbishop of Canterbury. He was born in North Italy, rose to be a famous lawyer there and came to Normandy as a teacher when he was about thirty-five. He very soon became dissatisfied with his successful career and he decided to retire from the world and live in obscurity in some lonely monastery. He chose Bec, which had then been founded only a few years before. Even there he was not content, and he was about to leave it for the life of a solitary hermit, when the Abbot persuaded him to stay and open a school at the Abbey. Before long it was among the most famous schools in Europe, and Lanfranc was to become a European figure, a great theologian, the intimate friend and counsellor of William. On his work as Archbishop of Canterbury the Church in this country was to a large extent founded. From his part in founding a school at the monastery of Christ Church, Canterbury, and the work of other monks from Bec at Westminster and St Albans (where too the traditions of Bec as a school and a monastery were followed) may be traced the mainstream of English education. It was not only Lanfranc that this country owes to the Abbey, for his successor at Canterbury was Anselm, another North Italian, a great saint and writer, who had been Abbot of Bec also.

No trace is left now of the Abbey which stood in the days of Lanfranc and Anselm, save some parts of later buildings and the name of a little village, which before long you may be reading in the newspapers, but I think that it is almost as true to speak of the Conquest of England as one by the Abbey of Bec, as by the Norman followers of William. At any rate its influence on our country is hard to overestimate, if we read History correctly as something more than the record of kings and battles they fought, important as these may often be.

But the most remarkable part of the whole story is that of the founding of the Monastery itself. You can only appreciate its strangeness if you can realise for a moment what its influence became, as I have tried to show you. Nowhere in History, I feel, can be seen more clearly the influence of apparently small events, of actions taken by men without their having any idea of their eventual consequence.

Bec was founded in about the year 1039 by a Norman called Herluin. He was of noble birth, a man of great physical strength and skill in arms, and for twenty years he fought as a follower of a famous Norman Count, Gilbert of Brionne. One day, when Herluin was thirty-seven years old, Gilbert led his followers on a raid into the district between Dieppe and Abbeville. There they were met in battle and decisively defeated. Many of Gilbert's knights were slain or captured. Herluin, in extreme peril, vowed that, if he escaped, he would never again devote himself to any other service than that of God. His escape decided him to leave the world and though for some months he did not cease to serve as a knight at Gilbert's court, he spent all the time he could spare from his military duties in fasting and prayer. He sought the advice of the priests and prelates, but at that time they were nearly all ignorant or worldly men and he could get no help from them. So eventually he withdrew to his own estate, where he built a chapel and spent his time laboriously learning to read. After two years he decided to visit a number of monasteries to learn what was the kind of life a monk should lead. There were then only some eight monasteries in Normandy so he penetrated further south into France. But he met further worldly behaviour and sometimes even rough treatment. His biographer, Gilbert Crispin, Abbot of Westminster, a monk who had been with him at Bec, tells us that one day Herluin was staying at a certain monastery where he was particularly disheartened by the life of the monks. Indeed he was in despair and on the point of abandoning his quest altogether. But that night, when the last service of the day was over, he stayed behind in the Abbey Church in prayer. He thought he was alone, but gradually in the darkness he became aware of another figure. It was one of the monks of the Abbey who had stayed behind to pray alone, and who too did not realise that the Church had another occupant. Together they remained throughout the night in prayer. No word was passed between them. But for Herluin this incident was conclusive. He gave up his intention to visit other monasteries, returned to Normandy, and with two others began to live his life as a monk in complete poverty and seclusion. The three worked all day farming the land and building a church. Herluin's mother lived near them and used to help in washing their clothes. It is little wonder that Lanfranc, wishing to turn from the world, saw in Bec a place where he would be able to live the life he sought.

Even more noteworthy is Herluin's insight in recognising that Lanfranc's true future lay in founding a great monastic school. From being a quite uneducated and unlettered soldier, he became a man with a genuine love of learning. He attracted to his monastery Anselm, the greatest thinker of his age. He was renowned for his power to inspire young men with a zeal for letters. And when his monastery became an intellectual centre of the greatest importance, with its sons ruling abbeys and churches on both sides of the Channel, he remained its undisputed leader. The great Lanfranc, when Archbishop of Canterbury, always showed towards him a reverent devotion.

Very rarely in History can we see a great movement spring so clearly from so small, so insignificant a source, a nameless monk praying alone in a darkened church. 'That monk's prayer', says one of the leading English medieval scholars of our time, 'may even be said to have changed the course of history.' Gilbert Crispin speaks of it as an example of that faith which is even greater than miracles. And in truth, this story brings us very near to the heart of things in History, where no distinction can be drawn between the miraculous and what is normally explicable. We may search but we can very rarely find the hidden sources of the great movements among men. But from this story – and there are other instances – we may learn that humility and simplicity often have consequences far beyond anything that we may imagine for ourselves, and far, indeed, beyond anything dreamed of by the man or woman concerned. They would not think of themselves as more than the agents through whom a greater power works in the world of men. 'The wind bloweth where it listeth, and thou hearest the sound thereof, but canst not tell where it cometh, or whither it goeth; so is everyone that is born of the spirit.'* It is in such ways, very, very rarely recognised and then perhaps only by chance, rather than in the great and spectacular events, that sometimes it is given to men to see in human history the finger of God.

* St John 3 v. 8.

A SERMON DELIVERED
ON 6TH MAY 1945

*Robert might well have deployed his favourite method of introduction –
'This really was one of the most curious of all sermons' – to describe what
follows. It was preached two days before V E day in an atmosphere of
feverish anticipation. Later sermons after the event dealt eloquently with
the meaning of victory and the sacrifices made for it. The life and legend
of St John may seem an odd theme at such an hour but there are many
overtones. It may have been meant to calm fermentations, probably
visible in a restless young congregation. It does nothing to diminish the
grandeur of the approaching moment. We can trace something of the story
of Germany from the Weimar Republic to 1945 in the story of the brigand
who threw down his arms and wept.*

WE ARE LIVING through one of the most tremendous months in the
history of the world and I have never felt it more difficult to decide
what I can say to you at evening service. For this moment, when we
stand at the very edge of a climax for which we have waited for so long
– when the whole world is in suspense – this moment does not seem
the time to try to express our feelings about the great crisis through
which we have lived. Instinctively, I feel, we wait for that climax to
come, before we can step back, even for an instant, to survey the
scene. So what I shall say to you will have no direct bearing, although
it may have some incidentally, on the great drama of which we are
witnesses. Let me take you for a moment into a back-water, which is
very far removed from the turmoil around us.

If you look at the beginning of a Prayer Book you will find a
calendar and against certain of the days of the year you will find
printed the names of certain saints. Some of these, printed in heavier
type or in italics, or in older editions in red, are the names of the great

saints whose memory is preserved by the special collects, epistles and gospels. The others are known as 'black letter saints' and a strange list they turn out to be. In fact no one quite knows why the compilers of the Prayer Book retained some out of the long list of saints commemorated in medieval times and rejected others. The compilers certainly seem to have been careless. One of the names, Saint Enurchus on September 7th, was simply a misprint for an obscure Saint Evertius.★ St Alban is commemorated on 17th June by mistake for 22nd June, because the second X of the day of the month in Roman figures was mis-read for a V. St Cyprian the Martyr was allotted the day of a little known name-sake, and one of the strangest survivals is that of today, 6th May. If you look in a Prayer Book you will see against it the words: S John Evangelist ante Portam Latinam, St John before the Latin Gate. I have no idea why this particular Saint's day was one of those retained.

'St John before the Latin Gate' commemorates an incident in the life of the Apostle, one that was not told until many generations after his death and which may safely be regarded as legendary. The story tells how St John was brought from Ephesus to Rome in a great persecution of Christians by the Emperor Domitian and just outside the city, by the so-called Latin Gate, was thrown into a cauldron of boiling oil and miraculously preserved. When the pictures are restored to the National Gallery after the War I hope some of you will see the remarkable painting by a very early Italian Master, called Margaritone of Arezzo, in which by the side of the Virgin and Child there is a small panel showing St John in the cauldron, supported by an angel, while his persecutors vainly stoke up the fire beneath it.

We might think for a moment of the man so strangely referred to, because St John the Evangelist is one of the most astonishing characters in the whole of History. The great difficulty in speaking about him lies in the uncertainty whether the Apostle was actually the author of the Gospel, the Epistles and the Book of Revelation which bear his name. Personally I believe that he wrote the Epistles and at least the main portion of the Gospel, but not the Book of Revelation. However, that is a question not suited to discussion here. It would be best to consider only what we can learn from the Gospels and the Acts of the Apostles, and that is strange enough.

Reference is often made to the extraordinary change which came over the character of St Peter after the death and resurrection of Christ.

★ See below, 'Meeting a Crisis: Patron Saints for Bibliophiles, Printers and Bookbinders'.

It is not generally realised that a change also came over St John. Because of the Gospel and Epistles ascribed to him, St John is usually thought of as always the quietest and most serene of the Apostles. Nothing could be further from the truth. I should say that he was almost as tempestuous and impulsive as St Peter himself. He and his brother James were called by Christ himself, 'Boanerges', 'sons of Thunder', or, as it has been paraphrased, 'the Angry Men'. When the people of a Samaritan village on one occasion refused to receive Christ and his disciples, the two brothers furiously called on him to summon down fire to consume them, as Elijah had done, and Christ rebuked them for their entire misunderstanding of his purpose. Yet this was he who was called the disciple whom Jesus loved, the man of whom Jesus said on the Cross to his own mother, 'Woman, behold thy son'. In the early days after Pentecost he is, with Peter, an acknowledged leader of the first Christians. Then he disappears from the story in the Acts of the Apostles.

But there is another story, one not recorded until over a hundred years after his death in any writings that have come down to us, though it is earlier than the legend of the Latin Gate and is a story I feel may well be true. At least there is nothing miraculous about it and it is entirely in keeping with the picture we have of the author of the Gospel and the Epistles. This tells how St John, then in his old age, once commended a young man to the care of a bishop in some town near Ephesus. Some time later, St John returned to this town and inquired of the Bishop about the young man. He learnt how he had fallen in with evil companions, had joined them in extravagant living and then in deeds of robbery and how he had at last joined a band of brigands and became their chief, 'the most violent, bloody and cruel of them all', haunting the mountains above the town. St John asked at once for a guide and rode off into the hills until he was seized by one of the robbers' sentries. He demanded to be taken to their leader who, when he saw the Apostle, shrank away from him. But St John called after him, 'Why dost thou fly from me my child; from thy own father, from one unarmed and aged? Have pity on me my child, fear not. Thou hast still hopes of life. I myself will give account to Christ on thy behalf. If need be, I will willingly endure thy death, as the Lord the death which he suffered on behalf of us. For thy sake I will give my own life in place of thine. Stand, believe; Christ has sent me.' And at these words the young man first stood still and then cast down his arms and wept. St John came up to him and embraced him and then led him back into the town where he restored him to the Church he had left.

I said that any relevance in what I have spoken of to the events of today would be only incidental. But we cannot consider the time when Christ lived and when his first disciples gave to the world His message without finding it relevant to our own problems, because it was from that time that there sprang the great ideals on which what is best in our civilisation rests, those which in fact we have been fighting for. And in times as critical as these we should recall to ourselves the Christ who was St John's master and is ours. When the two brothers wished to call down fire from heaven on the Samaritan villagers Jesus answered, 'Ye know not what manner of spirit ye are of. For the Son of Man is not come to destroy men's lives but to save them'. Already our minds should be turning to the duty that lies ahead of us, of bringing out of chaos a world where men can live at peace with one another. Christ, who made of the Son of Thunder the beloved disciple, alone can fashion us for that task.

Robert's source of inspiration in the Calendar of Saints may have been unconsciously prompted by the stories of the morning of 11th November, 1918, when the silence of peace fell across the trenches. Those French soldiers who had with them small books of devotion rushed to find the name of the Saint to whom they could give their thanks. They were reminded that it was the Feast of St Martin, the most beloved of all French Saints, whose name is enshrined in countless place names, churches and villages throughout the provinces of France.

A SERMON DELIVERED
ON 5TH MAY 1946

This sermon was preached one year after V E Day. Wartime austerities had continued into peacetime and shortages had no longer the moral support of defiant patriotism. The economic problems of Britain and Europe appeared to be almost insurmountable. Eastern Europe had passed into Communist control. The refugees and displaced persons numbered millions. It might be added too that in boarding schools at that time there were particular difficulties in storing adequate supplies of food and fuel during a system of rationing and controls that was dislocated nationally. Many older masters were physically tired by the double and treble roles they had filled during the War. Colleagues returning from active service into the pre-war hierarchies of the Common Room found it irksome to readapt to old ways.

'When Israel went out of Egypt, the house of Jacob from a people of strange language'. *Psalm 114.1*

AT THE beginning of Dante's *Purgatory*, we find the poet himself, who has climbed up a narrow passage from the very centre of the earth, out of the lowest depths of Hell, standing on the shores of an island mountain in the middle of the sea, which is Mount Purgatory. The dawn rises across the waters and then, in the far distance he sees a glowing light, which approaches swiftly. As it comes near him he sees that the light is an angelic figure, who with the strokes of his wings guides a little vessel. More than a hundred spirits were in the ship, the souls of men who had just died on earth, men who were secure from the pains of hell and who awaited their purification on the Mount of Purgatory before they could enter Paradise, and as the happy souls landed on the shore, he heard them singing with one voice the Psalm 'In exitu Israel', 'When Israel went out of Egypt'.

The story of the Exodus, the going forth, the deliverance of the Israelites from bondage in Egypt had always been taken as the crowning example of a deliverance. It may be taken, as Dante said elsewhere in a famous letter, either as a piece of history or as an allegory typifying the redemption of Man by Christ, or the conversion of the human soul, or the departure of the blessed from the slavery of worldly corruption to the liberty of eternal joy – There are many different ways in which we can read the Old Testament. In the Middle Ages men saw in the stories of Israelite history above all else allegories typifying the acts of Christ. Thus Moses and the Israelites crossing the Red Sea were taken as, in some sense, representing the Baptism of Christ. After the Reformation men came to look on the Old Testament as containing the total absolute and literal truth about nature, history and morality. I am not sure that that way of looking on it is not stranger to us now than the allegorical interpretation. At its best it produced the simple fervour of a book like Bunyan's *Pilgrim's Progress*. At its worst it took the barbarous practices in warfare of a primitive people and held them to justify the most cruel treatment of one's enemies. At the present day the Old Testament is studied with the eyes of the historian, the archaeologist and the anthropologist, and is seen to contain the story of the gradual development of a people who had a peculiar, an unrivalled genius, enabling them to lead the whole world towards religious truth. The Israelites, rightly understood, were the greatest of all pioneers. But this new insight into the meaning of the Old Testament should not cause us to forget that, as well as the utterances of the prophets and much fine poetry, it contains the best historical narrative that has ever been written, and further that, just because the Israelites were a profoundly religious people, the stories in it have, again and again, some simple moral lesson, which remains of the greatest significance to us today.

Take the story of the Exodus. We too have experienced a great deliverance. This is its anniversary today. But notice that in the story of the deliverance of the Israelites, their rescue does not for one moment mean that their troubles were over. They left Egypt only to find themselves in an inhospitable dreary desert, often without food, or water, so that they lost all hope for the future and even longed to return to the bondage from which they had come. They 'murmured' in the wilderness, 'Would to God we had died by the hand of the Lord in the land of Egypt, when we sat by the fleshpots, and when we did eat bread to the full.' God sent them manna from heaven and, according to the account in the Book of Numbers, they were still unsatisfied. 'We remember the fish which we did eat in Egypt freely;

the cucumbers and the melons, and the leeks and the onions, and the garlic; but now our soul is dried away; there is nothing at all, beside this manna, before our eyes.'

I do not think that it is difficult for us to read the lesson of this story. We too have had a mighty deliverance. Already we are liable to forget the mercies granted us, to murmur because things are still difficult. The lesson of the Book of Exodus is a hard one to learn and man has to learn it again and again. Deliverance from an evil bondage is a mercy, from some tyrannies it is so great a mercy that we can hardly estimate it, but deliverance never leads to an easy life. The story of Exodus is the story of men who continually fail to live up to their destiny, but men whom God continually forgives and helps again. It is the story of all men. And if we are prone to 'murmur', to think that peace ought to mean the fleshpots, we should do well to remember this story. As with so many Old Testament stories, the more closely we study it, the more profound and subtle we see it to be, for all its apparent primitive simplicity.

But there is another lesson to be learnt from the Exodus which is of even greater significance. It is one of the essential lessons of the whole of the Old Testament. For the Israelites, their deliverance from Egypt was the central point of their history. It was, in fact, the central point of *all* history. It proved conclusively that they were the chosen people called by God as his own for a peculiar destiny. And this belief, while it is perhaps the main reason why the Israelites were the greatest people of all ancient history, carried with it an immense temptation. It was to regard their election by God as His chosen people as enough in itself, to accept the privilege and to renounce the responsibility. The true greatness of the Israelites is seen when it is realised that they themselves produced the men who could understand the colossal error of which they were guilty, even though they failed to convince their fellow countrymen. The most difficult obstacle the prophets ever had to overcome was just this feeling of self satisfaction, of pride, which grew out of their memories of the Exodus. One man among them before all others recognised the truth. The prophet Amos in one terrible sentence undermined the whole foundations of the Israelites' pride: 'Have not I brought up Israel out of Egypt?' he reported God as saying. How often must the Israelites have heard those words before and how, as always, they must have preened themselves on hearing them. But Amos went on, 'and the Philistines from Caphtor? and the Syrians from Kir? Are ye not as the children of the Ethiopians unto me, O children of Israel, saith the Lord.' It is a most startling and original passage. God is seen as having chosen and as protecting with his love all peoples. And it may remind us of a further lesson which we may learn from the story of the Exodus. A deliverance can become a curse and not a blessing if we make it one. If we regard it simply as a means to divest ourselves of responsibilities, not to be even readier to accept them, above all if it leads to national pride and exclusiveness.★

A year ago today, we were finally delivered from a great tyranny. Even now we can hardly understand from what we were saved. And now looking out on a world which seems just as hard and difficult we must be ready not to 'murmur', not to forget to be grateful, not to give up hope or to think that we have done enough. We have to learn that in this life deliverance is always a new opportunity leading to new difficulties, and not an escape. We may learn much from this old story of hardships and weariness, of long waitings and disappointment, of ingratitude and human weakness, but also of heroic leaders and their trust in the divine purpose. We may remember that it was while they were wandering in the wilderness that God came down to the Israelites on Mount Sinai and in the supreme moment of their history, chose them to be the people to receive his Law.

★ The present political emancipation of Eastern Europe makes these thoughts seem as relevant as they were in 1946.

GERMANY

POTSDAM IN PRACTICE

Robert went out to Germany in May, 1947, as Educational Adviser to the Military Governor and Commander-in-Chief. This lecture was delivered many years later at an Anglo-German Conference in Oxford, which assembled to look back in retrospect on British Policy and its outcome. The opening section may seem to be a fairly prosaic and factual account of the main issues faced in reviving an educational system on the ruins of the Third Reich. A series of incidents are recounted which build up into a recognisable liberal pattern. Yet by the time we have made the surprising journey from Potsdam and Sanssouci to St George's in the East, Stepney, London, the narrative has become vivid and emotional.

It has been a strange experience to read this while the television screens have been filled with pictures of demonstrations in East Berlin, the flight of East Germans to the West, and the shaking and breaking of the foundations of Communism. In 1948, when the two systems of education finally parted company, the weapons in the hands of those on the Eastern side seemed so much stronger: state authority, dogma, armed force, police supervision. The weapons in the hands of those on the West were more imprecise, their use more inhibited: persuasion, camaraderie, exchanges and visits, dinner-parties, friendly encounters in school-rooms and common-rooms. But it is the quiet revolution that has had the victory.

One realises today, when the media seem always on hand to produce instant impressions of events and participants, that the materials necessary to re-create the onset of the Berlin Blockade in 1948 are scanty by comparison. This Address contains a personal account of certain moments which has a permanent historical value. A lighter aspect is the continual evidence of the conspiratorial glee with which Robert liked to evade official regulations. It was to reappear (more strongly than before) in South Africa.

As delivered in Oxford, the Lecture contained a mingling of German and English technical terms and place-names. The inconsistent mixture gives a sense of the amicable relations of survivors of that formative

period in modern German History and where the meaning is clear I have
kept to the original text.

'GERMAN EDUCATION shall be so controlled as completely to eliminate
National Socialist and militarist doctrines and to make possible the
successful development of democratic ideals.' I wonder how often
these words from the Potsdam Agreement will be quoted during our
deliberations. All things considered, I think it was a reasonably
sensible statement. At least it did not suggest that it is possible to teach
a nation to be democratic through its schools and universities. But this
is precisely what most people in this country directly after the War
believed should be done. For this reason there was coined the horrible
word 'Re-education' to express our policy in Germany (I never used it
myself and I did what I could to persuade others not to do so). What is
more, two of the occupying powers, the French and the Russians, also
believed it. But the British Education Branch did not. Its approach
was very different.

Perhaps I might say a word first on the policies of the other three
Powers. We met, of course, each month at the Educational Committee of the Allied Control Council. There we passed splendid
resolutions about 'democratic' education which did not matter at all as
we all had different ideas about what was meant by the word Democracy. In fact, I can only remember one discussion on a practical
question during any of the meetings I attended: whether members of
Youth Organisations in Germany should be allowed to wear uniforms. (Perhaps I may say that there was a strange arrangement in
Berlin in the period before the Air Lift. Every Sunday afternoon, a bus
took members of the British Control Commission to visit Potsdam. I
used to go almost every Sunday that I was in Berlin. But I am afraid
that I did not visit Sanssouci and the Neues Palais. I used to sneak off
by myself to see what I could find in the town. One Sunday I came
across a group of the Freie Deutsche Jugend wearing what to all intents
and purposes was a uniform. At the next meeting of the Committee I
mentioned this. At least I made my Russian opposite number Dr
Salutukin rather uncomfortable. I think we may ignore the Education
Committee of the Control Council.)

My impression was that in the eyes of the French, the German
school teacher with his narrow nationalist outlook had been the main
influence in creating the society which first accepted and then supported National Socialism. For them, therefore, the most important

needs were to have as many French teachers as possible teaching in the schools of their zone of Germany, and that they should control the training of the future teachers. The children who were to be the future teachers would, therefore, be chosen at the age of eleven and placed in separate schools, usually boarding schools, which would also be largely under French influence. The plan was that they should go on subsequently to Universities, which would also be largely under French influence. The plan was impressive, but apart from the fact that the French Zone was a small one, it depended upon a complete control by the Allies of German Education for at least ten or fifteen years – and there was never any real possibility of this.

The Russian policy was a great deal more realistic. I do not imagine that the Russians ever regarded the German teachers as capable of being reformed. The solution of the problem could only be a political one. If they could make Germany, or at least their zone, a Communist state, all the necessary educational reforms would follow, almost automatically. This, of course, they have succeeded in doing. Education in the DDR has become, in the sense of the term which the Russian representatives had in mind on the Education Committee of the Control Council, 'democratic'. The situation was well summed up for me once by a Pastor who had the duty, before the building of the Berlin Wall, of helping the Evangelical Church students who came over to the West. 'You must realise,' he said to me once, 'that these students know every movement of the Communist ritual dance. They have lived in a condition of perfected schizophrenia.' Now there was never any possibility of the Americans or the British adopting this policy.

I should not say that the differences between the Americans and ourselves were fundamental. They undoubtedly concentrated more on the educational headquarters, whether at 'zone' or 'Land'* level than we did, and they were rather readier to lay down the law. It is significant that they arrived in Germany after the War with a text-book on German History for use in Gymnasien† already written and printed. It was so neutral as to be hardly readable. I shall consider our way of dealing with text-books in due course. I remember that the American Land Commissioner for Bavaria suddenly declared one morning that in future no fees should be charged at German secondary schools. It was quite impossible in the economic circumstances of the time. I admired greatly the very astute way in which Herr

* Land in the sense of a constituent State, or administrative area.
† Schools corresponding to English Grammar Schools.

Hundhammer, the Kultus Minister in Bavaria,* dealt with the problem, setting up long series of committees to consider first how the change might be carried out – on a remarkably wide spectrum of subjects. One, I remember was on the use of projects in secondary schools and Herr Hundhammer said to me, 'You know, I think two teachers from Murnau on the Committee have very little idea what it is all about'. But I think we may claim that, in Dr Kohnen of North Rhine-Westphalia, we had for a time a Kultus Minister who was just as skilful in dealing with us. I remember it caused some difficulties that the Americans could see no reason why Bekenntnisschulen† should be preserved or why a University should have a 'numerus clausus'.‡ But I think our relations with the Americans were good; mine certainly were with the Director of their department during the second half of my time in Germany. We used to try to arrange to meet informally once a month. I remember once telling him that I thought they were giving the German Youth Organisations too much money. 'Yes,' he said, 'you may well be right. But do remember that you British have been occupying countries all your life. We have only done it once before, and then it was our own country after the Civil War – and look what a mess we made of it.'

The British Military Government fully controlled German Education in their Zone for only eighteen months. On 1st December 1946 there was issued what was known as Ordinance No. 57, handing over the right to legislate to the Land Legislatures, except on certain reserved subjects which did not include Education, the Military Government retaining the power of veto. At the same time the control of educational administration passed to the Land Governments, except on two points: the establishment of a 'numerus clausus' at the Universities and the status of the Bekennisschulen.

I should say that the three main tasks of the Education Branch at that time were first, actually getting the schools and administration started again – and in the Autumn of 1946, the Universities; second, the choice of Kultus Ministers and Senior Officials in the administration

---

* Dr Alois Hundhammer, Minister of Education in Bavaria, 1946–50. Deputy Prime Minister of Bavaria, 1964–9.
† Denominational schools.
‡ A system by which admission to University was dependent not on a simple pass but on achieving a higher average mark total in the Abitur (A-level). The statement is a gentle dig at the Americans. They had no experience in their History of a Kulturkampf or battles between Church and State over Education. Their Universities did not aim at making entrance as rigidly exclusive as possible. They could be forgiven for being totally baffled.

and often of Head Teachers – and later the first Rektoren of the Universities; and third the process known as De-Nazification. Of these, the first two were far the most important; the third, De-Nazification, the most difficult and irksome. As I had no responsibilities in Germany during that period, although I was fortunate enough to be able to see some of the work then, I can speak uninhibitedly and say that I feel sure that anything we were able to achieve in the educational field in Germany was mainly due to the way in which the staff of the Education Branch had set about their work at the start. We should not forget what things were like in those days. In Cologne 92 percent of the school accommodation had been destroyed. In Schleswig-Holstein only 162 out of 1550 primary schools were available and before long the influx of refugees doubled the population of the Land. I hope people in Germany now appreciate the immensely hard work and the courage shown by the German teachers and educational administrators in those days. Perhaps the difficulties helped. It meant that both sides were working together. In a very short time members of the Education Branch succeeded in convincing German administrators and teachers that they wanted to cooperate with them. They gained their confidence, they exerted an influence through their personal relationships, rather than by using their powers as the military rulers of a conquered nation. Their work was not spectacular, but their influence was to be seen from the Ministers at the top to the smallest schools in the country. To meet a Kultus Minister or a Schulrat* or a Rektor in the home of a British Education Officer – I may say that I do not believe that a single one of them paid the least attention to the various regulations against 'fraternization' – and listen to them discussing problems of policy, or to go into a small school with the local Education Officer and soon see him in earnest conversation with the Head Teacher about some shortage of text books or a leak in the roof of the school – well, many would say that it is all rather trivial, but it represented a definite policy, even if it was largely an unconscious one.

The next period may be taken as lasting from December 1946 to August 1949, when the first elections were held in the newly formed German Federal Republic. I should say that the British Education Officers in general found that their position was very little altered. They had been accustomed to offer advice rather than give orders and their advice was sought as much as it had been in the past. Moreover, the Länder Governments were feeling their way somewhat painfully

---

* The German equivalent of a Schools Inspector.

and the Kultus Ministers remained in very close touch with the senior officers of the Education Branch. It was remarkable how often the Kultus Ministers invited British officials to attend meetings of departmental committees which were considering education problems. On the British side it was regarded as natural to seek the approval of the German Educational authorities for any steps that were taken on British initiative. I can remember, for instance, attending a meeting of four Minister Presidents of the British Zone to gain their agreement to our setting up a Commission to consider the problem of German Universities. It was certainly not necessary for us to do this. The four Kultus Ministers of the British Zone used to meet once a month for a day or two in my house for informal discussions. I have no doubt that this was the most valuable time I spent each month. Until the Blockade and Air Lift began they were held in my office in Berlin. They stayed with me in my house and we always ended with a visit to the opera from which they were taken to catch the Military Train back to West Germany. When the awkward question, to which I have already referred, of uniforms for members of German Youth Organisations came up for consideration by the Education Committee of the Allied Control Council, I talked the matter over first with the four Kultus Ministers and was able to state the view which was much more theirs than that of the Military Government. But most of the time was taken up on purely practical problems, especially before the Währungs-reform*; on how to provide any text books at all for German schools and, immediately after it, on how to help students to remain at the Universities.

During this period the local governments were all engaged in discussing the question of Schulreform. It meant in practice the passing of legislation to set up a new educational system in each Land. In the autumn of 1947 the British Military Government took its one step towards controlling the kind of educational systems which would be established in its zone. It laid down four principles and declared that it would veto any legislation which disregarded them. These principles were that the status of Teachers' Training Colleges should be raised, that Secondary Education should be free, that no legislation should make the eventual adoption of the Sechsjährige Grundschule impossible, lastly that Bekenntnisschulen should not be abolished. I may say that the point of this last principle was simply not to disturb a compromise that had been established in the early

* Introduction of the new currency.

days of the Occupation on this vexed question. The compromise was of its nature a purely temporary one, enforcing a kind of local option on the question. Whether it was right for us to continue to enforce this compromise, I am not sure. I once said to the four Kultus Ministers that I felt that perhaps one reason why they were cautious on educational reforms was that they were always looking over their shoulders at the problems of the Bekenntnis-schulen. I asked them if they thought it desirable that we should cease to take any interest in the question and hand it over to them. 'For heaven's sake don't do that,' they said. 'We may be looking over our shoulders now, but if you did that we should turn right round.'

This Declaration was first suggested to me by two of the Kultus Ministers and it was fully discussed with all four of them before it was issued. I cannot say that I now think it was worthwhile. In any case, a year later we abandoned our Veto and the Declaration became invalid. It had, perhaps, a certain propaganda value and it gave some encouragement to those who advocated educational reforms. The principle about the Training Colleges was probably useful. The principle about Secondary Education meant nothing as it was in conflict with our policy adopted at the same time, of giving responsibility in the financial sphere to the German Economic Council at Frankfurt. The question of whether the Grundschule should last for four or six years produced in those days an extraordinary amount of heat in Germany.* The Declaration gave such very guarded support to the Sechsjährige Grundschule as to be almost worthless. (I remember at about this time being present at a discussion in Hanover when Herr Grimme spoke in favour of the Sechsjährige Grundschule and Professor Wolff of Hamburg in favour of four years. After a time I intervened to suggest they might consider a British compromise and do as was done in my country where we had a Fünfjährige Grundschule. At this both Herr Grimme and Professor Wolff agreed that any such solution was unthinkable!) This Declaration was as near as we ever came to

---

* This heated controversy had deep social connotations. A four-year Volksschule (Primary) Education meant that at ten years of age children from the more educated homes went on for the long nine-year course at the Gymnasium, leading to University and professional success. A large number of the others would spend four more years at the Volksschule and then enter the labour market. Prolonging the Grundschule from four to six years, prolonging comprehensive education, would – some hoped and some feared – give more children the opportunity to develop and prove their ability for the Gymnasium course. But the length and hence the quality of the Gymnasium course would be curtailed.

intervening in German educational politics, for the first three principles we supported were those advocated by the Social Democratic Party.

Can it be said then that we had no policy at all? If we were to endeavour in the educational field to 'make possible the successful development of democratic ideals' in Germany, and if we were to interpret democracy as a state of society in which the people of a country exercise their personal wills freely in determining their form of government and in choosing the rulers who will govern them, it was quite clear that to force educational changes on the German people would be wholly contradictory to that aim. What then could be done?

Perhaps I might return to the problem of De-Nazification.* It was an extraordinarily difficult, perhaps an impossible, task to decide which teachers should be forbidden to teach on account of their previous connection with the Nazi movement. Altogether 16,000 teachers in the British Zone were forbidden to carry on their profession. I remember once telling a prominent Social Democratic newspaper editor, Willie Eichler, something of the sense of helplessness I felt when faced with this problem, and I received some comfort from his comment: 'Don't be too worried. After all you have probably managed this better than the other occupying states. But you will never do it really successfully until you obtain the services of a particular person.' 'Really,' I said, 'and who is that?' He replied, 'The Archangel Michael'.

De-Nazification was all very well and I should say absolutely necessary, but it did nothing for those who were or had been Nazis, except to put them into positions without responsibility. But the problem of the ex-Nazis was not entirely neglected and, as practically nothing is known of this, I thought I might spend a moment on it.

Not long after I went out to Germany I was faced with the proposal to place all the Nazi leaders in the British Zone not sentenced to imprisonment on a small island in the North Sea called Adelheide. There they were to stay for the rest of their lives with their families, free except that they could not leave the island. I was summoned to a meeting at Lübeck to discuss this, along with other senior members of the Control Commission. I was asked to give my views. 'Well,' I said, 'I can only deal with the question of the education of the children of the Nazis. There are two alternatives. You could build a school for them

---

* A problem that now confronts Eastern Europe: what to do about the kleptocracy, informers, and secret police inherited from Communism.

on the island to which they would all go. When they reached the age to go to a University you would have to let them leave, and then, having been brought up inevitably with Nazi ideas, they would spread them throughout Germany. Or you could send them to school on the mainland, either staying with relatives or in boarding schools, and they would go back to Adelheide for the holidays. There they would be imbued each time with Nazi ideals and they would go back with them to school each term.' At this the British Chief of Staff said, 'I am going to ask each one of you in turn whether you think we ought to go on with the proposal for Adelheide.' Each one in turn said No. I have little doubt that they had made up their minds before, but I am glad that I played a part at least in defeating one of the most absurd proposals made while we occupied Germany.

Before I refer to another, and more constructive, effort, I might mention that it was decided in 1947 to release from camps where they were kept all Nazis below the age of twenty-one. It did no good to keep them with older and more committed Nazis who would certainly do all they could to keep their faith alive.

The one constructive effort was the establishment, at a place called St Michael's House at Blankenese near Hamburg, of a kind of conference centre. This had nothing to do with the Education Branch of the Control Commission. It was, in fact, wholly illegal. It was paid for out of Occupation Costs, although it did not fall into any category covered by arrangements about them. At this place all rations between Germans and English were shared equally, which was also illegal. We were supposed to be neutral in religious matters; nothing less neutral than St Michael's House could be imagined. For it was a definitely Christian Institution, run by an English priest (now a Bishop of the Church of England) and a German Evangelical Pastor together. There was nothing emotional or 'Pentecostal' about it. Those who went found they were taking part in really serious discussions on fundamental political questions. To this place we invited all the young ex-Nazis now free and, to use the common phrase, 'Category Six ex-Nazis': that is, allowed only to do manual labour. A great many accepted the invitation and I have good reason to believe that many were deeply influenced by their stay. Of course we could not talk about it. One day the Chief of Staff in Berlin asked me to come and see him. 'Can you tell me about a place called St Michael's House? I have just heard of it. It seems to me wholly illegal.' There was nothing for it, and I told him all about it. Now this Major-General was a devout Roman Catholic. After a moment's silence he said, 'Do you ever take any people from our side of the house?' 'Well,' I said, 'You don't make

it very easy for us. But I can assure you that there is not a Catholic
Bishop in West Germany who, if he knows of some ex Gruppen-
führer, who he thinks might benefit from a visit, will not send him to
us.' 'Really,' he said, 'That's very interesting; all right, don't worry.
You will hear no more about it.' And it went on for another six
months. Then in changed conditions it was clear that it could not be
paid for out of Occupation Costs any longer and it had to be closed.
But the young men who had been there, most of them ex-Nazis,
got together and raised money which they sent us and this kept it
going for another month. We call in England the past members
of a school, Old Boys. No Old Boys ever paid their place of education such a tribute as these young ex-Nazis paid to St Michael's
House.*

But the essential problem in Germany after the war was surely not
created by the ex-Nazis. I doubt whether the Potsdam Agreement,
when it referred to the complete elimination of National Socialist
doctrines, went deep enough. What was really needed was the development of a sense of personal responsibility for the affairs of the
state. I came to know a very remarkable German, Professor Kahle of
Bonn University, a most courageous opponent of the Nazis, who
eventually escaped to England. Some months after the Nazis seized
power he had cause to visit the Kultus Ministerium in Berlin. There to
his surprise he met two young men, recently Lektoren at Bonn, who
he knew were not Nazis. They were embarrassed and one of them
said, 'Please Herr Professor do not think we are Nazis. There are very
few in the Ministry. Some have been forced into it by the Government, but they are quite useless as administrators. It is people like us
who keep the Ministry going. We call ourselves "Spezis" (Spezialis-
ten).' It never seemed to occur to him that he was helping to 'keep
going' a regime which he professed to deplore.

I could give another example. One day I went to the University of
Göttingen. We had decided to set up a Commission, a German one
quite independent of the British Control Commission, to consider the
future of the Universities. I came to the conclusion that I ought to
explain (to the Senate of the University) what we were intending to
do. I did not expect a very favourable reception. When I finished I saw
they had chosen to answer me a most formidable antagonist, the

---

* 'Old Boys' bombarded with Appeals may raise an eye-brow at this. The hyperbole
is possibly excusable in so far as such ventures were unknown in the 1940s, the
impulse was spontaneous and the debt of gratitude was entirely a moral and not a
practical one.

philosopher Dr Nikolai Hartmann. 'Mr Birley,' he said, 'you seem to think that all the Professors at Göttingen were Nazis.' 'Not at all,' I answered. 'Of course they were not. The charge against them is something quite different. It is that they were quite ready to accept a regime the whole policy of which they knew to be based on academic nonsense.' And to this I received the astonishingly generous reply, which I have never forgotten: 'To that charge, Mr Birley, we have no answer.'

It is now very nearly thirty years since the ending of Nazi rule. It is sometimes difficult to recall the feelings one had in those years immediately after the War, when it was the one thing that seemed to matter. We realised that not all Germans had been Nazis, only a minority. But the great majority had accepted them. We could not eliminate this lack of a sense of personal responsibility by ourselves changing the educational system of the country or altering the constitution of the Universities or preparing anti-Nazi text-books. In the end there seemed to be three lines worth pursuing.

The first was to do everything possible to give the German teachers responsibility, to avoid the temptation to tell them what to do and then expect them to do what they were told. One of the obvious problems which faced the Education Branch was that of German text-books. Almost without exception those in use under the Nazis had to be forbidden, especially, as was to be expected, History books. I have already referred to the American solution of the problem. The British Education Branch issued no books of its own. Instead, it set up a text-book Committee of German educationists with two or three British advisers. All scripts of new text-books had to be sent to the Committee which returned them to their authors with comments if they had passages with blatantly or narrowly nationalist sentiments. This was, I felt – I had nothing to with starting it – true education. It was notable that when control over Education was handed over to the Land Governments in December 1946, the Committee continued to function without any changes in its constitution or procedure.

Along with this went the splendid work of a group of teachers of History at Brunswick, who published little handbooks, each one of which had on the title page the words '*Beiträge zum Geschichtsunterricht. Quellen und Unterlagen für die Hand des Lehrers.*'* They had, I believe, a great influence. The only credit that we can claim is that we supported

---

* 'Companion for the teaching of History. Sources and Materials for Teachers.'

them. Their leader was Dr Georg Eckert.* I am myself a teacher of
History and I can say that I regard Dr Eckert as the greatest figure of
my time in my own educational field. His recent death is a great loss to
many of us.

The second line that was pursued went back also to the earliest days
of the Occupation, when the Education Branch had done all it could to
bring forward those Germans who had not accepted the Nazis, to
persuade them to accept posts of responsibility and then to support
and encourage them. Opposition to the Nazis in Germany was more
considerable than most people realised, though, of course, it had been
quite unsuccessful. I worked with four Kultus Ministers. For most of
the time two of these were Social Democrats who had spent years in
Concentration Camps. Herr Grimme† of Niedersachsen and Herr
Kuklinski of Schleswig-Holstein. One was a lady, Frau Christina
Teusch of Nordrhein-Westfalen. She had been a member of the
Centrum Partie‡ in the Reichstag in 1933, had then left politics and
devoted herself to social work, often standing up to the Nazis. The
fourth, Senator Landehl of Hamburg, had been a Head Teacher, had
been dismissed immediately the Nazis seized power, and had spent the
next twelve years working as a printer. Would, I used to think to
myself, I have shown the courage that they had? For me to try to
preach Democracy to them would have been insulting. But one came
to realise that every liberal, humane and Christian German carried
with him the memory of an overwhelming defeat. These people
needed to feel that others were prepared to have confidence in them.
This could only be done through close personal relationships. The
great argument in favour of the British policy of deploying its
educational forces throughout the Zone and not concentrating them in

* Professor Dr Georg Eckert was a distinguished Professor of History at Brunswick
University and later Director of the International School Book Institute (founded in
1951). The significance lies in the involvement of a distinguished academic historian in
text-book preparation. Robert had a suspicion of History text-books, and rarely, if
ever, used them.
† Adolf Grimme was Prussian Minister of Education prior to the advent of Hitler. He
was Minister of Education in Lower Saxony 1946–49. From 1949–56 he was General
Director of the NordwestDeutsche Rundfunk (North-West German Radio). In 1945,
released from a prison camp, he turned up in Hanover unrecognised and asked at the
District Office about his friends. When he could not find them he went off without
giving his destination. Fortunately, someone in the Education Branch recalled the
name, a military vehicle was sent in pursuit and eventually he was discovered near
Hamburg. He was brought back to play a leading role in post-war Education. See
Arthur Hearnden: *The British in Germany*, p. 233.
‡ The Centre Party. Originally a mainly Catholic Party, hostile to Bismarck, strong
in the Rhineland.

the obvious seats of power, the capitals of the Länder and the Universities, as the Americans did, was that it made possible such personal relationships right through the whole educational system.

There was a third line of approach. Everything possible was done to encourage visits by German teachers abroad, especially to this country. This would have been quite impossible, of course, without the cooperation of people here. The difference in the attitude of the British after the Second World War from that adopted after the First was a remarkable phenomenon. In 1949 a Professor at the University of Münster told me that a quarter of the students there had been abroad since the end of the War. He himself had been one of the first party of German students to visit England after the First World War and that was in 1926, eight years after it had ended. Perhaps I might mention especially the arrangement under which young Lektoren from German Universities went for one year to a University in Britain, not as students but as members of the staff.

Particularly helpful, I believe, was the institution in the British Zone of short courses for German Secondary School teachers, held in Germany, to enable them to study the actual technique of teaching their own subject in company with teachers from Britain. In two years, from the summer of 1947 to the middle of 1949, sixty-three of these courses were held, attended by 2500 German Secondary School teachers, or one-fifth of those in the British Zone. But it should be realised that in those years most German Secondary School teachers were still older men and women, and it was generally the younger who came to these courses. In fact, almost half the Secondary School teachers in the British Zone under the age of forty-five took this opportunity to study the teaching of their subject along with teachers of another country, a record which surely must be unique in the history of Education.*

You will notice that I have said nothing about changes in the educational structure of Germany, comparable, for instance, with the arrangements made in the Soviet Zone to secure a proportion of children of workers at the Universities or the French insistence that the Abitur should be replaced by a written examination.† We made one attempt, however, which should be mentioned, the setting up of a

* Robert here paid tribute to the work of Miss Edith Davies, MBE, who originated and organised these courses. In her own Address to the Conference, Miss Davies quoted Adolf Grimme's remark in 1945: 'We stand before the void', adding, 'This applied to conquerors as well as conquered'.

† Not all subjects taken in the Abitur culminated in a written exam. Others were judged on continuous assessment etc.

German Commission to study the Universities and propose changes in them. (There were two foreign assessors, without votes, mainly to help contacts with other countries, Lord Lindsay★ from England and Professor von Salis of the Technical University in Zurich.) I think their Report was a very sensible and constructive one, but I cannot say that I think it had great influence. Not long ago a leading German educationist asked me if I had ever heard of a Report on the Universities which had come out in 1949. I admitted that I had heard of it. 'If only we had followed that Report,' he said, 'we might have saved ourselves many hectares of broken glass.'†

The Education Branch also did not become involved in German party politics, though I should say that most of its members found themselves in sympathy with the Social Democrats. Once, however, the Youth Section did become involved. The work of this section was inevitably somewhat detached from that of the rest of the Branch. One of its greatest successes was to persuade the various German Youth Organisations, especially the Catholic ones and the Social Democrat Falken, to work together. The compact was celebrated by a lunch given by the Land Commissioner of Nordrhein-Westfalen, a Major-General, who had once been a prominent Boy Scout. In his speech he said that he felt sure that we were all agreed on one point; that what we really wanted of any boy, be he German or British, was that he would grow up to be a good Christian Democrat. It took some time to persuade the leaders of the Falken after lunch that he had *not* meant what they thought he had.

On the whole, however, the British Army gave splendid support to the Education Branch of the Commission. I sometimes think that perhaps the most important step in the history of Education in the British Zone was Field Marshal Montgomery's order, not long after the end of the war, that in future no schools were to be taken over by the Army or the Control Commission. Once, however, there was real trouble about this and I tell the story as an example of some parts of the history of the Education Branch which naturally received no publicity. In 1947 it was decided to set up a boarding school for the children

★ Master of Balliol.

† The Report, partly through the highminded influence of Lord Lindsay, advocated certain tutorial and pastoral features of British universities, seeing preparation for intelligent citizenship as one element in University education. This conflicted with the conservative view that Universities were places solely for research and the pursuit of knowledge. The student riots of the late 1960s might have been less violent if the Universities had kept pace with social change. The smashing of University windows, as a symbol of the need to allow fresh air into the places, was carried out with German thoroughness.

of members of the Control Commission and the place chosen for it was what he had been during the War the Headquarters of the German Navy at Plön in Schleswig-Holstein. Up till then it had been occupied by the Royal Engineers. It was decided that they should be moved to an island in the Plöner See and this meant turning out a German boarding school which came under the Kultusministerium of Schleswig-Holstein. I protested as strongly as I could but without avail. The order for the moves was issued. And then I made a discovery. As a young man, the Direktor of the School had taught at an English Public School, Tonbridge, and the British Military Governor, Marshal of the Royal Air Force Sir Sholto Douglas, had been a boy there. So I wrote the Air Marshal a letter in which I gave once more all the arguments against closing the School and ended by saying it was particularly unfortunate because the Head Master had been for a time a Master at Tonbridge and he was successful in spreading the ideas he had learnt there throughout the schools of Schleswig-Holstein. (I may add that I told the Kultusminister in Kiel that he must support me in this.) The next thing that happened was that I was summoned to a meeting of the Chiefs of Staff at Hamburg. I went in and the Air Marshal spoke to me very severely. He was not used, he said, to having his orders questioned after they had been issued. 'However, gentlemen,' he said, turning to the Chiefs of Staff, 'I have heard recently that this school is in the position to make a unique contribution to German Education. I have decided, therefore, to change my mind. The Sappers will go to Flensburg.'

What the British educational policy could mean in those days was brought home to me most vividly by a simple incident. It took place not in the British Zone but in Berlin. Practically nothing I have said about Allied control of Education in Germany as a whole before August 1949 can be taken as applying to Berlin. For one thing Berlin, until it was forcibly split by the Russians on November 30th, 1948, was a single unit. It had a City Council, the Magistrat, controlled by the Allied Kommandantur with its Education Committee. Agreement had to be reached between all four occupying powers or nothing happened at all. A School Law was passed by the Magistrat in 1947 and eventually accepted by the Allied powers after a most prolonged game of diplomatic chess over the continued existence of the Bekenntnis-schulen. Agreement, however, was quite impossible on the teaching of History, a significant issue as it was here that the ideological differences between East and West were most apparent. Another point of difference which was never resolved was that of the status of the Universities in the City. The Russians insisted that the University of

Berlin, now called the Humboldt University, should come under
the control of the Administration of their Zone, not of Berlin, which
they had no right to do under the inter-allied agreements. In reply we
kept under our control the Technische Universität of Berlin-
Charlottenburg, which was in our Sector. In March 1948, three
students were expelled from the Humboldt University after they had
written anti-communist articles in a journal. The other students
protested with such success that the three were allowed back. But I
remember their saying that protest would not be so successful a second
time and that the only answer would be a new University. They were
quite right. It may be remembered that the Blockade of Berlin began
the day after it had been announced, on the evening of June 23rd, that
the new West German currency would be introduced into the three
Western Sections of Berlin. That night Ernst Reuter, who had been
elected Regierende Burgermeister* of Berlin, though the Russians
vetoed his appointment, along with three other political leaders (Herr
Neumann, Dr Peters and Dr Suhr) dined with Mr Creighton and
myself to discuss the question of founding a new University. I
suggested that we had better break off our discussion to listen to a
broadcast which we knew would be critical in the history of Berlin.
But they refused. 'That's all right,' they said. 'We were given copies of
the announcement before we left. We haven't had time to read it yet.
They are in our coats outside.' So four of the leading Germans in West
Berlin never heard the announcement which immediately brought on
the Blockade. They had something more important to consider, the
future of the youth of their City. From that moment I had no doubt
that we in West Berlin would win.

It is not always appreciated that for five months after the Blockade
began Berlin still remained an administrative unit. Towards the end of
November we became fully aware that the Russians would soon split
the City. It was one evening at that time, just before six o'clock, that I
was rung up at my office in the Fehrbellina Platz by a lady, Frau Dr
Panzer, who was responsible for the Secondary Schools of Berlin. She
spoke from her Department's Headquarters which were in the Russian
Sector. 'Mr Birley,' she said, 'the most dreadful things have happened
today. May I see you at once?' This was awkward as at half-past six I
was due to read a paper at my house to a Berlin Literary Society on the

---

* The Lord Mayor. Both Professor Ernst Reuter and Professor Dr Otto Suhr were
Lord Mayors of Berlin (Reuter died during the Blockade, 1948–9). T. R. M.
Creighton was for some time Head of the Education Branch in the City. Professor
Peters was a CDU member of the Berlin Town Parliament.

third scene of the Fourth Act of *Othello*. However, I suggested that we should both go straight to my house, where we might have a few minutes together before the meeting began. Unfortunately she was delayed and arrived at the same time as my guests. I still feel appalled at the thought that she had to sit through my paper, the discussions which followed it and then wait while we had refreshments. It was nearly half-past nine before the last guest left and I was able to ask her what had happened.

A few days before we had invited to Berlin Mr Lester Smith,* one of the leading figures in English educational administration, to look at the schools and then give a talk on what to do with a new School Law once one has one. All the officials in the education administration of the Magistrat and all the Schulrate had been summoned to listen to him. When he had finished he left to catch a plane at Gatow and then, immediately after, before the meeting broke up, in stalked the Russian Deputy Military Commandant of Berlin, with a revolver in his holster, and addressed the meeting. His speech was very violent and full of threats. He said that he knew quite well that money which should have been spent on Education was being used instead for the so-called Luftbrüche, the new air station at Tegel, and the Sturm Polizei. He added that the Russians knew quite well who were the supporters of educational reform and who were not and that the latter could expect no mercy.

She had taken shorthand notes of the speech and as she read them to me it became quite clear what it portended. The Russians had made this violent demonstration in order to frighten the educational administration into remaining with them when the Spaltung† we were all expecting took place.

'And then', she concluded, 'came the most Nazi moment I have known since the end of the War.' I asked her what she meant. 'A complete silence.' The remark was extremely significant. What happened after that I learnt mostly later on from others who were present. The silence was broken by Frau Dr Panzer who got up and made a reply which from all accounts was a magnificent performance. She began by telling the Russian General that he had no right, even if he were the representative of an Occupying Power, to bring his revolver into an educational meeting. She went on to tell him that he was lying, that he knew he was lying and, which she said was particularly insulting, that he knew that they knew he was lying.

* Dr W. D. Lester Smith, Director of Education for Manchester.
† The division of Germany.

The effect of her speech was to ruin completely the impact of the General's intervention. A few minutes later he went out of the room, leaving the argument to be continued, rather miserably, by the Communist members of the administration. It did not last long. I have no doubt that the future of Berlin education depended on that moment when she broke the silence and answered. If she had not done so, I do not believe that most of the educational administration and the Schulrate would have come over to the West, when the Spaltung came three days later, and with them eight hundred out of the eleven hundred students and all but two of the Professors and Lektoren of the Pädagogische Akademie,★ which, as it was attached to the Humboldt University, was under the control of the Russians.

My first action was to summon to my house members of the Education Branch in Berlin to inform them, as we had certain steps prepared to take immediately the Spaltung occurred. It was not until after midnight that I was alone with her again and able to ask her the question I had been wanting to put to her ever since I heard her story. 'Why did you do it?' The answer was immediate and may seem surprising. 'St George's in the East, Stepney.' She was referring to a Secondary Modern School in a very poor part of East London, a very remarkable school with an exceptional Headmaster.† We had arranged for her to spend four weeks in England a few months before. She had visited this school and had been deeply impressed by it. When she had returned to Berlin she said to me once, 'If I could have in Berlin three schools like St George's in the East, I could revolutionise the education of this city.' What it meant, of course, was that at that moment of crisis she felt that she could not cut herself off – not from anything so grandiloquent as Western Civilisation or the Free World – but from a particular school in London and the friends she had made there.

I have related this incident in some detail because it seems to me to sum up well our educational policy in Germany. First, this lady had been chosen by us for an important educational post because we knew that she had shown herself staunch in resistance to the Nazis. She had been caught distributing underground Social Democratic leaflets and had been condemned to a concentration camp, from which she had

★ College of Education.
† The Headmaster was Mr A. Bloom. He would not have envisaged that the way in which he conducted his school in Stepney would one day influence important events in Berlin. This element of chance in History and the unforeseen effects of idealism echoes the story of Herluin and the Abbey of Bec. St George's was closed in 1963 during educational reorganisation.

escaped during an air-raid. At the end of the War she was in the British Zone. She had become the personal friend of members of the British Education Branch in Berlin. We had been able to bring her into touch with British schools and teachers so that she really felt that she was a member of the same family, if I might put it in that way. What we had never attempted to do was to 're-educate' her, to teach her Democracy. That would have been an insult.

SOUTH
AFRICA

*Robert was Visiting Professor of Education at the University of
Witwatersrand for three years from 1964 to 1966. Even with his considerable knowledge of international affairs he had not expected the
Apartheid system to break in so constantly and harmfully in everyday life.
The most striking impression he gained was of the strength of White Liberal
opposition, which felt ignored by world opinion which regarded all Whites
as natural supporters of domination. There is not space here to describe all
the facets of Robert's involvement in education and politics in the Republic.
He taught in Soweto and other townships, sat on the governing bodies of
independent schools and gave moral and practical support to students and
teachers in the universities, who often risked their careers and personal
liberty by espousing causes denounced by the authorities. On a return visit
in 1970 he and Elinor attended a late-night group meeting of medical
students in Natal. Steve Biko was present and they talked far into the night,
as much about English literature as politics. Not long after, Robert said to
Denis Healey, who was going out to speak at Durban, that he thought the
most important person for him to see was, 'an African medical student as I
felt sure that in thirty years time he would be Prime Minister of South
Africa'. Denis Healey did seek out Steve Biko – this was before* Cry
Freedom *and the fame which Biko posthumously acquired – and said he
agreed. When Robert spoke at the Memorial Service for Robert Sobukwe in*

St Paul's Cathedral, he quoted from Steve Biko, 'who', he said, 'will remain for the rest of my life a companion'.

Relations with Nelson Mandela's family were even closer. When Winnie Mandela was sent to the remote hutments of Brandfort under the Banning Order, Elinor arranged for the despatch of shrubs and plants with which to enliven the dismal surroundings of Hut No. 802. She and Robert helped to ensure the care and education of the two Mandela daughters. When Winnie heard of Robert's death — she had no access to news or information and read of it by chance in an old newspaper in the back of a car that happened to be passing through — she wrote:

I am simply stunned with shock and deep sadness at not even having known about it . . . One of my greatest dreams was that of a huge re-union between him and Nelson, who never forgot to mention you in each one of his letters from time immemorial. As you know, to us we have lost a very dear member of the family. I do not even know how I'm going to get this letter to you. I simply pray God that someone passes by because it will never get to you from Brandfort. Nelson has been extremely heart broken by the tragic news. We had not stopped dreaming of the day he would meet Uncle Robert.

Only an expression that Robert used so frequently — 'probably one of the most remarkable things that has happened' — is adequate to describe this conjunction of a world that embraced the Foundation of a medieval King, Henley, Lord's, court dress for Speeches and the treasures of College Library, with the prisoner of Robben Island.

THE STATE AND EDUCATION

In 1959 the Government of South Africa, in a totally mis-named 'Extension of University Education Act', forced racial segregation on the English Universities. (Non-white students had never been accepted at the Afrikaner Universities.) Every year the students of Witwatersrand, Johannesburg and also at Natal arranged a lecture on Academic Freedom. At Witwatersrand at the end of the lecture (and there were two thousand present when Robert gave the Address in 1970) the audience would rise and repeat the declaration first made at the General Assembly of the University in 1959: '. . . It is our duty to uphold the principle that a University is a place where men and women without regard to race and colour are welcome to join in the acquisition and advancement of knowledge . . .' The strength of white liberal opposition is evidenced by this tradition, though coverage of South African affairs in the media still gives an almost wholly Black v. White picture of the situation. 'The State and Education' was the Inaugural Lecture given by Robert on the 16th June 1964 on his appointment as Visiting Professor of Education. It is relatively cautious as befits an Inaugural Address, but it concludes with a description of opposition to State control in Germany which must have signalled very clearly what he saw as the role assigned to him in South Africa. Gloucester Grammar School, referred to in the second paragraph, enjoyed a monopoly of education in the city. Two of its schoolmasters brought an action for loss of earnings when someone endeavoured to found a rival establishment. Justice Thirning declared that the Common Law Court could not try the case as it was a matter for the Ecclesiastical Courts.

IT IS, I BELIEVE, customary for a Professor, when delivering an inaugural lecture, to make a proper obeisance of respect to his immediate predecessor in the chair. I am in some difficulty about this, for a Visiting Professor has no predecessor to refer to. I hope I may substitute for a person a book. This book, with the title, *The Open*

Universities in South Africa,★ is no doubt well known to many of you. I admire it for its purpose and for the style in which this purpose is presented. It is not, I think, inappropriate for me to refer to it. I can say that it was due to this little book and the stand for Academic Freedom of which it was the expression that I am now in South Africa and addressing you. For it was my appreciation of what the University of the Witwatersrand stood for then and what it stands for now that made the invitation I received from it to come as a Visiting Professor quite irresistible. My only complaint is that I cannot escape from feeling some embarrassment in speaking on a subject, 'The State and Education', which has been so well dealt with in this book already. I shall try to deal with it from the point of view of an historian, albeit a very amateur historian. And I shall draw occasionally on my own experience. For, although I have spent most of my life in very pleasant waters where the State does not interfere with education at all, for two and a half years after the war, when I was responsible for education in the British Zone of Germany and the British sector of Berlin, I suppose it might have been said without very much exaggeration that in this field I was the State myself.

A history of the relations between the State and Education would have to give most of its space to events in the last two hundred years, for it is only during this period that governments have played more than a rather fitful part in the provision and control of education. Before then education was generally regarded as the concern of the Church. Not only in England, but throughout Western Europe, the great dictum of Mr Justice Thirning in the Gloucester Grammar School case of 1440 would usually have been accepted without much question, 'Le doctrine et enformation des enfants est chose espiritual'. When the State took a hand by building schools or universities, or, more often, by encouraging their foundation, it was generally because the government of the day was lending its support to some religious denomination. Churches, whether they are established Churches or rival denominations or sects, have had a different aim in education from that of the State. The best expression of this that I know is to be found in the answer of the Headmaster of a Roman Catholic School in England not long ago to a gushing parent who asked him to tell her what his school educated boys for. His very succinct reply was, 'For death, madam.'

A school or university controlled by the Church, however, could

---

★ A publication produced by the Universities of Capetown and Witwatersrand as a result of a conference on the value of non-segregated Universities.

have other aims as well. When some religious leader, such as Luther in his *Letter to the Burger-masters of Germany on behalf of Christian Schools* or John Knox in his *First Book of Discipline*, advocated the provision of schools by the secular power, they had in mind the preparation of the pupils for life as well as death. But in the very great majority of cases the religious aim came first. The Massachusetts Law of 1647, establishing an elementary school in every town of fifty householders and a Grammar School where there were a hundred, is often taken as one of the first examples of the State itself making provision for education. But the wording of the Law shows that it was religion that the State legislation had primarily, though not, it is true, exclusively in mind.

> It being one chief piece of that old deluder, Satan, to keep men from the knowledge of the Scriptures, as in former times by keeping them in an unknown tongue, so in these later times by persuading them from the use of tongues, that so at least the true sense and meaning of the original might be clouded by false glosses of saint seeming deceivers – that learning may not be buried in the grave of our fathers in the Church and Commonwealth, the Lord assisting our endeavours – It is therefore ordered that every township in this jurisdiction, after the Lord hath increased them to a number of fifty householders, shall then forthwith appoint one within their town to teach all such children as shall resort to him to read and write . . .

During the sixteenth and seventeenth centuries, however, as the power of the State increased, there were repeated instances of governments being prepared to intervene in education, not only in support of some religious denomination, but for purely secular ends. Thus we find King Henry VIII bringing victory to the Grecians at Oxford against the Trojans, who were resisting the introduction of Greek into the University curriculum. In the 1530s and 1540s the Archduke Ferdinand of Austria even went so far as to appoint royal officials to enforce regular lecturing at the University of Vienna and to lay down detailed regulations about the instruction to be given to the students. Princes, especially in Germany, began to found their own universities, mainly no doubt as a kind of status symbol, but also to ensure that young men would be trained for the administration of the State in the way they wanted.

The Church had been working in this field for so long, that when the State eventually marched in to claim it as its own, a conflict was inevitable. An immense new battle-front appeared in the long struggle between Church and State. The contest is far from over. Since the end of the last war it has caused acute political crises in France, Germany,

Italy, Belgium and Holland. I can well remember the anxious days when it seemed that inability to reach agreement on the status of the Confessional Schools would wreck the efforts being made to draw up the Constitution of the German Federal Republic. But this is a question which has been exhaustively studied by historians already. I wish to consider rather some of the causes and effects of the gradual assumption by the State in Western Europe and America of the duty to provide education itself for the people. But in such a study we should never forget the rival claims of the Church, constantly asserted and defended and continually influencing the decisions of governments and peoples.

It is not surprising that the earliest example since classical times of the direct intervention of the State in education should be found in the thirteenth century. It was then that Christian theology came to terms with Greek philosophy and made possible the civilisation to which we now belong. With the discovery of the works of Aristotle the State became, as it were, self-conscious; men began to consider what the State was there for. I refer to the creation of the University of Naples by the Emperor Frederick II in 1224. Far from being an instance of the State supporting the Church in its educational task, it was founded in direct opposition to the Church. It had no faculty of theology. Its purpose was to produce trained lawyers and administrators for Frederick's kingdom of Sicily and his subjects in that kingdom were forbidden to resort to any other university. However, in spite of the fact that St Thomas Aquinas studied there, Frederick's university is of little importance in the history of education. Once Naples and Sicily had been conquered by Charles of Anjou, forty years after its foundation, it became a university controlled by the Church. Frederick II, who it has been claimed was the most remarkable figure in European history between Charlemagne and Napoleon, was in this, as in so many other ways, before his time.

It is almost always impossible to say with any certainty of any new idea in politics or sociology that a certain moment was the moment of its birth. But if one studies the early appearances of the idea, appearances which were only transitory and seemingly futile, one can often learn a great deal by considering what were the fundamental assumptions of the author who produced the idea so long before its due time. What one has to wait for is for these assumptions to be generally accepted: only when this has happened has the new idea some chance of being accepted also. I felt that it might be interesting – more interesting at least than producing an historical sketch of the development of State education – to consider first three books written in the sixteenth century which advocated State control of education, such as was quite impracticable at the time, and to see what were the underlying assumptions of their authors. We shall find brought out in them all the main principles which eventually governed such State control and also the problems which it was to create. Of these three books, one made a considerable impression at the time it was published: the other two passed quite unheeded. In fact, one of them did not appear in print until over three hundred years after it was written.

The Dialogue between Reginald Pole and Thomas Lupset was written in about 1535 by Thomas Starkey, Master of Corpus Christi College, Cambridge, but not published until 1871. Starkey wished to see administrative burdens laid on the government, which no government at the time could possibly have borne. It was to organise agriculture, regulate rents, abolish poverty, and codify and simplify the Common Law. He advocated also compulsory education for all children from the age of seven and the establishment of schools by the government, which would pay for the education of the most promising scholars from them at the universities, which were themselves to be reformed by the State. These favoured pupils were to be selected by specially appointed 'conservators of the common weal'. When we turn to consider his underlying assumptions about the State we find that he appreciated that any such control by the government would be impossible under an absolute monarchy; it could only be accomplished if power were in the hands of a Council, approved by Parliament. Although his attitude was essentially aristocratic, he realised, or at least sensed, that a government strong enough to do what he wanted would have to be more broadly based than the government of his time. Above all, he had an optimistic belief in the efficacy of education which foreshadows the views of the philosophers of the eighteenth-century Enlightenment. 'This good education of youth in virtuous exercise', he said, 'is the ground of the remedying of all other diseases of our politic body.'

The most remarkable of the three books was the *Dichaearchiae Henrici regis Progymnasmata*, published about 1556, by Raoul Spifame, a mysterious figure of whom little is known. There is some evidence that the book was written when the author was in a lunatic asylum. It takes the extraordinary form of 309 royal edicts, which he imagines to have been issued by King Henry II of France. They are so persuasive that several eighteenth-century historians believed that they were genuine. They cover almost every aspect of social and economic life in astonishing detail: control of agriculture and of the ownership of land, town planning, the codification of the law, the responsibility of the

State to provide work for the unemployed, the establishment of isolation hospitals for infectious diseases, the obligation laid on publishers to deposit one copy of every book in the royal library, the provision of bands in public parks – he seems to think of everything. He goes much further than any other sixteenth-century writer in his educational programme. There were to be schools in every parish with compulsory attendance from the age of six, and free education, at least for the children of the poor. The most prophetic part of the book was his insistence that education was a right which could be claimed by all. When we consider his fundamental assumptions we find that he faced squarely the question of the position of the Church. It was to come wholly under the State. All ecclesiastical privileges were to be abolished and the salaries of the clergy were to be fixed and paid by the State, which would also establish a pension fund for them.

Jean Bodin's *Six Livres de la Republique*, published in 1576, was, in contrast, a book the importance of which was recognised at once. An absolute and perpetual power, he believed, must belong to the State, and there are passages in the book which suggest that he held that this should rest on some kind of popular sovereignty, though he never developed the idea. What was really original in Bodin was the assumption, implied throughout the book, that the existence of the State was in no sense due to divine will; it existed to fulfil the needs of men. When we read of the duties which Bodin lays on the government, we are hardly surprised to find that the complete organisation and administration of education was one of them. And he introduces a new principle of the greatest importance for the future. He realised that the State, if it was to perform all these duties, must be united. He saw in its control of education the means whereby the State could give society the unity of sentiment once, but no longer, provided by the Church.

Already, when considering these three writers, we have met almost all the main questions which the provision of education by the State has raised during the last two hundred years: the need for a basis for State sovereignty stronger than that provided by the Divine Right of Kings; the need for the State to assert that sovereignty over the Church; the belief that the State existed to meet human needs, of which education was one; the concept of education as a human right; the necessity for financial assistance from the State for individual children if that right was to be granted; the optimistic belief in the value of education to solve political problems; and finally the idea that the State should use the education it provided to promote unity.

During the eighteenth century we can see men beginning to accept the principles of which these writers had been the prophets. The most important developments before the French Revolution were in Germany. The subsequent rise to greatness of the kingdom of Prussia has led historians to single out for attention the institution of the system of compulsory education there by Frederick William I in 1717. But he was only following the example of other German princes. As early as 1619 a decree of Duke Ludwig V of Hesse had made education compulsory for all children in the State of Hesse; it was said of Gotha under Duke Ernst the Pious, who had made attendance at schools obligatory in 1648, that the peasants in his principality were better educated than noblemen elsewhere. What made the Prussian example so important was that its rulers showed that they were ready to remove education from the control of the Church. This was even more evident in the sphere of the university. It was from the German universities of this period that all modern universities derive. Of them I shall have to say something in due course.

Before the Revolution of 1789 there was nothing to show in France in any way comparable to the educational movement in Germany. But what manifested itself in that country was a belief which was of even greater importance for the future. This was the belief in the efficacy of education, derived largely from the philosophical writings of John Locke. His picture of a child's mind as a 'yet empty cabinet', waiting to be furnished, seemed to lend to education an importance not appreciated before, at least since the days of Plato and Aristotle. It was, no doubt, a highly dangerous idea, giving rise only too easily to a facile optimism. We cannot but smile when we read how Turgot, the statesman whose proposals for reform might have prevented the Revolution if he had been given proper support against the vested interests of his time, once solemnly told King Louis XVI that if he only introduced universal education, 'in ten years your nation will be no longer recognisable'. Jean-Jacques Rousseau was for once forced to speak in terms of practical politics by being asked in 1769 to suggest a new constitution for Poland. He found himself obliged in the end to admit that the only practical step would be to establish a national system of education, as this would eventually turn even the Poles into a people capable of creating a stable State. But, though we may smile, we have to admit that it was this absurdly optimistic opinion which did most to persuade men to regard the provision of education as one of the inescapable duties of the State. King Louis XVI might ignore the advice of Turgot; the popular leaders of 1789 could not.

It is not surprising, therefore, that we find in the French Constitution of 1791 a specific statement that it was the duty of the State to establish a system of public education. It is with a clause in this Constitution that the history of relations between the State and Education in modern society may be said to begin. 'There shall be created and organised a system of public instruction common to all citizens and free in respect of those subjects which are indispensable to all men. Schools of various grades shall be established according to need throughout the whole kingdom.'

The attempts by the French Assemblies during the Revolution to bring this clause into effect are a story of repeated frustrations. Education laws were introduced into the National Assembly in 1791 and into the Legislative Assembly in 1792, but both bodies were dissolved before they were passed. A law introduced into the Convention was dropped on the fall of Robespierre. It was not until 1795 that the Directory actually established a national system of public instruction, but it only did so on paper and little or nothing was done. Napoleon, indeed, by his law creating the Imperial University of 1806 established secondary education in France on a firm enough foundation to last until the present day, but he was not in the least interested in primary education. It was not until 1833 that a system of primary education, which was to endure, was started in France and not until 1895 that a system of free education provided by the State, as enacted in principle in the Constitution of 1791, was finally achieved.

Why was there this long delay? Similar delays were experienced by other countries. Governments in France believed in the provision of free education by the State. Why was it not provided? The reason was the same as that which has frustrated all similar experiments in the past, bringing some of them to nothing at all and causing others to amount to very little: in Massachusetts and the New England colonies, in Scotland and in the principalities of Germany, including Prussia. No one yet appreciated that the provision of free education for all children made demands on the State which were far greater than any that had ever been made on it before. It was only possible if the State had a financial and administrative system which could ensure that schools were not only built, but maintained. It was to the great credit of the French government in 1833 that it did more than state a principle; it decided how the necessary funds were to be raised, mostly from local taxation, with subventions, where necessary, from central funds. Still, other States before France in 1833 had not been wholly unmindful of the fact that education must be paid for. What made the French Education Law of 1833 successful was the fact that France during the Revolution had already created a system of local administration which could be used to sustain this immense new burden.

Matthew Arnold, who understood the need for a popular system of education better than anyone else in England in the nineteenth century, never spoke more wisely than when he said in 1868, 'The real preliminary to an effective system of popular education is, in fact, to provide the country with an effective Municipal organisation.'

Before the eighteenth century it was the view of most men that education for the working classes was not only unnecessary, but positively dangerous. This was stated very firmly in Richelieu's *Political Testament*, the most influential political document on the continent of Europe of the seventeenth century. He saw in too much education something which would ruin agriculture and make it impossible to recruit soldiers, for, he said, they could only be found if there were enough ignorant men, who alone could be expected to follow a military calling. In the social conditions of the time there was a good deal to be said for this view. It was held by many well into the nineteenth century, especially when to the fear that labourers might get above their station was added the fear that education might lead to political unrest, a danger which Richelieu had also appreciated. Popular disaffection, wrote Lord Wilton in *Fraser's Magazine* for December, 1830, might be credited to 'the march of education, to the malign nastiness of schoolmasters, to the spurious morality of the present day, and the dangerous influence of Mr Henry, now Lord Brougham, and cheap libraries.' When one reads the impassioned pleas of writers of the eighteenth-century Enlightenment for education, it is always as well to discover whom, in fact, they meant to be educated. They almost always excluded the working-classes. It is true that sometimes the belief that education should be provided for all children for religious reasons conflicted with this view. The charitable organisations which founded and maintained a remarkable number of schools for poor children in England during the eighteenth century were tortured by this dilemma. On the one hand the schools were necessary to save the country from the danger of Popery and the children from growing up to be a menace to society; on the other hand every care was taken to ensure that the children were not taught so much that they would become dissatisfied with their lot as hewers of wood and drawers of water.

In time, however, the hewing of wood and the drawing of water became a more complicated business, and it came to be realised that the new techniques of industrial production made necessary rather more education for the worker. Moreover, if members of the poorer classes were to take part in government through the exercise of the vote, it was arguable that they would do so more wisely if they had received some education. 'We must educate our masters', in fact. But Robert Lowe never made this classic utterance, which is always attributed to him. Nor, for that matter, did anyone else. What he said, in the debate on the Second Reform Bill which gave the vote to the urban working-classes in 1867, was something a good deal more banal: 'I believe it will be absolutely necessary that you should prevail on our future masters *to learn their letters.*' If one probes into the minds of many in the eighteenth and nineteenth centuries who advocated a system of national education, one will find only too often that their reasons were prudential ones and that they did not want the provision of popular education to go any further than was absolutely necessary. This attitude was superbly expressed by Wordsworth in some lines from *The Excursion*, which must surely be regarded as one of the supreme examples of bathos in all literature.

> O for the coming of that glorious time
> When, prizing knowledge as her noblest wealth
> And best protection, this imperial Realm,
> While she exacts allegiance, shall admit
> An obligation, on her part, to *teach*
> Them who are born to serve her and obey;
> Binding herself by statute to secure
> For all her children, whom her soil maintains,
> The rudiment of letters.

Some, no doubt, would have gone rather further. They felt that in a democratic State the people must receive at least enough education to make them a satisfactory check on the government. One of these, Thomas Jefferson, declared in his *Notes on the State of Virginia*, written in 1781, 'In every government on earth is some trace of human weakness, some germ of corruption and degeneracy, which cunning will discover and wickedness insensibly open, cultivate and improve. Every government degenerates when trusted to the rulers of the people alone. The people therefore are its only safe depositories. And to render even them safe, their minds must be improved to a certain degree.'

'To a certain degree.' Even Jefferson was not prepared to go very far. In the end all these various prudential reasons in favour of popular education have done little to advance it – in fact they have often retarded it – in comparison with another, which has been the dynamic force in the slow progress towards its establishment since the days of the French Revolution. This force has been the principle of equality. It was stated first by the French statesman, mathematician and philosopher, Condorcet, in his Report when he introduced his Education Law before the Legislative Assembly in April, 1792. The purpose of his law, he declared, and of the educational system it would set up, was 'to establish among the citizens an equality in fact, making real the political equality recognised by law.' It was expressed with the greatest possible force by Matthew Arnold in 1871. Already Disraeli had told England that it formed 'two nations, the Privileged and the People'. Matthew Arnold went further than Disraeli. He showed what the division into two nations, or as he would have put it into three, really meant. This passage has claims to be the most revolutionary statement made by any Englishman in the Victorian era. Once its truth, its absolutely shocking truth, was accepted, educational equality in England became inevitable.

> What the middle class sees is that splendid piece of materialism, the aristocratic class, with a wealth and luxury utterly out of their reach, with a standard of social life and manners, the offspring of that wealth and luxury, seeming utterly out of their reach also. And thus they are thrown back upon themselves – upon a defective type of religion, a narrow range of intellect and knowledge, a stunted sense of beauty, a low standard of manners. And the lower class see before them the aristocratic class, and its civilization, such as it is, even more infinitely out of *their* reach than that of the middle class; while the life of the middle class, with its unlovely type of religion, thought, beauty, and manners, has naturally in general, no great attractions for them either. And so they are thrown back upon themselves; upon their beer, their gin, and their *fun*. Now, then, you will understand what I meant by saying that our inequality materializes our upper class, vulgarizes our middle class, brutalizes our lower. And the greater the inequality, the more marked is its bad action upon the middle and lower class.

All those who live in a country where equality of education has not yet been achieved should ponder on this devastating passage, making, of course, the necessary changes in the picture to fit it to the social conditions of their own country and their own time.

I cannot in this lecture refer to more than one or two educational problems to see what light they throw on the question of the relation between the State and Education. Among them is the question of the organisation of secondary education. The abortive French Education Law of 1791 drew a distinction between the education which was indispensable for all, to be provided free, and that which was a preparation for professional life, for which fees would be charged. We may see here in embryonic form the common distinction between elementary or primary and secondary education. One of the results of the acceptance of the principle of educational equality has been the demand for, and in due course the provision of, what is sometimes styled 'secondary education for all'. The question then arises inevitably whether this secondary education should be given to all children (other than those who go to a private school) in some kind of common school, as in the United States, for instance, or in this country, or in schools distinguished from one another by the ability or interests of the pupils, as is still usual in England or Germany. No one can reasonably suggest that this is something which can be left to each secondary school in the State system to decide for itself. The decision is one that must be made by the State authorities; whether national, provincial or local does not affect this issue. The question will no doubt be settled largely on social grounds, though it is bound to affect the kind of education that is provided. In fact, it is now-a-days usually impossible to keep separate social and educational factors in dealing with educational problems. Another issue where the State intervened in the affairs of educational institutions was that of the imposition of religious tests at the Universities of Oxford and Cambridge. These two Universities were forced to become 'open' ones by a series of Acts of Parliament. Few would now hold that the State made an unjustifiable incursion on the Academic Freedom of the Universities by doing so. The change was not carried through for educational reasons, but again for social ones.

It is only if this fact is appreciated – in the modern State governments are bound to interfere, if that is the right word, with educational institutions, and this interference is often going to affect the education they provide – that it is possible to make any realistic study of the two questions which have become matters of vital importance in the sphere of education during the last two centuries. These are, first, the question whether the State has the right to control the teaching provided in educational institutions, or at least to interfere with it, and, secondly, whether teachers, by virtue of the fact that they influence the minds of young people, should stand aside from the political struggles of their time. May I draw your attention to the fact that I have been deliberately using the term, 'educational institutions', for I very much doubt whether Academic Freedom can be preserved in the universities of a country if it has been abandoned in the schools. Naturally one must make allowances for the fact that the minds of pupils at school are less mature than those of students at a university. When dealing with this, as with any other aspect of the question of Freedom, one should not lose sight of Common Sense.

It is necessary to emphasise this point. One of the commonest lines of attack by those who oppose Freedom, whether in writing or speaking or teaching, is to use the argument of the *reductio ad absurdum*. They point to some example of the exercise of this freedom which is clearly a breach of the law or of ordinary morality or decency, and from this they infer that any freedom of expression is dangerous. But the great advocates of the Freedom of the Press, for instance, have never upheld the view that this freedom is absolute. Having had the honesty to accept this limitation, they have inevitably laid themselves open to the charge that they have given away their case. But it is just as absurd, just as much a *reductio ad absurdum*, to say that because there must be some restraints on the press, no freedom should be allowed to it at all.

The case against Academic Freedom was never stated more decisively than by Napoleon in 1805. 'Of all political questions,' he said, 'that of education is perhaps the most important. There cannot be a firmly established political state unless there is a teaching body with definitely recognised principles. If the child is taught from infancy that he ought to be a republican or a monarchist, a Catholic or a free-thinker, the State will not constitute a nation; it will rest on uncertain and shifting foundations; and will be constantly exposed to disorder and change.'

We should not underestimate the force of this argument. What it amounts to is this. In any secular state the government, whatever form it takes, must act according to some principles. On these it must decide what the secular needs of the community are and how they shall be met. Can it be expected to allow its children, in the schools and universities it maintains or helps to maintain, to be taught what contradicts these principles? Is there not even something cynical in allowing this to happen?

I should say at once that it is almost impossible for an Englishman to face this issue squarely. For him the freedom of academic institutions has been taken so completely for granted for so long that he does not feel it necessary to defend it. H. A. L. Fisher, President of the Board of Education just after the First World War, once told me that, while he had held that position, he had always been careful never on any public occasion to praise or condemn any book in case it might be thought that the Government was recommending or disapproving its use in schools. Nothing shows more clearly the attitude of Englishmen towards this problem than their resolute refusal to believe that any problem about Academic Freedom could ever arise at all. When we consider the history of the world during the last hundred years, their

complacency seems almost incredible. Occasionally they recognise
dimly that the situation might arise when a government would try to
control the content of education. But if this happened, the remedy was
obvious, to change the government. In his great speech in the House
of Commons on 30 July, 1833, introducing a motion in favour of the
provision of compulsory education, John Roebuck attempted to face
the issue. 'If the State or Government cannot be trusted, it is a proof
that the Government is a bad one; if so, get rid of it, reform it, make it a
good one.' Thirty years later Matthew Arnold, who at least knew
something of what was happening in other countries, was to show the
same complacency. 'Any exaggeration of the action of the State in
France,' he wrote, 'furnishes no reason for absolutely refusing to
enlarge the action of the State in England; because the genius and
temper of the people of this country are such as to render impossible
the exaggeration which the genius and temper of the French people
rendered easy.' A few thinkers, such as Price and Godwin, showed
themselves aware in the eighteenth century that it might not be as
simple as that. Only John Stuart Mill in a moment of apocalyptic
vision saw precisely what the danger was, when he wrote in his 'Essay
on Bentham' in the *Westminster Review* of 1838:

> Is it at all times and places good for mankind to be under the absolute
> authority of the majority themselves? We say the authority, not the
> political authority merely, because it is chimerical to suppose that what-
> ever has absolute power over men's bodies will not arrogate it over their
> minds – will not seek to control (not perhaps by legal penalties, but by the
> persecutions of society) opinions and feelings which depart from its
> standard, will not attempt to shape the education of the young by its
> model, and to extinguish all books, all schools, all combinations of
> individuals for joint action upon society, which may be attempted for the
> purpose of keeping alive a spirit at variance with its own.

An Englishman would be well advised to turn to some thinker from
another country if he is to find a valid defence of Academic Freedom.
He is more likely to find there someone who will take the problem
seriously. This defence was never more cogently or more eloquently
stated than in the great Report on Education presented by Condorcet
to the National Assembly on April 20 and 21, 1792.

> Freedom of teaching constitutes, in a sense, one of the rights of the human
> race . . . Since truth alone is useful and since any error is an evil, by what
> right would any power, no matter what it might be, dare to determine
> what is truth and what is error? Moreover, a power which has served as the

basis for enacted laws, would attack directly the freedom of thought, would contradict the purpose of every social institution, namely, the improvement of the laws, which necessarily follows from conflicts of opinions and the spread of enlightenment . . . For that matter, the French Constitution makes such independence our rigorous duty . . . Should we, in reality, have respected the inalienable independence of the people, if we had permitted the government to fortify any particular system of belief with all the weight which universal instruction could give it, and would not the power which would arrogate to itself the right to choose our opinions have undoubtedly usurped a portion of the national sovereignty?

This passage from one of the finest statements ever made about education deserves careful analysis. All that I can do now is to point out that it lays down two principles and it is on these that the defence of Academic Freedom in a modern society must be based.

The first principle is that one of the very demands which the State exists to supply is the demand for the freedom of the individual to search for Truth. It is taking away from man an inalienable right if he is prohibited from doing so. He becomes something less than man or, at least, an incomplete man. One of the gifts he has received from God must then, to use Hamlet's phrase, 'rust in as unused'. The second principle is that the State which refuses to allow the search for Truth will be a less efficient State than the one which permits it. This is an exceedingly difficult principle for many to accept. We may note the contrast between Napoleon's words and those of Condorcet. For Napoleon a State which allowed freedom of teaching would be 'constantly exposed to disorder and change'. To any government which thinks it has found the ideal solution to its problems, change is sure to seem something to be avoided at all costs. But we know that in individual men a belief that one knows all the answers, a refusal to pay heed to criticism, a determination to ensure that one does not even hear it, are taken as signs, not of intelligence, but of stupidity. Exactly the same is true of governments. All history teaches us how stupid governments can be. The historian, looking back on the disasters into which governments have led people by this kind of arrogance, is tempted to exclaim in despair with Schiller, 'Mit der Dummheit kämpfen Götter selbst vergebens.' (Against stupidity the gods themselves struggle in vain.)

Condorcet, on the other hand, believed that change was necessary, for how could laws ever be improved without change? And this improvement, he held, could only come out of 'the conflict of ideas'. That was the great lesson taught to the world by the Greeks: that Truth, unless it comes from divine revelation, comes out of a dialectical encounter. An Englishman can at least claim that this principle was never more finely expressed than by an English writer, John Milton. 'Let her and Falsehood grapple; who ever knew Truth put to the worse, in a free and open encounter?'

The tradition expressed in Milton's words has indeed been in grave peril in many countries during this century. In February, 1948, I had the misfortune to be in Prague during the Communist *coup d'état*, spending most of my time with men who knew that their lives' work was being destroyed. One evening just after the *coup* was over, I was talking with Professor Vocadlo, the Professor of English at Prague University, and he told me that he had been asked to sign a document stating that he approved of the changes made in the constitution of the University, changes which destroyed completely its Academic Freedom. He had refused to do so. 'How was I to sign such a statement,' he said, 'I, who teach my students about Milton and Shelley?' I asked him if this meant that he would be dismissed. He said that that was certain, but he added that he did not think that this would happen at once. 'After all,' he said, 'I am a double blue.' I knew what he meant. On his wrist were tattooed the two numbers he had had as a prisoner in both Buchenwald and Auschwitz.

'Who ever knew Truth put to the worse, in a free and open encounter?' It is not true, of course. Milton disregarded the prejudices, the stupidity and the gullibility of men. But at least we know that without such an encounter there is no chance of discovering Truth at all.

It is the duty of a university to force men to face the Truth. In an age when the State is more powerful than ever before in history this is more than ever its responsibility. For a State in which this free and open encounter is feared and therefore prohibited is bound to come to disaster. It will be unable to see what is happening. It will be unable to decide on the changes in policy made necessary perhaps by economic evolution, changes in methods of production or the organisation of industry, or perhaps by changes in the minds and attitudes of men, as when new classes or races attain political consciousness. To face facts is often an exceedingly painful process. Unless men are taught to do so by an education which allows unpopular or unfashionable views to be expressed and defended, one can be sure that governments will shrink from doing so.

Now it is obvious that during the twentieth century the principle of Academic Freedom has been subjected to some devastating onslaughts. Of these the most serious have been its total suppression in Soviet Russia and in the Communist satellite states, its suppression in

Germany under the Nazis, and the witch-hunt in the United States carried out by Senator McCarthy and his followers. From the first of these we cannot be expected to learn much. A supporter of Communist theories of the State is bound to reject the principle of Academic Freedom; one who does not accept them will not be influenced by the Communist example. From the other two we can learn a great deal. In the time available I can only consider one and I shall attempt to see what lessons can be gained from a study of the collapse of the German universities before Hitler.

To the student of the history of education the failure of the German universities to offer any resistance to the Nazis may well seem almost inexplicable. Germany can claim with every justification to have created the modern university. The foundation of the University of Halle in 1692 was one of the decisive moments in the history of European civilisation. Christian Thomasius, now almost entirely forgotten, was among the foremost thinkers of the second half of the seventeenth century and his name should be held in reverence by all those who believe in Academic Freedom. A native of Saxony, he found himself in serious trouble for criticising a book by the Court preacher in Denmark. The Danish government demanded that he should be punished and in 1690 the Elector of Saxony forbade him to lecture and threatened him with prosecution. Thomasius left Leipzig for Prussia and the Elector Frederick III allowed him to lecture at the Academy of Halle. Two years later, under his influence, Halle was raised to the status of a University and he was its first Professor of Jurisprudence. It was laid down in its statutes that it was to be free to members of all denominations and that it was to work for the conciliation of all Christians. Halle was, in fact, the first true 'open university'. Its influence in Germany was immense and was to lead to the foundation in 1737 of the University of Göttingen, which has been called the first modern university, where the study of medicine and natural sciences was substituted for that of orthodox Protestant theology and scholastic philosophy, where the study of the classics was carried on in such a way as to prepare men for a life of political and administrative activity, where historical research was directed towards the study of the development of civilisation and of the economic and social conditions of the past, where the students were expected to study contemporary politics, and where seminars were held in which the current newspapers were discussed. The contrast with the picture of Oxford University in Gibbon's *Autobiography* is certainly embarrassing for an Englishman. Or we may look forward to the days of Wilhelm von Humboldt and the founding of the University of Berlin in 1809. Von Humboldt insisted that the University must serve the German nation, but that it could only do so if it was granted administrative autonomy and its professors liberty to teach as they wished. Almost without exception the American professors who laid the foundations of freedom in the universities of the United States paid tribute to the inspiration of the universities of Germany.

'The French University has no liberty,' wrote Matthew Arnold, 'and the English Universities have no Science; the German Universities have both.' *Lehrfreiheit*, freedom of inquiry and freedom of teaching, was regarded as the hall-mark of the German profession. The very term, Academic Freedom, is a translation from the German, *Die akademische Freiheit*. Academic Freedom was, in its origin, not an English but a German concept. How is it possible to explain why the German universities put up no resistance to the rise to power of a political party which they knew was bound to destroy their freedom?

We may note first that *Lehrfreiheit* in Germany was regarded as the prerogative only of the universities, not of the schools. After the failure of the Revolution of 1848 the last vestiges of freedom were lost in the schools. Bismarck, when addressing a meeting of schoolmasters, said once, 'As teachers, you do not only represent the Ministry of Education, but the Government itself.' Moreover, the privilege of Academic Freedom in the universities was only enjoyed on sufferance. The German universities had never been independent corporations like those in England. Oxford University had been defined in the early eighteenth century in a telling phrase as 'that English Avignon or independent ecclesiastical State in the heart of the Kingdom of Britain'. It had needed State intervention on more than one occasion to shake the English universities out of their torpor, but they had never lost their legal independence. The German universities were either the creation of Princes or had been taken over by them at the time of the Reformation. It was in the great days of Thomasius, who once defined Halle as a place of 'unfettered freedom, yes, freedom, which is the very life of the spirit and without which human reason is as good as dead', that Christian Wolff, the disciple of Leibniz and, after him, the greatest figure of the Enlightenment in Germany, was summarily dismissed from that University by King Frederick William I, who had disapproved of one of his lectures. In 1792 a new legal code in Prussia stated specifically that the universities were institutions of the State. Whenever during the nineteenth century there was a reaction towards absolutism, the German universities were made to appreciate their position. The expulsion of the Professors from Göttingen in 1837, the famous Göttingen Seven, for protesting against the illegal revocation of the Constitution of Hanover by King Ernst August, is often taken as the decisive defeat of the cause of Freedom in the German universities. After 1871 under the Empire, however, there was little to show that the *Lehrfreiheit* of the professors was endangered by the government. The professors had become a branch of the civil service and a highly privileged branch at that. They had no wish to jeopardise their position and politically they almost invariably supported the government. Only once was it necessary to crack the whip, in 1890, when Dr Leo Arons, a Privatdozent at the University of Berlin, was dismissed for making speeches in support of the Social Democrats. It is true that the Philosophical faculty of the University protested, but in their protest they admitted that university teachers were not 'free and independent citizens' and that as members of a State institution they ought to accept a special code of behaviour.

There was a deeper reason, however, why the German universities came to take up a position of neutrality in all matters outside the realm of the university itself. For they came to hold that any participation in political affairs involved their compromising their personal dedication to the search for truth and the pursuit of learning. This point of view was expressed with the utmost clarity and force by Friedrich Paulsen, perhaps the greatest of all historians of education.

> Scholars cannot and should not engage in politics. They cannot do so if they have developed their capacities in accordance with the demands of their calling. Their business is scientific research, and scientific research calls for constant examination of thoughts and theories in order to harmonise them with the facts. Hence they are bound to develop a habit of theoretical indifference towards opposing sides, a readiness to take any path in case it promises to lead to a theory more in accordance with the facts. Now, every form of political activity, and practical politics particularly, demands above everything else a determination to follow *one* path that one has chosen. Political activity . . . produces a habit of mind that would prove fatal to the theorist, the habit of opportunism.

Never was the principle of the Ivory Tower more brilliantly expressed. But it led to the general adoption of an attitude of complete irresponsibility and, in the end, to the paradoxical position that Academic Freedom made it seem improper to oppose a political party which was clearly bent on destroying it. It meant that the professors and teachers at the universities felt no call to criticise political tenets which they knew to be false or, morally, wrong. It was a far cry from the statement of Nietzsche, that 'the sincere professor has always been the bad conscience of society'.

I have suggested before that it is no longer any use trying to separate educational from political and social issues. The only way to defend educational principles today is very often to enter the political arena. The members of the German universities seem to have thought that they could preserve their own freedom while freedom was destroyed in all other spheres of national life. Their hope was vain and they should have realised that it was.

In a great speech at the re-opening of Marburg University after the war Professor Julius Ebbinghaus, the Rektor, showed even more clearly where the German universities had failed.

> One fact remains unfortunately all too true. The German universities failed, while there was still time, to oppose publicly with all their powers the destruction of Wissenschaft and of the democratic state. They failed to keep the beacon of freedom and light burning during the night of tyranny so that it could be seen by the entire world.

But actions speak louder than words. I have little doubt that the most significant incident in Germany since the war – it is certainly the most encouraging – was the political crisis in the Land or Province of Lower Saxony in May, 1955. Because it coincided with a General Election it attracted little attention in the British Press. An election in Lower Saxony had resulted in a victory for an alliance between the Christian Democrats and a Refugee Party. The latter were granted two seats in the Cabinet, one of them the post of Minister of Education, and for this they chose an undoubted Nazi, the only Nazi to be appointed to a Cabinet post in Germany since the war. The immediate result was the resignation of the Rektor and the whole Senate of Göttingen University. The students organised a three-day strike to express their solidarity with them. Then the Rektors of the Technische Hochschulen of Hanover and Brunswick resigned. Messages of protest came in from Teachers' Associations all over Western Germany. After ten days of acute crisis the Minister resigned. It was, perhaps, the greatest victory for Academic Freedom in any country during the last twenty years. It was not the only one. We may remember also, for instance, the resistance of Harvard University and some other universities and colleges in America to the imposition of 'Loyalty Oaths' in the days of Senator McCarthy. We may certainly add the resolution, passed by twenty-nine votes to two of the staff of the Natal Medical School, that they would resign if the Separate

University Education Bill of 1957 were passed without the omission of the clause removing the School from the authority of the University of Natal.

These were victories. But all history teaches us that in the unending struggle for Freedom there have been defeats which, by inspiring its defenders in the future, have been as significant as any victories. The finest statement in defence of true Academic Freedom that I have ever read was made by a defeated man. Kurt Huber, Professor of Philosophy at Munich University, was one of the greatest teachers of philosophy in modern Germany. Students from many faculties attended his lectures. He was the leader of a group of students, styled the White Rose, who resisted the Nazis in Munich during the last war. Early in 1943 they were all arrested and Huber, along with the others, was tried by the People's Court, convicted and beheaded. A draft has survived of his 'final statement' and it is possible, though by no means certain, that he actually delivered it at his trial. It begins with the words:

As a German citizen, a German university teacher, and a man of political conviction, I regard it not only as a right, but as a moral duty to help shape the destiny of my country, to uncover and oppose manifest evils . . . [and it ends] They have taken from me the title and rights of a professor, my doctorate, bestowed with the highest distinction, and have reduced me to the level of the lowest criminal. But no trial for high treason can rob me of the inner worth of a university teacher, of one who openly and courageously proclaims his philosophy of politics and life. The implacable march of history will justify my aims and actions; of that I am firmly convinced. I pray to God that the spiritual energies which Germany possesses may be released in time among my countrymen. I have acted in accordance with an inner compulsion. I accept the consequences in the fine words of Johann Gottlieb Fichte:

And thus you are to act,
As though the destiny of German life
Hung solely on your deeds and you,
And you alone were held accountable.

THE BEGINNING OF IT ALL

Robert's Speech in 1966 in Cape Town to the Black Sash, a society of white ladies dedicated to non-violent demonstrations against Apartheid, was ingenious. He knew that the Special Branch of the Police attended the Conference and a violent attack on Apartheid would mean, if not deportation for him, at least trouble for the members. So he cast the Speech as an entirely historical account of a Parliamentary Debate of 1792, academic in tone but, to those with ears to hear, full of overtones also, relevant to the current situation. Moreover, the Speech assured his listeners that in spite of the outcome of the 1792 Debate, when advocates of the Slave Trade won the vote, the foundations of triumph had been laid. The Black Sash was part of a tapestry of freedom. The historical dimension showed that they had partners in earlier generations and others would come forward in the future. This was certainly one of the finest of the countless lectures and speeches that he gave in South Africa.

MY AIM IN this address is to introduce to you a speech, one made 174 years ago in the House of Commons at Westminster, one of the greatest speeches ever made there, though largely forgotten, I think, today and not often referred to in South Africa now. I can imagine no audience to whom I should rather introduce it, for in a way the work which you do springs from the ideas which are to be found in it. You will be able to appreciate, in a way which the academic historian cannot do, the force, the revolutionary force, of these ideas. I hope, then, that you will accept what I say as an offering on my part, a way of expressing admiration for your ideals, your very brave stand for them and the work that you do in their service.

No one, as far as I know, has ever made a full historical study of the origins of colour-prejudice. It is quite a recent phenomenon in human history. It is true that one may find paintings in Ancient Egypt which caricatured the captives they made from the Negro tribes who lived to the south of them, though they seemed to think the shape of their lips more caricaturable than their colour. But, then, they made similar caricatures, as a way of expressing their sense of superiority, of the captives they made in raids on the northern shores of the Mediterranean. There is no evidence of colour prejudice among the Greeks. They looked down on all those who were not Greeks and styled them Barbarians, but they did not differentiate between Barbarians of different colours. When St Paul in a tremendous sentence showed how Christianity destroyed the barriers between different races or groups – 'Where there is neither Greek nor Jew, circumcision nor uncircumcision, Barbarian, Scythian, bond nor free; but Christ is all, and in all' – he never mentioned 'whites' and 'blacks' for the very good reason that the distinction would have added nothing of significance to his statement. The introduction of Scythians certainly was significant, for they were regarded as the most degraded of Barbarians. But they were white, not black.

It may surprise some people in South Africa that, as is shown in the classic work by the Principal of my University, *Race Attitudes in South Africa*,* there was no colour prejudice among the early Dutch settlers at the Cape. Colour prejudice, as he explains, is one of the signs of a strong group consciousness. There was naturally from the start a very clear distinction between the settlers on the one hand and the native population and the slaves imported from Asia on the other, and this coincided with the colour difference. But well into the eighteenth century the Dutch settlers drew a distinction in their minds between blacks who were free and those who were unfree. The distinction then was originally one of status. In much the same way when, as a consequence of their sea voyages, Europeans began to come into more than very occasional touch with Negroes, they regarded them as inferior beings because they had no developed civilisation and, above all, because they were defenceless, but not because they had a different colour.

In attempting to determine when this particular manifestation of group-consciousness, the emphasis on colour as a mark of distinction, appeared, one might think that a study of Shakespeare's *Othello* would be helpful. But it raises as many problems as it solves. It has been argued that Othello was made out to be a black in order to make Desdemona's marrying him even more unnatural. Did not Othello himself hint at this?

> Haply for I am black,
> And have not those soft parts of conversation
> That chamberers have . . .

* Professor Ian Macrone.

But it has also been pointed out that there is no trace of colour consciousness in the relations between the Venetian nobility and Othello. One has to remember that Othello is 'black' in the play for the very simple reason that the plot was taken from an Italian play in which he was a Moor. I could say that in this play Shakespeare shows something of that extraordinary ability to see – or rather to feel – both sides of a question, which we can find also in *The Merchant of Venice*. Obviously this is an anti-Semitic play, and yet it contains one of the most moving onslaughts on racial discrimination to be found in all literature: 'Hath not a Jew eyes? hath not a Jew hands, organs, dimensions, senses, affections, passions?' But I should say that there is enough in *Othello* to show that some kind of colour-consciousness was at least beginning to appear. One finds this also in *The Merchant of Venice*. The Prince of Morocco in this play is regarded as no unworthy suitor for the hand of Portia, and, in fact, she goes so far as to say that he

> . . . stood as fair
> As any comer I have looked on yet
> For my affection.

But his opening words to her are

> Mislike me not for my complexion,
> The shadowed livery of the burnished sun,

and when he makes his choice of the wrong casket and leaves with his attendants, she says,

> A gentle riddance. Draw the curtains, go
> Let all of his complexion choose me so.

It seems significant though that when Shakespeare came to depict a savage from the West Indies in *The Tempest*, he never referred to his colour. Perhaps even more significant was the fact that in productions of *Othello*, the Moor of Venice was played as a Negro until the early years of the eighteenth century, when it came to be felt desirable for him to be no more than brown-skinned. By that time England had certainly become colour-conscious. It really would not do for the hero of a play to be, as Iago put it, 'sooty'.

The reason for this is not far to seek. England had become involved in the slave trade, bringing Negroes from Africa to America and the

West Indies. For a good many years she had very little interest in this particular article of commerce, but in 1663 a new Charter for the Africa Company gave it a monopoly in the English traffic in slaves, the Company engaging to supply the modest total of 3000 slaves a year. What made England the country more involved in it than any other was the Treaty at the end of the War of the Spanish Succession in 1713, which gave her the monopoly of the supply for the Spanish colonies in America. By 1770 British ships were carrying about 50,000 slaves a year across the Atlantic; or about half the total supply. By 1800 about six-sevenths of all the slaves from Africa were transported in ships coming from the port of Liverpool alone. Never before the days of the Nazis, I suppose, have so many men and women been treated with such inhumanity as were the Africans who were seized or bought to be transhipped to the Americas. It seems astonishing that ordinary men, who were not themselves concerned with the trade, were so ready to support its continuance, even when people appeared who were ready to tell them of all the horrors it involved. We can learn a good deal, I believe, from the supporters of the Slave Trade.

Among those who were unhappy about it early in the eighteenth century was the poet, Alexander Pope. His lines in his *Essay on Man* were an early expression of the disquiet some Englishmen felt. (In them the word Indian refers to the West Indian Negro; his native land is Africa.)

> Lo! the poor Indian, whose untutor'd mind
> Sees God in clouds, or hears him in the wind;
> His soul, proud Science never taught to stray
> Far as the solar walk, or milky way;
> Yet simple Nature to his hope has given,
> Behind the cloud-topt hill, an humble heav'n;
> Some safer world in depths of woods embrac'd,
> Some happier island in the watery waste,
> Where slaves once more their native land behold,
> No friends torment, no Christians thirst for gold.

The Christians did indeed thirst for gold. But it would be a great mistake to think that it was only those directly concerned, the West Indian planters or the Liverpool merchants, who for this reason supported the Slave Trade. A great many people had a direct interest in maintaining it. These lines by Pope were themselves based on some in one of his earliest poems, 'Windsor Forest' which was written in 1713, the very year when England gained the monopoly, which was then granted by the government to the Africa Company. The sentiments

Pope expressed did not prevent him from investing some of his money in the Company. And going beyond that, it came to be believed that the prosperity of England depended on the maintenance of this lucrative trade.

The next step was inevitable, the quietening of consciences. The Bible came in very useful, especially the Old Testament. The great evangelical preacher, George Whitfield, wrote in 1751, 'As for the lawfulness of keeping slaves, I have no doubt, since I hear of some that were bought with Abraham's money, and some that were born in his house. I also cannot help thinking that some of those servants mentioned by the Apostles, in their epistles, were or had been slaves. It is plain that the Gibeonites were doomed to perpetual slavery, and though liberty is a sweet thing to such as are born free, yet to those who never knew the sweets of it, slavery perhaps may not be so irksome.' And then, with unexpected candour, he comes to the real point. 'However this be, it is plain to a demonstration; that hot countries cannot be cultivated without negroes.' (It is only right for me to add that one of the strongest opponents of the Slave Trade was another and even greater evangelical preacher, John Wesley.) But the best ways to quieten one's conscience were first to get oneself to believe that the slaves enjoyed their treatment and were really very happy, and then that they were essentially an inferior kind of being to whom the ordinary rules governing human treatment did not apply. To believe this was made much easier by the convenient fact that they were of a different colour.

The debate that gradually developed in England may well be illustrated by considering the views of two men who were as closely connected as any two men ever have been: Samuel Johnson and his biographer, James Boswell. 'The wild and dangerous attempt which has for some time been persisted in to obtain an act of our legislature,' Boswell wrote,

to abolish so very important and necessary a branch of commercial interest, must have been crushed at once, had not the insignificance of the zealots who vainly took a lead in it, made the vast body of the Planters, Merchants and others, whose immense properties are involved in that trade, reasonably enough suppose that there could be no danger . . . To abolish a status, which in all ages God has sanctioned, and man has continued, would not only be robbery to an innumerable class of our fellow-subjects; but it would be extreme cruelty to the African Savages, a portion of whom it saves from massacre, or intolerable bondage in their own country, and introduces into a much happier state of life, especially now when their passage to the West Indies and their treatment there is humanely regulated. To abolish that trade would be to "Shut the gates of mercy on mankind".

One could hardly go further and after reading such hypocrisy it is almost a relief to listen to someone who felt it quite unnecessary to employ any whitewash, like the London Alderman who declared in the House of Commons in 1790, 'The abolition of the [Slave] Trade would ruin the West Indies, destroy our Newfoundland fishery, which the slaves in the West Indies support by consuming that part of the fish which is fit for no other consumption, and consequently, by cutting off the great source of seamen, annihilate our marine'.

Dr Johnson, of course, is regarded as the very type of English Conservative. But it is a great mistake to imagine that all those who attacked this system, so firmly established by custom, so necessary, as most people thought, to preserve English prosperity – to imagine that they were radicals, or as we should say today 'liberals' or perhaps 'anti-anti-Communists'. For it was of Dr Johnson that we are told that 'upon one occasion, when in company with some very grave men at Oxford, his toast was, "Here's to the next insurrection of the Negroes in the West Indies"', and who once wrote, 'The laws of Jamaica afford a Negro no redress. His colour is considered a sufficient testimony against him. It is to be lamented that moral right should ever give way to political convenience.'

Boswell wrote of 'the insignificance of the zealots who vainly took a lead in it', that is, in the attempt 'to abolish so very important and necessary a branch of commercial interest'. They must have seemed very insignificant to themselves when they set out to destroy the system. When the Society for the Abolition of the Slave Trade was formed in 1787 it consisted of only thirteen men. It is interesting to consider how two of the most famous of the thirteen men came to take up the cause. Thomas Clarkson was a student at Cambridge and in 1785 he entered for a Latin Essay prize on the subject, 'Is it lawful to make men slaves against their will?' Two years before a group of six Quakers had decided to agitate against the Slave Trade and, when Clarkson set about his task, they had just published a book by an American Quaker, Anthony Bezenet, on the condition of the slaves in the British Colonies. They approached the Headmasters of Winchester, Eton, Harrow, Westminster and Charterhouse to ask if they might distribute copies to the boys in their schools. I do not think it is known what reception they had, but I like to think of two of my predecessors being embarrassed in this way. Clarkson, in search of material, obtained a copy and read it, and he made considerable use of it in his essay. He won the prize and had the distinction of reading it publicly in the Senate House at Cambridge. Then he mounted his horse to ride home to London, and as he did so he could not help thinking about his essay. 'I stopped my horse occasionally, and dismounted and walked. I frequently tried to persuade myself in these intervals that the contents of my essay could not be true . . . Coming in sight of Wades Hill in Hertfordshire; I sat down disconsolate on the turf by the roadside and held my horse. Here a thought came into my mind – that if the contents of the essay were true, it was time some person should see these calamities to their end. Agitated in this manner, I reached home.' He is the only man I know of who was persuaded to change his whole course of life by something he had written himself. Before long he discovered that there were some others, though only a very few, who were as agitated as he was.

William Wilberforce came to the same conclusion very differently, but here again one can see the extraordinary influence of a handful of people. In 1787 he was twenty-eight years old and a rising Member of Parliament, which he had entered immediately he became of age. He disliked the Slave Trade, but it did not particularly distress him. And then one day he was invited to stay by a married couple, Sir Charles Middleton, a great Admiral, and his wife, who a few years before had travelled home from the West Indies with a young clergyman, and he had told them something of what he had seen in the slave plantations. He was a guest there as well and the three of them pressed the young Member to raise the issue in Parliament. They were not the only influences brought to bear on him. He also met Clarkson and some others. He began to be interested and he started questioning merchants in London who traded with the West Indies. They were quite ready to talk, for as Wilberforce said, '"the trade" had not yet become the subject of alarming discussion'.

Now Wilberforce's great friend in the House of Commons, a young man of almost exactly the same age as himself, was the Prime Minister, William Pitt, who had reached this position at the astonishingly early age of twenty-four. Pitt, of course, knew of his friend's new interest and, for that matter, he too was unhappy about the Trade. And then, one day in 1787, as they sat together 'at the root of an old tree', Pitt said to him, 'Why don't you, Wilberforce, give notice of a motion on the subject of the Slave Trade?' So the battle came to be joined. We know a great deal about the man who founded the movement for the Abolition of the Slave Trade and I must admit that I find it fascinating to be able to see, as one can only very rarely, the first minute beginnings of a movement which was to accomplish what must have then appeared almost impossible. Nowhere in History can one see more clearly what can be done by intensely strong moral convictions. The movement which led to the ending of the Slave Trade was the greatest of all instances of what can be achieved by moral protest.

Wilberforce proposed this motion, after much careful preparation, in May 1789, in a very great speech, lasting three hours. The issue cut right across the normal lines of party division. He was supported not only by Pitt, the Tory Prime Minister, but also by the two great leaders of the party in opposition, Fox and Burke. But most of Pitt's cabinet were firmly against him on this issue and it was quite impossible for him to make it one of government policy. Preliminary successes, such as the passing of Wilberforce's original motion that the Privy Council should investigate the question of the Trade, and of a Bill which limited the number of slaves a ship might carry, made those who supported the Slave Trade realise that they must rouse themselves. In 1791 Wilberforce brought the matter to a head and moved a resolution 'for leave to bring in a Bill to prevent the further importation of slaves into the British islands in the West Indies'. He noted the result in his diary, 'Resumed debate and badly beat'.

He tried again next year. By that time fate seemed to be on the side of the planter. People were beginning to be afraid of the French Revolution and all that it implied, and the argument that abolition was an attack on Property seemed a very cogent one. A slave insurrection on the French island of San Domingo, in which appalling atrocities were committed on both sides, made men fearful of anything which might excite the slaves on the British islands. The leaders of slavers' interests in the House, of whom the most important was Pitt's greatest friend and closest colleague in the cabinet, Henry Dundas, were skilful. When on April 2nd, Wilberforce moved his resolution: 'That it is the opinion of this Committee [that is the House of Commons in Committee] that the trade carried on by British subjects, for the purpose of obtaining slaves of the coast of Africa, ought to be abolished', they did not oppose it directly. They moved a very cunning amendment, of which I shall tell in due course.

It was a tremendous debate, a battle of the giants. Wilberforce began with an excellent speech, in which he concentrated on two points, that the Slave Trade was intolerable and that its abolition would not ruin the planters. He was succeeded by two champions of the Trade, one the Member for Liverpool, who made all they could out of the rebellion in San Domingo and its resultant horrors. And then Dundas spoke. His speech was a remarkably clever one. He made no attempt to defend the Slave Trade; he was all for abolishing it. But were they being practical? And were they not in danger of forgetting the importance of defending the rights of individuals? Would it not be better to proceed carefully by means of regulations, which would ease the situation? They should promote breeding among the slaves – this would make new purchases from Africa less attractive; they should improve the conditions of the slaves and do something to educate their children. In this way, he believed, the trade would in the end die out. He appealed to all 'gentlemen of the moderate or middle way of thinking'; he asked them 'to reduce the question to its proper bounds'.

He was succeeded by one of the greatest debaters in the House, one of the greatest the House of Commons has ever known, Charles James Fox, a violent enemy of the Slave Trade. He let fly at Dundas for his appeal for moderation. Was there to be moderation in robbery, murder, pillage and destruction? To him it seemed that these regulations would prove to be a foundation to preserve the Trade, not for some years to come, but for ever. He concluded by summing up his views on the Slave Trade. 'I believe it to be impolitic: I know it to be inhuman. I am certain it is unjust. I find it so inhuman and unjust that, if the colonies cannot be cultivated without it, they ought not to be cultivated at all.' It was magnificent, but it may not have been wise. Many members were already frightened by what was happening in France, very near to them. After all, this vehement speech was made by someone who had said of the taking of the Bastille, 'how much the greatest event in the history of the world, and how much the best'.

Dundas answered him in the most effective way possible. In a few sentences he moved his amendment to the resolution. It could not have been a simpler one. It just inserted into the original resolution the word, 'gradually'. The Slave Trade 'ought to be gradually abolished'.

The next speaker was a young man, already a junior member of the government, who was one day, as Lord Liverpool, to be Prime Minister for fifteen years. He welcomed the amendment and had some ideas of his own. Slave-owners who promoted a higher birth-rate among their slaves might benefit financially; female slaves who had five children, provided they reached the age of seven, might be freed; every ship which brought from Africa more young women than men might receive a bounty, for the islands should be encouraged to produce their own slaves.

It was now after half-past five in the morning and then Pitt rose to speak. I have an idea that he realised that Fox's vehement outburst might have done more harm than good, and he began very cautiously. After all, he suggested, the supporters of the amendment had condemned the Slave Trade. 'Mankind', he said 'in general, are now likely to be delivered from the greatest practical evil that ever has afflicted the human race – from the severest and most extensive calamity recorded in the history of the world.' (It was not quite what Dundas and his friends had meant, of course.) He then said that they ought to consider carefully whether gradual would be more effective than immediate abolition. With all this preliminary part, I think I need not deal. His apparent determination to take his opponents seriously must have been deliberate. It made the second half of his speech all the more startling. 'I beg pardon', he said, 'for dwelling so long on the argument of expediency.' All the arguments which were drawn from it pleaded more loudly and more strongly for an immediate, than for a gradual abolition.

'But now, sir, I come to Africa.' With these words a new chapter in History was opened. For the opponents of the Slave Trade up to that point had thought in terms of the West Indies. After all, in the year 1792, the European world knew very little of Africa. There were the Portuguese colonies, but they did not extend more than two hundred miles or so from the coast. There were some 15,000 Dutch Settlers at the Cape. There were some isolated posts and strips of territory in West Africa. The states of North Africa were in the control of the Barbary Corsairs. Something was known of Egypt, but it was thought of as part of the Ottoman Empire. Africa then was, as has been said, little more than a coastline. No one concerned himself with what happened beyond the coastline, except to be aware that some of the slaves that were purchased must come from there. Whitfield used to refer to the slaves as Ethiopians. To Pitt it was given to see further.

> Long as that continent has been known to navigators, the extreme line and boundaries of its coasts is all with which Europe is yet become acquainted . . . As to the whole interior of that continent you are, by your own principles of commerce, as yet entirely shut out: Africa is known to you only by its skirts. Yet even there you are able to infuse a poison that spreads its contagious effects from one end to the other, which penetrates to its very centre, corrupting every part to which it reaches.
>
> But now, Sir, I come to Africa. That is the ground on which I rest. Why ought the Slave Trade to be abolished? Because it is an incurable injustice. How much stronger then is the argument for immediate, than gradual abolition! [He dealt with the specious argument that it was a necessary evil.] The origin of evil is indeed a subject beyond the reach of human understandings; and the permission of it by the Supreme Being, is a subject into which it belongs not to us to enquire. But where the evil is a moral evil which a man can scrutinise, and where the moral evil has its origins with

ourselves, let us not imagine that we can clear our consciences by this general, not to say irreligious and impious, way of laying aside the question.

But his gaze was turned by now in a prophetic vision, on the whole continent of Africa. He saw the temptation which the traders laid in the way of the African peoples to sell their fellow-creatures, leading to misery throughout all Africa. 'Do you think nothing of the ruin and the miseries in which so many individuals in Africa are involved in consequence of carrying off so many myriads of people? Do you think nothing of their families which are left behind? Of the friendships, attachments and relationships that are burst asunder? . . . What do you know of the internal state of Africa?'

He turned for the moment to deal with what many felt to be one of the strongest arguments against the Abolition of the Slave Trade, that if Britain abandoned it, it would not mean that other countries would do so. 'How, Sir,' he exclaimed, 'is this enormous evil ever to be eradicated, if every nation is thus prudentially to wait till the concurrence of all the world has been obtained?' He considered also the argument that there was 'something in the disposition and nature of the Africans themselves, which made it impossible to civilise them.' He quoted an example which had been given of African barbarism and then coldly quoted from the laws of the West Indies which established death as the penalty for any slave who ran away and left his master for more than six months. 'Let the house now contrast the two cases. Let them ask themselves which of the two exhibits the greater barbarity. I hope, therefore, we shall hear no more of the moral impossibility of civilising the Africans, nor have our understandings and consciences insulted, by being called upon to sanction the slave trade, until other nations have set the example of abolishing it.' And then, in words which were long remembered, he drove his point home. 'There was a time, Sir, which it may be fit sometimes to revive in the remembrance of our country when . . . the very practice of the slave trade once prevailed among us. Slaves . . . were formerly an established article of our exports. "Great numbers", [he quoted from a contemporary historian] "were exported like cattle from the British coast and were to be seen exposed for sale in the Roman market."' He listed what he called 'those sources of slavery', such as debtors or prisoners taken in war, and added,

Every one of these sources of slavery has been stated, and almost precisely in the same terms, to be at this hour a source of slavery in Africa . . . These circumstances, Sir, furnish the alleged proof that Africa labours under a natural incapacity for civilisation . . . that Providence never intended her to raise above a state of barbarism, that Providence has irrevocably doomed her to be only a nursery of slaves for us free and civilised Europeans . . . Why might not some Roman senator, reasoning on the principles of some honourable gentlemen and pointing to the British barbarians, have predicted with equal boldness, 'There is a people that will never rise to civilisation – there is a people destined never to be free – a people without the understanding necessary for the attainment of useful arts; depressed by the hand of nature below the level of the human species; and created to form a supply of slaves for the rest of the world?'

We, Sir, have long since emerged from barbarism – we have almost forgotten that we were once barbarians – we are now raised to a situation which exhibits a striking contrast to every circumstance, by which a Roman might have characterised us, and by which we now characterise Africa.

He glanced at the long history of his country, how 'by a progression slow, and for a time almost imperceptible', it had become pre-eminent in commerce, the arts, philosophy, science and

all the blessings of civil society . . . in the possession of peace, of happiness and of liberty . . . under the guidance of a mild and beneficent religion . . . protected by impartial laws . . . living under a system of government . . . which has become the admiration of the world . . . From all these blessings, we must for ever have been shut out, had there been any truth in those principles which some gentlemen have not hesitated to lay down as applicable to the case of Africa.

I trust we shall no longer continue this commerce, to the destruction of every improvement on that wide continent, and shall not consider ourselves as conferring too great a boon, in restoring its inhabitants to the ranks of human beings. I trust we shall not think ourselves too liberal [it is interesting to see this word of such ancient lineage, associated through many centuries with the great human qualities of freedom and generosity, now used for almost the first time in a political sense] if, by abolishing the slave trade, we give them the same common chance of civilisation with other parts of the world, and that we shall now allow to Africa the opportunity, the hope, the prospect of attaining to the same blessings which we ourselves, through the favourable dispensation of Divine Providence, have been permitted, at a much more early period to enjoy. If we listen to the voice of reason and duty, and pursue this night the line of conduct which they prescribe, some of us may live to see the reverse of that picture, from which we now turn our eyes with shame and regret. We may live to behold the natives of Africa, engaged in the calm occupations of industry, in the pursuits of a just and legitimate commerce. We may behold the beams of science and philosophy breaking in upon their land which, at some happy period in still later times may blaze with full lustre; and joining their influence to that of pure religion, may illumine and invigorate the most distant extremities of that immense continent. Then may we hope that even Africa, though last of all the quarters of the globe, shall enjoy at length, in the evening of her days, those blessings which have descended so plentifully upon us in a much earlier period of the world. Then also will Europe, participating in her improvement and prosperity, receive an ample recompense for the tardy kindness (if kindness it can be called) of no longer hindering that continent from extricating herself out of the darkness which, in other more fortunate regions, has been so much more speedily dispelled.

The House by now was listening to him spellbound. For the last twenty minutes, Wilberforce said afterwards, he had really seemed to be inspired. The dawn had now broken over London and as he came to these words the rays of the rising sun streamed through the windows of St Stephen's. Pitt turned towards them and with what must be the most superb use of quotation in all oratory, and obviously quite impromptu, he exclaimed,

> Nos primus equis oriens afflavit anhelis,
> Illic sera rubens accendit lumina vesper.

(The quotation comes from one of the *Georgics* of Virgil – 'On us the rising sun first breathes with her panting steeds; there glowing Vesper is kindling his evening rays.')

In his concluding words he showed again that it was Africa, not just 'the extreme link and boundaries of the coasts', but the whole of Africa, of which he was thinking.

It is in this view, Sir, – It is as atonement for our long and cruel injustice towards Africa, that the measure proposed by my honourable friend most forcibly recommends itself to my mind. The great and happy change to be expected in the state of her inhabitants is, of all the various and important benefits of the abolition, in my estimation, incomparably the most extensive and important.

I shall vote, Sir, against the amendment; and I shall also oppose to the utmost every proposition, which in any way may tend to prevent or even to postpone for an hour, the total abolition of the slave trade: a measure which, on all the various grounds which I have stated, we are bound by the most pressing and indispensable duty, to adopt.

But Pitt was not successful. Immediately he sat down the House divided, and the amendment was carried by 193 votes to 125. Nine months later England was at war with France and soon the problem of the Slave Trade seemed to have been forgotten. Those who supported it began to find themselves associated with the Republicans in France. A noble lord in a debate three years later exclaimed,

> And what does Abolition of the Slave Trade mean more or less than Liberty and Equality? What more or less than the Rights of Man? And what is Liberty and Equality and what the Rights of Man but the foolish fundamental principles of this new philosophy? . . . All being equal, blacks and whites, French and English, wolves and lambs, shall . . . promiscuously pig together, engendering a new species of man as the product of this new philosophy, a nondescript in the order of human beings.

But I think we can see now that, after Pitt's speech, the Slave Trade was doomed. Fifteen years later it was abolished and twenty-six years after that all the slaves in the British Colonies were freed.

But it was even more important that this great speech opened up to Britain, and in due course, to all Europe, the problem of Africa. With that problem we, of European stock, are still grappling. What should strike us particularly is how at the very beginning the problem was considered, not as an economic one, or even as a political one, but as a great moral issue, a question of right and wrong. And it is because I know that I am speaking to people who look on the problem of Africa today in exactly the same way that I have been so glad to be granted the opportunity this evening to recall to you this speech. You, in all you do, are echoing the ideals and the prophetic words which are to be found in it.

THE FOUNDATIONS OF THREE TOTALITARIAN REGIMES

This essay is based upon a lecture given to a Conference of Chaplains in Institutions of Higher Education in September, 1975. It was published subsequently on behalf of the Christian Institute Fund of which Robert was Chairman and which helped to pay the costs and alleviate problems of Christians in South Africa whose opposition to Apartheid had invited persecution. The treatment of the theme is therefore concerned with Totalitarianism and Religion and the dilemmas of convinced Christians under repressive regimes.

As I AM intending to say something about what seems to me to be – or have been – the essential foundations of three Totalitarian regimes, Nazi Germany, the Communist States and South Africa, I had better explain what right I have, if any, to do so. I knew Germany first in 1922 during the inflation, when I spent over three months in the summer between school and university, wandering about Central Europe by myself. I visited Germany quite often after that and I knew it before the Nazis and under the Nazis. Then in 1946 I was asked by the Ministry of Education to go to Germany for six weeks to look at the educational work we were doing there and this led to my being in charge of this work for two and half years from early in 1947. Except when I was in South Africa I have visited Germany once or twice every year since then, usually twice in a year and sometimes more often.

I should explain at once that I have never been to Russia. My contact with Communism was a very strange one. I had to work with the Russians, of course, in Germany. Except in one place this meant very little. Each of the four occupying powers carried out its own policy in its Zone as it liked. The monthly meetings of the Allied Control Council were of no real significance. The one exception was Berlin.

There the situation was quite different. Berlin was politically a unit until it was split by the Russians in December 1948. There was a single German administration which could do nothing without the approval of the Allies and the four Allies had to agree or nothing happened at all. I spent for two years endless hours playing chess – for this is what it seemed like – with the Russians and it taught me a great deal. And may I add that I have visited East Berlin once or twice a year since then.

As for South Africa, I went out there first for a month in 1962 to help a committee which had been set up to consider the educational needs of the country, but treating it as *one* problem not as five separate ones – Afrikaners, English, Africans, Indians and Coloureds. One result turned out to be three years as a Professor of Education in the University of the Witwatersrand in Johannesburg, from the beginning of 1964 to the end of 1966. I have been out there three times since then and spent three months there, mostly at the University of Cape Town, in 1974.

I first began to turn this question over in my mind ten years ago when I was in South Africa. Pastor Niemöller was out there and Dr Beyers Naudé, the Director of the Christian Institute, invited him to come and meet some of us privately. We wanted particularly to ask him about the support given by Christians in Germany to pastors of the Confessional Church who lost their posts under the Nazi regime. I remember at first feeling fascinated as two periods of my life seemed to come together – and then I became aware of an essential difference. One might put it figuratively. The inspiration of Nazism came from the Devil, that of the regime in South Africa from a perverted Christianity.

I think, though, that it would be as well to realise that there are certain similarities in all totalitarian regimes. Of these, two seem to me to be of special importance. The first is the social phenomenon expressed once in a letter by Lord Acton (and almost always mis-quoted), 'All power tends to corrupt: absolute power corrupts abso-lutely'. The other is the phenomenon sometimes called collective psycho-pathology. A few years ago, Mr David Astor, the Editor of the *Observer*, Professor Norman Cohn and myself went out to Ger-many to see Dr Heinemann, then Minister of Justice in the Federal Republic, to ask him if we could send out a fully trained psychiatrist, who could speak perfect German, to interview ten ex-Nazis who were serving sentences of life imprisonment. This would mean, of course, that the number of deaths for which they were responsible would have been at least in four figures, if not five. He understood what our aims were and agreed to help us. As a result, one of the ablest of British psychiatrists, Dr Henry Dicks, went out to Germany and in his book, *Licensed Mass Murder*, he describes his meetings with eight Nazi criminals. He writes, 'These studies support the view I have come to, contrary to my expectations, that the eight SS killers were not simply primitive, impulsive psychopaths.' And again, 'With the dubious exception of two of them, none of these SS men would have been likely to become "common murderers" in normal conditions.' The psycho-pathology was, in fact, 'collective'. I came across what seemed to me to be a similar manifestation two years ago in southern Africa. I stayed at a hotel in Gaberone, the capital of Botswana, a hotel which was also a gambling resort. It was ten miles from the frontier with the South African Republic and was full of people, mostly Afrikaners, from across the border. That they should be glad to get away and have a flutter, impossible in their own country, seemed to me not unnatural. But another phenomenon seemed to me more significant. At the back of the hotel was a swimming pool, which I could see from my bedroom window. In this many of the visitors were enjoying themselves and with them in the pool were 'blacks'. Fifteen miles away this would have been something for them quite unthinkable.

Obviously it is also important when considering any kind of regime to think of the historical causes for its acceptance by society. This, of course, necessitates a long and complicated study, but I cannot altogether ignore them.

Let me begin with Nazi Germany. I think one can trace two kinds of causes for the appearance and triumph of Nazism in that country, though I am well aware that I am going to be guilty of a gross oversimplification. The first one might call 'immediate', the other more fundamental. I consider most important among the immediate causes the fact that Germany, during just over ten years before the Nazis gained absolute power, had had two appalling experiences. The first was the astounding inflation of the years 1922 and 1923. This seemed completely to undermine all good sense and tolerance. Perhaps the effect may be illustrated by a story I remember being told when I was in Germany during that period. 'There were two brothers. The elder brother stayed at home with his father, looked after the family business carefully and competently, saved money for the future and placed it in government securities. The younger brother went off to the city and wasted his substance on wine, women and song. Then came the great inflation. The family firm went bankrupt; the elder brother's savings became completely valueless. But the younger brother had kept the empty bottles of his drinking bouts in the cellar.

These he was able to sell at a very considerable profit. He then went home and rescued his elder brother.' Germany rescued itself from the inflation with remarkable skill and determination. In five years, in spite of reparations, she made a great economic recovery. Then came the Wall Street crash of October 1929 and the ensuing world slump. By the beginning of 1933 there were six million unemployed in Germany. I can remember at that time hardly ever meeting a student who thought he would get a job. Any solution seemed worth considering.

I give two more fundamental causes. The first I might call the militarization of Germany. Except for the glorious rising against Napoleon and the sudden outburst then of national feeling, the first fifty years of the nineteenth century were a disastrous period for Germany: the creation after 1815 of a still divided country, the utter and ignominious failure of the Revolution of 1848. Then came Bismarck and in his famous speech of 29th September 1862 were two sentences – 'The great questions of the day will not be settled by speeches and resolutions of majorities but by iron and blood', and, which seems to me even more significant, 'What Germany wants of Prussia is not her liberalism but her might'. The marvellously successful confirmation of these sentences were the wars of 1866 and 1870–1871. And the effect was perfectly illustrated in this extract from the autobiography of the great German dramatist Gerhart Hauptmann.

The German victory of 1871 by means of the Prussian-Potsdam principle caused this to be regarded as the sole way of salvation, and so led to its general strengthening as much as possible. The schools, with their reserve officers as teachers, felt the first results of this, and the pupils had to adapt themselves to it. Thus when the teacher entered the classroom, the boys sprang from their seats and stood stiff and tense until the command 'Sit' rang out in cutting tones. The manner in which instruction was handed down from the teacher's desk exactly resembled the teaching methods in the army. Thus did Jurich bellow forth religious instruction, asking questions from the New Testament, such as 'What did St. Paul say?' 'How did the disciple John put it?' 'What did Christ teach in the Sermon on the Mount?' At the same time, if a boy was slow to answer he would haul him up by the tip of his ear as far as he could short of tearing off his ear. Simple terms, good nature, friendly encouragement of the pupil, were ruled out as sentimentality: they were regarded as soft, effeminate. For behind the teacher as his driving force stood not Lessing or Herder, Goethe or Socrates, but the Prussian noncommissioned officer.

The second, I should suggest, was the development of German romanticism. This, of course, is a very large subject in itself. Let me simply give three quotations from three very prominent Germans of the nineteenth century, which will, I think, serve to show what I mean. First, Johann Gottlieb Fichte, who lived from 1762 to 1814, one of the ancestors of Existentialism, whose 'Addresses to the German Nation' in 1807 and 1808 did so much to awaken German Nationalism:

> What spirit has an undisputed right to summon and to order everyone concerned, whether he is willing or not, and to compel anyone who resists, to risk everything including his life? Not the spirit of the peaceful citizen's love for the constitution and the laws, but the devouring flame of higher patriotism, which embraces the nation as the vesture of the eternal, for which the noble-minded man joyfully sacrifices himself, and the ignoble man, who only exists for the sake of the other, must likewise sacrifice himself.

Second, Richard Wagner. I am not thinking only of his operas, though they certainly played a part. But let me take this description by him of the German of the old days:

> In rugged forests, in the long winter, in the warmth of the fire upon the hearth of his castle chamber towering aloft in the air, the German indulges long in the memories of his forefathers, he transmutes his home-bred myths of the gods in legends, manifold and inexhaustible.

And third, Nietzsche, who declared once that 'almost everything we call higher culture is based upon the spiritualising and intensifying of cruelty.' I take these sentences from his most famous work, *Also sprach Zarathustra*, the classic work on the ideal of the Superman.

> This new tablet I put up for you, my brethren: Become hard! Man must be trained for war, and woman for the relaxation of the warrior; all else is folly. You say that a good cause will even sanctify war! I tell you, it is a good war that sanctifies every cause.

The obvious manifestation of this romanticism was the Wandervögel movement, the great German youth movement of the early years of this century. Of this a very perceptive German historian, Joachim Fest, has written, 'In spite of all revolutionary claims, the Wandervögel movement was fundamentally escapist. What purported to be a revolt against the dullness and dreariness of the bourgeois world was at bottom a retreat into a special state of mind not seeking to change the world but despising it.'

I think it might be said that Nazism was a combination of the militarism and the romanticism making use of the opportunities presented by the national experience of a slump, following a quite appalling inflation.

One day, after a visit to Germany during the Nazi period, I went on to Prague. There I met at the University a Professor of Philosophy, Dr Mathesius, a very remarkable man. I let fly about the Nazi rule in Germany, its appalling cruelty. 'Yes, yes,' he said, 'of course Hitler is a devil. But remember that he entered an empty room.' And he added, 'Don't forget too that Hitler has offered these young men the greatest bribe he could put before them. He has asked them to sacrifice themselves.'

I believe that what he said was profoundly true. But to understand the incredible success of Nazism in capturing a nation, one must inevitably take into account the astonishing magnetic power of Adolf Hitler. This will, perhaps, illustrate it. On 27th January 1932 he made a speech to the Industrie Klub in Düsseldorf which is, I think, one of the turning points of modern history. The Nazi Party was in great difficulties and almost bankrupt. With this speech he won over the industrialists of the Ruhr and the Rhineland. A year and three days later he was Chancellor.

Two of my greatest friends are a German business man and his wife.* This will show you what kind of people they are. When the British forces invaded Germany, the Dutch Government in exile asked us to keep a special look out to protect them, for, they said, they had helped many members of the Dutch resistance movement to escape. The lady told me once that for the last two years of the war she never went anywhere without a phial of poison in her handbag because she felt that, if she were arrested and tortured, she might betray her friends. As an industrialist her husband attended the Düsseldorf meeting. That night he returned home and his wife has told me that he was in an extraordinary state, muttering to himself, 'It's horrible, it's horrible. The man's a wizard.' Next morning he could tell her about the meeting. He said that he had had the utmost difficulty in restraining himself from promising financial support to the Nazi Party, as all others present did, except for one friend of his. I know the speech well and it seems hardly credible, but what Hitler actually said never had much significance.

* Herr Hans Milchsack who died in 1984. His widow, Dame Lilo Milchsack, Hon. DCMG, is one of the very few recipients of this honour from a foreign country. It was bestowed in appreciation of her work on behalf of Anglo-German friendship.

I was very interested in this occasion and when I went to Düsseldorf in the years after the war, which I did very often, I was always trying to find someone else who had been there and was prepared to talk about it. And then one day I came across an elderly waiter who understood just what I was talking about. 'That was a wondeful day for me,' he said. 'When the Führer came he was presented with a bouquet of flowers, I was in charge of the cloaks and the flowers were left with me. All the wives of those men who went upstairs came to me and asked me if they could smell the Führer's flowers. I charged them a Mark each.'

But what was the real foundation of this extraordinary regime? I do not think one can learn much from Hitler's speeches. He was prepared to say anything. I give this as a quite outstanding example. It comes from what is known as 'The Testament of Adolf Hitler'. These were records of monologues by Hitler during the last days of his life, written down by Martin Bormann. This is an extract from 13th February 1945, ten weeks before his suicide.

> If I lose the war, the shifty, the shamefaced Jew will disappear and will be replaced by a Jew vainglorious and bombastic; and the latter will stink just as objectionably as the former – perhaps even more so. There is, then, no danger in the circumstances that anti-Semitism will disappear, for it is the Jews themselves who add fuel to its flames and see that it is kept well stoked. Before the opposition to it can disappear, the malady itself must disappear. And from that point of view, you can rely on the Jews: as long as they survive, anti-Semitism will never fade. In saying this I promise you I am quite free of all racial hatred.

This is enough to show us, I should say, what was the foundation of Nazism. It was evil, cruel, destructive, and selfish. Above all, it was destructive. Destruction can be worshipped. It can even *seem* to be creative. 'I want a violent, domineering, undismayed, cruel youth', Hitler said once. 'Youth must be all that. It must bear pain. There must be nothing weak or gentle about it. The free splendid beast of prey must once more flash from its eyes. I want my young, strong and beautiful. In this way I can create the new.'

If I had to choose one moment when Hitler – and therefore Nazism – showed most fully what it was I should take a passage from a book by Hermann Rauschning, entitled *Hitler Speaks*. He was for a time a Nazi leader in Danzig, who defected in 1935 and wrote two books attacking the Nazis. He refers to difficulties in the Baltic town of Stettin in 1933, where there was a revulsion against the cruelties of the SS and complaints by the Nationalist Party supporters of Hitler. Goering had to order an investigation. One day when Rauschning was present, Hitler was informed of this.

The occasion [Rauschning wrote] was my first experience of Hitler's paroxysms of rage and abuse. He behaved like a combination of a spoilt child and an hysterical woman. He scolded in high, shrill tones, stamped his feet and banged his fist on tables and walls. He foamed at the mouth, panting and stammering in uncontrollable fury: 'I won't have it! Get rid of all of them! Traitors!' He was an alarming sight, his hair dishevelled, his eyes fixed, and his face distorted and purple. I feared that he would collapse, or have an apoplectic fit.

Suddenly it was all over. He walked up and down the room clearing his throat and brushing his hair back. He looked round apprehensively and suspiciously, with searching glances at us. I had the impression that he wanted to see if anyone was laughing . . .

'Preposterous,' Hitler began in a hoarse voice. 'Haven't you ever seen a crowd collecting to watch a street brawl? *Brutality is respected.* Brutality and physical strength. The plain man in the street respects nothing but brutal strength and ruthlessness – women too for that matter, women and children. The people need wholesome fear. They *want* to fear something. They want someone to frighten them and make them shudderingly submissive . . . Why babble about brutality and be indignant about tortures? The masses want that. They need something that will give them a thrill of horror.'

After a pause, he continued in his former tone: 'I forbid you to change anything. By all means punish one or two of these men, so that these German Nationalist donkeys may sleep easy. But I don't want concentration camps turned into penitentiary institutions. Terror is the most effective political instrument. I shall not permit myself to be robbed of it simply because a lot of stupid, bourgeois molly coddles choose to be offended by it . . .' No one ventured to put any questions. 'I don't want to hear anything more about this,' Hitler said in conclusion. 'It's your business to see that no evidence about such cases leaks out. I cannot allow such absurd trifles to break in on my work. Anybody who is such a poltroon that he can't bear the thought of someone merely having to suffer pain had better join a sewing-circle, but not my party comrades.'

I think one can go further. Hitler was never more contradictory in what he said than when talking about the Christian religion. A very self-conscious seeking for a return to an old German paganism was to be found before the Nazis appeared. Ludendorff was a protagonist of the new cult. Later we find a special kind of wedding service devised for members of the SS. Rosenberg in his famous book, *The Myth of the*

Twentieth Century, attacked Christianity as a soft humanitarian creed which supported the equality of different races, but Hitler never really approved of Rosenberg. But there certainly were moves towards an organised faith in opposition to the Christian religion, though it was played down during the war for fear of dividing the German people. If they had won the war we should have heard a great deal more of it.

In the autumn of 1946 I visited the town of Brno (or Brünn) in Czechoslovakia. Above it stands a great castle on a hill, the Spielberg, which had been a prison for political captives under the Habsburg Emperors. During the last war it was the Headquarters of the Gestapo in Moravia and a place of unimaginable cruelties. In the castle was a chapel and I once found a photograph of it as it had been, with its conventional baroque ornaments and a picture of the crucified Christ hanging above the altar. It had been turned into a chapel of the new Nazi religion and after the war it had been left untouched, except for the removal of a bust of Hitler. Where the altar had been was a great block of granite, on the front of which was carved an iron cross, on which was painted a swastika. On this new altar was a book-rest and on this a copy of the new bible, Hitler's *Mein Kampf*. Above the altar was fixed to the wall an immense stone figure of an eagle with its talons stretched out below it, swooping downwards. On it was painted a lightning flash so that it really seemed to be swooping down on one. On the wall were metal rings to hold torches, the only lighting for the services, the Wagnerian torch.

Very little has been written of this new religion. I once heard of a similar chapel for the SS in West Germany which was immediately destroyed when overrun by the Allies. But some account of the new 'National Reich Church' is to be found in an unexpected source, a book called *It's Your Souls We Want*, published in New York in 1943 by Stewart W. Herman junior, who had been pastor of an American Church in Berlin from 1936 to 1941. I have never seen this book, but it is quoted in a very well known one, W. L. Shirer's *The Rise and Fall of the Third Reich*. 'This Church', Herman said, 'had thirty articles, beginning with one claiming the right to control all churches in the German Reich, and with one saying 'it is determined to exterminate irrevocably . . . the strange and Christian faiths imported into Germany in the ill-omened year 800', and another forbidding the publishing and dissemination of the Bible. Three other articles read:

18 The National Church will clear away from its altars all cru-
cifixes, bibles and pictures of Saints.

19 On the altars there must be nothing but *Mein Kampf* (to the

German nation and therefore to God, the most sacred book) and
to the left of the altar a sword.

30 On the day of its foundation, the Christian Cross must be
removed from all churches, cathedrals and chapels . . . and it
must be superseded by the only unconquerable symbol, the
swastika.

(He is certainly mistaken in saying that the National Reich Church was
Rosenberg's creation.)

Let me turn now to the second of my regimes, that of the Communist
states. I have explained the limitations of my experience. It happened,
however, that the particular contact I had with the Russians and with
the German Communists who supported them was one which inevitably taught me a good deal about the Communist philosophy. The
great question in Berlin Education in the years just after the war was
that of a new school law. On this, as I have explained, agreement
among the four occupying powers was essential. The most important
question was whether the secondary schools should be *Gesamtschulen*
(we should say Comprehensive Schools), with an eight-year range, or
highly selective *Gymnasien*, as in the old system. In the end the
Communists and Social Democrats got their way with the former
arrangement. An even more difficult question was whether religious
instruction should be allowed in the schools. Here in the end, the
Communists gave way and two hours a week were allowed for this, to
come either at the beginning or the end of the school day, *Eckstunden* as
they were called, 'Corner Periods'. Even more difficult was the
question whether Church Schools might be allowed to continue. To
tell the truth I did not think that this was so very important, as there
were not many of them, but I knew that all hell would be let loose in
the Rhineland if we gave way on this point. It was necessary to
threaten to veto the whole Bill to get what we wanted here.

There was, however, one point on which agreement was impossible: the teaching of History. And in the endless arguments we had
about this I realised more and more clearly that we were dealing with
something to them quite fundamental. I said that we should not mind
if history according to the Marxist dialectic was taught in some
schools. (Of course, we realised that it would be in the schools in the
Russian sector.) But we were not prepared for it to be compulsory in
all schools. So in the end no history was taught in Berlin schools until
the Russians split the city in December 1948. (At least officially none

was taught. I knew quite well that it was in the Russian sector and – I might put it this way – I never made any inquiries about it in the British sector.)

The best short summary of the Communist theory of History I have ever read comes in the speech from the dock made by Bram Fischer in South Africa.* 'The Marxist approach', he said, 'explains in rational terms why at different times in man's history, different economic and political forms of society have existed. It also explains why one type of society must of necessity give way to a new and higher form. History therefore becomes something which can be naturally understood and explained. It ceases to be a meaningless conglomeration of events or a mere account of great men wandering in haphazard fashion across its stage.' We may recall, too, the famous outburst of Dimitroff, the Bulgarian Communist accused of having been responsible for the Reichstag fire in 1933: 'The wheel of history moves slowly on to the ultimate, inevitable, irrepressible goal of Communism'. Or, to express it a little differently, *Rude Pravo*, the Czechoslovak Communist Party newspaper, warned dissident intellectuals after the publication of Charter 77, several of whom had been arrested, 'those who lie on the rails to stop the train of history must expect to get their legs cut off'.

One must be careful about using the term 'Marxist'. Marx was not nearly as doctrinaire as he has sometimes been made out to be, and he quite often changed his mind. But what matters is what people in Communist countries think he said. And one thing seems to me to stand out in Marxist and Communist thinking: you knew that you were bound to win. The dialectical process was inevitable. If so, why not just fold one's hands and sit back and wait? But that is not the way men's minds work. It is the greatest encouragement to action to know that you are going to win.

Marx, of course, was a man of his age and it was an age which believed in progress. In a sense what he did was to re-interpret this belief so that it meant something to the working man. But for many it is something much more. It is a passionate conviction. And for many, many others it has become an established conviction, which one does not feel passionate about but which one has come completely, in a sense automatically, to accept.

What brings this out very clearly is, I think, the belief in the eventual 'withering away of the State', the inevitable reaching of a final goal.

* The grandson of a Prime Minister of the Orange River Colony and a Queen's Counsel, at his trial under the Suppression of Communism Act in 1966.

The classic statement of this is in the *Communist Manifesto*: 'In place of the old bourgeois society, with its classes and class antagonisms, we shall have an association in which the free development of each is the condition of the free development of all.' In a rather earlier work, *The German Ideology* of 1846, Marx had shown what an essentially romantic picture it was. 'In communist society, where nobody has one exclusive sphere of activity, but each can become accomplished in any branch he wishes, society regulates the general production and thus makes it possible for me to do one thing today and another tomorrow, to hunt in the morning, fish in the afternoon, rear cattle in the evening, criticise after dinner, just as I have a mind, without ever becoming hunter, fisherman, cowherd or critic.' It is true that as time passed Marx became rather less certain about this and in his prophesying about the withering away of the State he had to call to his aid the development of automatic machinery and the drastic reduction of the working day, both products of a bourgeois society. Lenin certainly believed in the withering away of the State. Stalin at the Sixteenth Congress of the Communist Party in 1930 stated, 'We believe in the withering away of the State and to keep on developing the power of the State in order to prepare for the withering away of the State – that is the Marxist formula.' He was quite right of course. It *is* the Marxist formula. But I wonder how many people now living in a Communist society really believe in the Withering Away of the State, except perhaps as a far-distant eschatological dream.

One can speak I think, of the essential foundation of Communist Society as an alternative faith. This may seem an absurd way of describing a theory based on an entirely materialist view of life. I became very friendly with one of the leading German Communists in Berlin. We got on well together in our discussions, but there was one thing he would not allow me to say. When I referred to his Communist Faith he would reply angrily, 'It's not a Faith. It's an intellectual conviction.' But I felt sure I was right. He had been educated at a Jesuit School in the Rhineland. I did not feel that, in one sense, he had jumped very far.

I turn now to South Africa. The totalitarian state there is essentially an Afrikaner creation. If the English had remained on top, it would be a different kind of state now. That is not to say that the English are not largely to blame, but I shall deal with that in due course.

Professor Pistorius, Professor of Greek at the University of Pretoria, an Afrikaner, in a book published in 1957, called *No Further Trek*, said of his own people that it should be realised that the Great

Trek may have been an heroic adventure, but it took place because, faced with very difficult social and political problems, they found a solution in physically moving away from them. And, he continued, throughout our history we have taken the same line. We have moved away. Now we can move no further: so what do we do? We move the problem. And that is what Apartheid is, a moving of a problem out of sight. But there is more to it than that. The first thing to realise is that the policy of the government in South Africa and of the 'whites' is based on fear. I was once asked by an Afrikaner journalist in Pretoria what I thought of his people. I replied that, allowing for some splendid exceptions, I divided them into two classes. The first, quite a small one, I called the Thousand Years' Reich men. Hitler's Reich only lasted for twelve years but that was neither here nor there. The others I called the 'Aprés nous le déluge' men. 'I see,' he said. 'You mean that we are being very selfish towards our grandchildren.' 'Well', I said, 'you have put it much better than I have. But that is what it comes to.' 'In our heart of hearts,' he said, 'we all know that'.

One might make a comparison between South Africa and Sparta. In Sparta there was the clearest possible distinction drawn between the Spartans, who were invaders of Dorian stock, and the subject race of Helots, descended from the original non-Dorian inhabitants of the country. The economy of the country was maintained by the Helots. Cultural separation was complete. Intermarriage between the two races was illegal and hardly thought of. Sparta could never allow freedom of thought or expression; this would endanger the discipline and safety of the garrison. And, what is most significant is that in Sparta, in the middle of the city – and only in Sparta among all Greek cities – there was built a temple to Fear. Plutarch, an admirer of Sparta, explained it. 'For they worship Fear, not as they do supernatural powers which they dread, deeming it hurtful, but because they know that their whole form of government is based on and largely maintained by fear.' There is a temple to Fear in the middle of South Africa.

The result is a regime continually on the defensive. This was well shown in a discussion which took place in 1956 between Mr Strydom, the Prime Minister, and Dr Verwoerd, the Minister of Native Affairs, on one side, and representatives of the Christian Council of South Africa on the other. The subject was migrant labour, which even the Dutch Reformed Churches have agreed to be a canker at the heart of South Africa. Dr Verwoerd, as one might expect, dealt with the matter very skilfully. The Prime Minister does not seem to have spoken until the end of the discussion, when he said a few words, ending with these, 'The government shares with the Churches a concern for a stable life, but it must always be remembered that it is the first duty of the South African government to preserve white civilisation.'

'If you give him an inch he will take an ell.' This becomes the motto of every defensive regime or society. It explains some very strange things in South Africa. While I was out there Mr Basil D'Oliveira, a South African Coloured, came out to Cape Town to coach coloured boys at cricket. A Coloured cricket club decided to have a dinner in his honour. They then had the very nice idea of inviting to the dinner a certain Mr Tom Reddick. Mr Reddick had once played cricket for Middlesex and had come out to South Africa as an ordinary immigrant, and, in easier days, he had coached Mr D'Oliveira when he was a boy. But they had to get special permission from the authorities to invite a white man to their dinner. In due course they received the answer, 'Yes, Mr Reddick may attend the dinner – provided he does not eat.'

Could anything be more ridiculous? But at almost the same time a similar decision was made. An admirable organisation in Cape Town, the Association of Jewish Women, used to hold every year at Christmas time, a party in the City Hall for handicapped children of all races. Local entertainers gave their services and there were refreshments. Then, quite suddenly, just before one of the parties, they received a communication from the authorities informing them that in future the parties might only be held on three conditions. First, white and non-white children must enter the Hall by separate entrances. Second, white and non-white children must sit in separate parts of the Hall. And third, refreshments might be served to the white children only.

The position of the Church in South Africa is one which is difficult for a foreigner who does not know the country to appreciate. I refer, of course, to the Dutch Reformed Church and the Afrikaners. (There are, in fact, three Dutch Reformed Churches in South Africa, the Nederduitse Gereformeerde Kerk (NGK), the Nederduitsch Hervormde Kerk (NHK) and the Gereformeerde Kerk, usually called the Doppers. The first of the three is much the largest. The Doppers, though small in numbers, have great influence.) The link between the Nationalist Party and the Government on one side and the Dutch Reformed Church is very close indeed. One of the turning points of South African history in this century was a meeting in 1941 when the leaders of various Afrikaner Nationalist groups issued a declaration giving the policy of the Afrikaner Front. This Declaration was received enthusiastically by Dr Malan, then leader of the Nationalist

Party, who became Prime Minister when they came to power in 1948. He promised that the policy would be vigorously pursued by the Party. The Declaration pledged its support for 'a free, independent, Republican, Christian-National State, based on the word of God, eschewing all foreign models . . . with a Christian-National educational system . . . and the strongest emphasis on the disciplining of the people.' In 1948 the Institute for Christian-National Education published its policy document, which was accepted by the Nationalist party which gained power a few weeks later. This stated that, 'Afrikaans-speaking children should have a Christian-National Education, for the Christian and Nationalist spirit of the Afrikaner nation must be preserved and developed. By Christian, in this context we mean according to the creeds of the three Afrikaner Churches; by Nationalist we mean imbued with the love of one's own, especially one's own language, history and culture.'

Even more significant, perhaps, are two statements drawn up, one by the NGK in 1951, the other by the Doppers in 1961. The former dealt particularly with political issues. Here are a few extracts from a summary of the statement:–

The humanist ideal of a world state must be rejected as contrary to Scripture and an attempt to achieve world peace outside the Kingdom of Heaven.

The franchise is a treasure which should belong only to those who are of age politically and are able to use it responsibly before God. The Bantu does not fulfil these requirements and therefore will not be able to use this right correctly . . . Not only undeveloped groups, but all those who are openly in rebellion against God, such as the Communists, should not be given the vote. In a Christian state, therefore, the necessary qualification is not only that a man should be of age, but that he should be a Christian . . . Only the Christian political faith is valid and no anti-Christian philosophy should be given the right to form political parties.

Where political life is threatened by doctrines born of unbelief – powerful in Liberalism, much stronger in Democracy, and most dangerous in Communism – it is without doubt the duty of Christians to try to become the strongest political factor in the country and to establish a Christian Government.

And here are extracts from the statement of the Doppers.

The love of one's neighbour in no way excludes the protection of one's own interest. It is in complete accord with the Scriptures that people should protect themselves for their God-given calling. He who is nothing to himself is also nothing to others. In any particular circumstance we must judge whether self-sacrifice or alternatively self-preservation is in the best interests of one's neighbour . . . From what has been said above it follows that every nation is called to protect its national identity, to develop it positively and so correspondingly fulfil its own nature and God-given cultural task to the glory of God and the blessing of the whole world . . . It therefore follows that races and nations mixing as a principle and rule in church circles must be rejected. It is not beneficial to the Church. It pleased the Lord that on the day of Pentecost each one praised His great deeds in his own language (Acts 2:11).

It is not exactly what is in the Bible, but that does not matter. The Bible can always be used. I remember once meeting an Anglican priest who worked at a small town in the Northern Transvaal, where his congregation was only a small one, most of the white inhabitants being Afrikaners and members of one of the Dutch Reformed Churches. One day he was asked to join a Brains Trust of which the Pastor of one of these churches was Chairman. Someone asked whether there was anything in the Bible which could be used in support of mixed marriages. He was on the point of saying 'Yes, look at the Book of Ruth', when the Chairman spoke: 'Certainly not,' he said. 'Look at Moses. He married a Midianite. That is why he never reached the Promised Land. And look at Samson and Delilah and, above all, at Ahab and Jezebel.' (Is there, in fact, anything in the Bible to show that that was why Moses did not reach the Promised Land?) The Head of the Police in Johannesburg said not long ago that it was perfectly reasonable for them to use criminals for police purposes. After all, was not Rahab a harlot? But worst of all – and one of the most dreadful things I have ever read – is the story in Canon Gonville ffrench-Beytagh's autobiography. He was Dean of Johannesburg from 1965 to 1972, was arrested, tried and convicted under the Terrorism Act but his conviction and sentence were quashed on appeal. He was being questioned by interrogators after his arrest. They had told him that they were practising members of the Dutch Reformed Church. They were asking him about the Church's attitude towards the South African Immorality Act, which prohibits sexual relations between Europeans and non-Whites. '"Surely you know," they said, "that sexual relations between Black and White are forbidden in the Bible?" That I flatly denied. They reiterated that I would find it in the Old Testament. I asked them what they meant. "Well," they replied, "don't you remember that it says in the Old Testament, A man may not mix his seed with that of the animal?"'

The great South African symbol is the laager, the defensive encampment made with the ox-wagons of the Great Trek. (It is significant that the extreme Afrikaner movement of the war years, which openly supported the Nazis, was called the Ossewabrandwag, the Ox-Wagon Sentinel.) The essential foundation of the South African regime is Christianity used as a defensive barrier, a laager.

Let me say a word on another totalitarian regime with which I am familiar, that of Rhodesia. Here the essential foundation seems to me to be something different. It is simply an exaggerated form of the evils of a Consumer society. It is materialist, but not the way a Communist society is. There is nothing philosophical about it. It is based on the enjoyment of, and the wish to continue enjoying, a very comfortable existence. There are two statistics about Rhodesia which seem to me very significant. The first is that of the White inhabitants, two-thirds live in two towns. It is a remarkably urban society. The other is that about a quarter of a million Whites have over 120,000 domestic servants, which is surely a world record. And I should say that the same is true of the great majority of the English in South Africa. They often support the Government, but they are hardly represented in it. They do not belong to the Dutch Reformed Church. But they are comfortable and well-off and they are very ready to accept a regime which maintains their position. But it would be a mistake to think they are all respectable members of the Middle Class. The strongest supporters of the Government in South Africa are the White workers, defending their very privileged position in industry.

As I have said, all totalitarian regimes have much in common. Anyone who has had experiences of both Nazi Germany and present-day South Africa is not likely to be surprised by this quotation from a speech by the present Prime Minister of South Africa in 1942.* 'We stand for Christian Nationalism which is an ally of National Socialism. You can call this anti-democratic principle dictatorship if you wish. In Italy it is called Fascism, in Germany National Socialism and in South Africa Christian Nationalism.' I think it is very interesting to compare the art in modern totalitarian states. There are extraordinary similarities. Those who know them might make a comparison between the Soviet War Memorial at Treptow Park in Berlin and the Voortrekker Monument near Pretoria, completed in 1949. I once remember reading in the course of a single week two statements about pop music. One came in a book about Youth Organisations in the Soviet Bloc. The author had repeatedly been told that pop music was an invention of the monopolo-capitalistic world deliberately infiltrated into the Communist world in order to corrupt the Youth. The

* B. J. Vorster.

other came in the report of a speech by the Secretary of Education for the Transvaal in which he said that pop music was an invention of the Communist world deliberately infiltrated into the Free World in order to corrupt the Youth.

Communism: this is undoubtedly the most formidable opponent. It is based on an interpretation of history which must be taken seriously and has, in fact, much to contribute to its understanding. To my mind it has one very great weakness. It is based on an over-simplification of human society. To take an example, I feel myself that the greatest turning point in European society since the Graeco-Roman world was the successful attempt in the thirteenth century to reconcile Greek philosophy and the Christian religion. I believe that our modern society rests largely on this and, as they perhaps can never be wholly reconcilable, it explains some of the tensions in our society as well. I do not see how this achievement can possibly be fitted into the framework of the Marxist dialectic.

But surely the greatest lesson to be learnt by Christians is that they must recapture the belief that Hope is a virtue. Faith, Hope and Charity: Christians will believe that Faith is a virtue; many more that Charity or Love is; but what of Hope? Either it becomes merely a way of expressing a general acceptance of a belief in Progress, as it did in the last century, or it is regarded as a kind of futile optimism. What it can mean as a virtue was made clear to me when, just after the end of the war, I was shown a letter written by someone who had been in a Nazi concentration camp and had survived. In this letter he spoke of how strange it was that he had been able to endure 'the horror and squalor' of that camp.

How can I explain it? In that monotonous, flat, mauve country near Breslau, with eagerness I used to watch the sunrise. On clear nights I would wait for Orion. Every bush and every tree were something rare for me. Once I came across a rabbit hole and I used to stand by it for long periods at a time and I was happy when at least for a moment, I could catch sight of the rabbit's family. I clutched at living realities to convince myself that I myself was still alive. In that there was some kind of urge to hold onto something, to snatch at some support. I cannot say that religious certainty gave me support of that kind, though it comforted me by representing my situation as a state that was not abnormal for a Christian. I had a little missal with me; I used to read it to my comrades, especially to one with whom I shared my palliasse. A strange thing: in the service for almost every day it spoke of persecution, and in every one despair was overcome by hope. I was myself astonished at that. That victorious hope!

> On the day that I was released, I had read in the service, 'contra spem speravit', and in that hope, in spite of everything, was a truly comforting thing. [Contra spem speravit – Who, against hope, believed in hope.]

I think we must consider also what has happened in the Communist world with the abandonment of freedom. It has been abandoned quite deliberately, as Stalin explained so cogently. The answer comes, I think, in one of the two passages of modern writing which I have read which have made the greatest impression on me. It comes from one of the Note-Books of Albert Camus, published in 1965 some years after his death.

> I have the liveliest taste for freedom and for every intellectual, freedom ends by being identified with freedom of expression. But I quite realise that this concern does not come first with a great number of Europeans because justice alone can give them the material minimum they need and that, rightly or wrongly, they would willingly sacrifice freedom for this elementary justice. [I had better explain that when Camus spoke of Justice here he meant Social Justice, fair treatment by society.] I have known this for a long time. If it seemed to me necessary to defend the conciliation of justice and freedom, it is because, in my opinion, in this resided the last hope of the West. But this conciliation can only be accomplished in a certain climate which today appears to be almost Utopian. Shall we sacrifice one or other of these values? What are we to think in that case?
>
> After an interval of two thousand years, we shall watch Socrates' sacrifice repeated time and time again.

There is, I think, a hard lesson in this. If, in order to destroy social injustice, men abandon freedom, then quite inexorably they create a new social injustice in its place. I believe the real significance of what is sometimes called the Prague Spring of 1968 was that it was a definite attempt to bring about the reconciliation Camus had hoped for.

South Africa: the finest people in that country are, in my opinion, Afrikaner members of the Dutch Reformed Church who do *not* use Christianity defensively. I used to meet them as members of the Christian Institute of Southern Africa. They fearlessly challenge their own society by finding in Christianity an inspiration to face the need for constructive change and so to find a non-violent solution of the appalling problems of their country. Anyone can discover what that inspiration is by reading a book recently published, *The Trial of Beyers Naudé*; he is the Director of the Institute. In this book will be found a sermon he preached in September 1963 on the text, 'We must obey God rather than men'.

Now I know, there are many who would say today, that now is not the time to speak out, even though there are many things that are unjust and morally indefensible; now is the time to remain silent and to stand by your people.

Brothers and sisters, however well-meant such a viewpoint may be, do not we as Christians understand that such an attitude is born of fear and that fear is a sign of unbelief? Do we not confess and believe that if we obey God in everything, according to his Word, we can also leave our future and the future of our people safely in his hands? Whose kingdom comes first, the Kingdom of God or that of our people? What is more important, that we will all stand together or that we will stand with God? And what does it mean, to stand with God, except that we should claim the kingship of Jesus Christ over all people, thus also over our people, also as it concerns our ecumenical and race relations. And when we as Nederduitse Gereformeerde Kerk fear or refuse to do this boldly, then we fail our people, then we commit treason against our people.

If NG Kerk does not understand and exercise more deeply this obedience demanded by God, then we will suffer endless loss and sorrow. Not only will we lose or frustrate the best intellectual and spiritual forces in the ranks of our ministry; not only will we lose the trust of thousands of our members who are seeking biblical light on the controversial questions of church and state, kingdom and nation, colour and race, and not finding it now in their Church. But even more than this, our Church is in the process of irrevocably alienating the hearts of our daughter Churches and is closing the way for her witness to the Churches of Africa. If our Church continues with this deliberate and fear-inspired process of isolation, with its tragic withdrawal from the Holy Catholic Church in South Africa, in Africa, we will spiritually wither and die.

Oh, my Church, I call this morning in all sincerity from my soul – awake before it is too late. Stand up and give the hand of Christian brotherhood to all who sincerely stretch out the hand to you. There is still time, but the time is short, very short.

I might give the following incident as evidence that there is an answer. I think one of the most tragic events of the last few years in southern Africa was the murder of Eduardo Mondlane, the founder of Frelimo. He once told me that he had been born at Lourenco Marques. When he was six his father had moved with his family to Louis Trichardt, a town in the northern Transvaal. There he had been to an African school in the African location and he did so well that he gained a bursary to my own university, the University of the Witwatersrand in Johannesburg. This was before the present Nationalist Government came into power and the University was very ready to take African students, which was quite legal. He was due to take his final law examination in November 1948. In March the Nationalists won the election and formed a government. In May he was expelled from the country and he went back to Lourenco Marques. The University sent a young lecturer there with the Law Examination papers and instructions to hire a room in a hotel and invigilate him. He took the examination and passed very well. When he heard that I came from Wits he was very excited. He asked after members of the staff whom he had known and he told me this story. He ended by saying to me, 'That is the reason why, when I address the new recruits among my Freedom Fighters, as I always try to do, I tell them to remember that they are not fighting "Whites"; they are fighting tyrants.'

Nazism: this seems to me the most difficult as we surely find in it the nearest to the ultimate Evil in human History. The only answer is as near as we get to the ultimate Good. I have no doubt what is the piece of writing during my own life-time which has meant most to me. It is a letter by Dietrich Bonhoeffer written from prison on the 16 July, 1944. It is too long to quote in full, but here is the ending:

> The only way is that of Matthew 18:3, i.e. through repentance, through *ultimate* honesty. ('Except ye be converted and become as little children, ye shall not enter into the kingdom of heaven.') And the only way to be honest is to recognise that we have to live in the world *esti deus non daretur* [as if we assume the non-existence of God]. And this is just what we do see – before God! So our coming of age forces us to a true recognition of our situation *vis à vis* God. God is teaching us that we must live as men who can get on very well without him. The God who is with us is the God who forsakes us. (Mark 15:34: 'My God! My God! Why has thou forsaken me?') The God who makes us live in this world without using him as a working hypothesis is the God before whom we are ever standing. Before God and with him we live without God. God allows himself to be edged out of the world and on to the cross. God is weak and powerless in the world and that is exactly the way, the only way, in which he can be with us and help us. Matthew 8:17 ('That it might be fulfilled which was spoken by Esaias the prophet saying, "Himself took our infirmities and bare our sicknesses".') makes it crystal clear that it is not by his omnipotence that Christ helps us but by his weakness and suffering. This is the decisive difference between Christianity and all religions.

And to show the full nature of the paradox I may point out that earlier in the letter Bonhoeffer had said that if the recipient of the letter had shortly to preach a sermon he might consider one of seven texts for which he gives the references. Here are five of them . . . 'He verily is my strength and my salvation: he is my defence, so that I shall not greatly fall', 'I am thine, O save me', 'The Lord hath appeared of old unto me saying "Yea, I have loved thee with an everlasting love; therefore with loving kindness have I drawn thee"', 'O Israel, fear not: for I have redeemed thee; I have called thee by thy name; thou art mine', and 'Lo I am with you always, even unto the end of the world'.

May I conclude with a personal memory? One day in 1946 I visited a camp in the British Zone of Germany where two hundred Nazi women, most of them wardresses of concentration camps, were being held before trial. It would not be unreasonable to claim that never before have two hundred such dreadful women been gathered together in one place. They were in the charge of a Sergeant, who was a woman. She had to help her two or three girls and there were sentries round the camp. As we walked across the camp she said she had no idea why she had been chosen for this post. She said she had never had anything to do with prisoners before. 'But I've learnt one thing,' she said. 'The really important thing is to keep up your prisoners' morale.' I found that she had been spending her own money on buying lipstick and rouge for the prisoners, 'My prisoners' as she always called them. If you had seen their faces!

She asked me if I could get her a piano. I said I thought I could, and I asked, 'Does one of your girls play?' 'Oh no,' she said, 'It's not my girls, it's my prisoners. I've learnt one thing about the Germans. They're a very musical people. I am sure some of my prisoners can play the piano, and it would be so good for them, you know. It would take their minds off things. And the only instrument I have is a cello and we haven't got a bow.' We walked on further. She said she thought the best thing of all that she could do was to get them to act plays. 'That really takes their minds off things. And it's good for those who watch too.' She was in a state of great excitement. She had persuaded the authorities to allow her to arrange for some of her prisoners to go off next day to a neighbouring camp of male Nazi prisoners awaiting trial to act a play there. They would go in a bus, accompanied by guards. The play was a very well-known English play and she had got one of her prisoners to write a new translation of it. (This prisoner, I may add, was Lord Haw-Haw's widow.) The play was *Charlie's Aunt*.

It was far-and-away the most incongruous thing I have ever known in my life. I have sometimes told this story to people with some experience of politics and I find the response varies. A good many feel that she was quite mistaken. These dreadful criminals should not have been treated in this way. For myself I can only say that Life for me has never been quite the same again since I met that Sergeant.

ROBERT KENNEDY

In 1966 Robert Kennedy visited South Africa. As the American Press Corps was excluded from covering the mission, these notes and impressions are of interest in recalling the charismatic effect which the Senator exerted over the younger generation before his tragic assassination. The letter of thanks which follows, draws a parallel between the party after Kennedy's speech in Johannesburg and the party in Berlin the evening before the Blockade began in 1948. The hosts to whom the letter is addressed were Clive and Irene Menell. Clive is a prominent business man in Johannesburg; Irene, a leading member of the Progressive Party. Both became very firm friends of the Birleys during the time of Robert's Visiting Professorship.

THE KENNEDY VISIT has roused the most intense excitement here, and this has been enhanced by the incredibly ham-handed performance of the government. By delaying the granting of his passport, refusing entrance to his newspaper correspondents and finally refusing to meet Kennedy himself they succeeded, as nothing and no one else could have done, in concentrating on his visit the attention not only of South Africa, but of the whole world. His speech at Cape Town made a very great impression, and was matched by the very great numbers who attended the Affirmation Ceremony and the ovation which he received before and after. His speech at Durban was also good, although according to observers, the audience was less responsive; the students there seem to have had less support from their Principal and academic staff. By the time Senator Kennedy got to Johannesburg he had had two gruelling days with only a few hours' sleep each night and a schedule for each day which had literally not a spare minute. On Wednesday, when he was due to fly up from Durban, his plane was late and he was never able to make up the hour he lost, so arrived late for his speech in the Great Hall.

I don't know about the Cape Town and Durban arrangements, but the organisation of the White Students Representative Council was absolutely first rate. They had about 1500 tickets to dispose of and about 7000 applications. Being in some ways rather unworldly, they told us they were slightly shattered by the number of people who considered themselves their old friends, and by the Black Market rate offered, R10 per ticket! Only 800 tickets were available for students, and at least 1000 of them camped outside the office all night to get them. The SRC took great touble to see to it that Indian, Coloured and African students had a good share (they would not have been allowed to queue for them) and a representative of each group got a seat on the platform. They also arranged for the proceedings to be relayed to some lecture rooms and broadcast outside by loud speakers over the main entrance. There was a crowd of about 4000 people there by the time Kennedy arrived. Thanks to Robin Margo who knows all about my ear we had very good seats right up in the front so I was able to hear practically everything.

The space between the platform and the front row was crawling, literally, with pressmen and cameramen: I have never seen so many in one spot, and they moved about almost entirely on hands and knees. I don't know where they could have put the American pressmen if they had been allowed in. We sat a longish time, but the pressmen's activities kept everyone fairly happy, and the people in charge of the lighting kept turning it on the main door, which made us all think that he was coming any moment. Incidentally, it is interesting how playing about with lights, especially spotlights, can build up the sense of excitement and anticipation. When he did arrive he was given a standing ovation which went on for several minutes. Rather a nice thing happened just before. Lawrence Gandar (the *Rand Daily Mail* Editor) and his wife walked in, and quite spontaneously the whole packed hall broke into unprompted applause. It was the best possible tribute and no one could have more deserved it. K's speech was good, but being the third in three days on virtually the same subject it had not quite the impact of his first to Cape Town. But he spoke directly and naturally without any of the usual politician's over-emphases, and had a very good line in asides. But he did make it very clear that he realised what a tough time the students have been and are having and how courageous they are, and conveyed unmistakably that he intended to see that students in other parts of the world should realise it too.

After that he answered questions quite skilfully. After leaving the hall he then had another standing ovation; at the entrance he stopped again to say a word to the people outside, about 5000 of them. We slipped out by a side door, as Clive, with whom they were staying, was having a small party for them to which he asked us. This was easily the best thing that happened. He had got round about twenty of the best singers from Union Artists (the people who did *King Kong*) to come and perform. They were all there when we arrived, in a state of tremendous excitement, dancing to while away the time in an absent-minded sort of way. They have got a new European (I think English) trainer, caller Exley, a very nice man, quite young, with a very nice wife. He said it was the first time he has worked with African performers and he has never enjoyed anything so much in his life: because they put the whole of themselves into all that they do, and their musical feeling is incredible.

When the Kennedys arrived they really got going; first a very accomplished solo on some sort of trumpet with drums and guitar accompaniment, and then two superb choruses (I think from their new musical *Sikalo*). They are pretty good when they sing anything, but when it is their own music the emotional force is overwhelming; and yet it never adversely affects the technical side of the singing, the phrasing, the rhythm, and so on. I have never heard anywhere else human voices with the kind of organ tone that these Africans have. It was completely intoxicating and at the end of it we were almost as exhausted as the singers, if not more so. After that they sang 'Nkosi sikelela Africa', which is pretty well guaranteed to reduce any hearer to tears. After that K. suggested the American Marchers' song, 'We shall overcome' which was just about the biggest anticlimax you could imagine, as it is an exceptionally dreary tune on about three notes, consisting of those three words and practically nothing else. However the Africans with their usual good manners did their best with it, and it wasn't too bad. K. was very good with them all, talking to them and laughing with them without any over-heartiness. The party went like a bomb until about two o'clock and ended up with everybody jigging while the Africans sang.

There is no doubt that the visit has had a tremendous effect on the students' morale, and not only theirs, but the Profs, Liberals, Black Sash and all, and we are all bustling round with new ideas about how to keep up the battle. The students particularly have had a pretty stiff time lately with a lot of public vilification in the National Press and the Radio, and also private intimidation: visits from the Special Branch, warnings by Police to their parents, refusals of passports and so on. This has really put new heart into them. I think K. really was impressed by them and that he really will see to it that America knows how well NUSAS [National Union of South African Students] is doing, even if the English remain uninterested. I think the Nats have ensured that happy result by refusing entry to all the US newsmen, who are not used to this treatment and are out for blood. A satisfying thought.

June 1966

Dear Clive and Irene,

I simply cannot tell you how grateful I am to you for asking us to your house on Wednesday evening. It was a quite unforgettable evening.

That's an easy thing to say, perhaps. One has evenings with an exceptionally good party which one does not forget. And there are evenings which one remembers for some purely personal reason, like the evening when I met the whole school at Eton in School Yard just before I left and said good-bye to them, or, for that matter, the evening when I proposed to Elinor – immediately after we had been to a performance of *Othello* as she sometimes reminds me. But I have only known one other evening in my life which I can really compare with last Wednesday's. That was the evening of 23 June 1948.* This was the day before the Blockade of Berlin began. That evening I had to dinner Ernst Reuter, the Mayor of Berlin, and the three leaders of the main political parties in Berlin to discuss the founding of a new University in Berlin in the Western half of the city. The famous University of Berlin was in the Russian sector and had become quite impossible. I knew that at nine that evening the British Military Commandant was going to announce on the wireless the introduction of a new currency into West Berlin and this would lead to an immediate blockade. I tried to get them to stop our discussions and listen to him, but they would have none of it. To found a new University and save the youth of Berlin was more important.

From that moment, I felt sure that we should win. In the end we relied entirely on the reaction of the people of Berlin. I don't think it is generally known that we took the steps which caused the Russians to blockade Berlin, quite aware that on paper the Russians were bound to win. We (that is about twenty on the British side in Berlin who were in the know) believed that the Americans would wake up in time and send enough aircraft – which they did with a vengeance a month later.

* See page 90. This account and the reference to morale explains his optimism a little more fully.

But the question was whether the ordinary people of Berlin would stand the strain. I was quite convinced after that evening that they would.

Anything much more different from my staid and earnest dinner party in Berlin eighteen years ago than the exciting party at your house last Wednesday it would be hard to imagine. But essentially it had the same effect on me. The situation in Berlin then was altogether different. Then we knew that a few months would settle it one way or another. I don't think any of us contemplated then a blockade lasting for as long as eleven months. Here in South Africa one faces a very, very long haul. But I left your house feeling in the same way quite sure that it will work out all right in the end. I think it was the combination there of the African singers and those students and the absolutely natural companionship and the shared enjoyment and excitement which had this effect on me. Of course, I know there is a subtle alchemy which some hostesses have which makes a party go. This does *not* entail the hostess pushing herself forward and 'throwing people together'. It is something much more subtle than that. Probably one of the chief ingredients is that everyone should completely trust the hostess. I told Mrs Kennedy that I was sure that there were no other two people than you two who could have laid on that party.

At any rate you gave us the most memorable occasion of our time out here. It was incredibly exciting and enjoyable. It was also the perfect finish for Kennedy's very remarkable four days in South Africa. I am still feeling intoxicated by it and I am quite sure that my memory of it is never going to fade. I cannot get over the fact that at the age of *sixty-two* I should have had such an experience.

Yours ever
Robert Birley

IN PARTIBUS INFIDELIUM

*This paper was given after Robert's return from Johannesburg to the UU
(United Ushers), a Schoolmaster Society whose members are drawn
from many of the major Public Schools. The atmosphere is always
relaxed and this account of teaching experiences in African schools is
geared to stimulate post-prandial discussion. In Orlando High School,
referred to at the outset, Robert founded the first school library in Soweto.
The plaque bearing his name survived the school riots of 1976, though
many other parts of the buildings were destroyed. The title of the paper
was a phrase applied to national Catholic bishoprics in lands long held by
the Turks. A near rendering would be: 'A Ministry in the Lands of the
Infidel'.*

It was in a classroom in the African school known as Orlando High
School in Orlando, an African township of Johannesburg, that I heard
the most unexpected remark ever made to me when I have been
teaching. I had not been out in South Africa for long. A week or so
before I had been taken on an official sponsored tour of some African
schools in Johannesburg and one of them was this school. There I had
whispered to the headmaster the question whether he would let me
come and take a class one day in History and I had received an
enthusiastic whisper of assent. I realised that this would be illegal, but I
thought it was worth asking.

My experience of schools, that is of teaching in schools, has been a
very limited one. I taught for a fortnight at Bradfield when still an
undergraduate, at Eton and Charterhouse and for two months at St
Paul's School, Concord, New Hampshire. That is four in all. I have
also taken odd lessons here and there. But to this meagre list of four, I
can now add Orlando High School as well. I gave odd lessons in a
great many schools in South Africa for Whites, Africans, Coloureds
and Indians. I used to go and take a class at Orlando whenever I could.

Mr Kambule, the Headmaster, who always called me 'Prof', spoke of me as a regular member of his staff, sometimes very indiscreetly, but then one of the most endearing things about Mr Kambule was his readiness to be indiscreet. I suppose I had better face the question of how I got away with it. The authorities must have come to know what I did. I was never sure whether they knew what I said in some of my lessons. Mrs Helen Suzman, who forms the one-woman opposition in the South African Assembly – for the official opposition, the United Party, is no opposition – once warned me that every senior class I took in any school would certainly include at least one informer. I think she must have been wrong. I know I puzzled the authorities because the Head of the Security Police in Johannesburg once said to someone, who repeated it to me, 'That man Birley, we simply do not know what to do about him'. But I have little doubt what my protection was. I was immensely respectable. In any case, I got away with it, though hints were sometimes dropped to me by those in authority and towards the end of my time sometimes more than hints.

But I must get back to the remark which so surprised me. I ought not to have been quite so surprised; in a sense the remark was prepared for.

It was a Matriculation Class of about thirty-five children, boys and a few girls, the top class in the school. They had questioned me about the British Empire (my efforts to persuade them that it was now styled the British Commonwealth were unavailing). 'Please Sir,' one of them said at one point, 'we know all about the Durham Report. Can you tell us something about Lord Durham?' It was not easy to describe convincingly to a class in an African township of Johannesburg a man who was one of the most aristocratic figures in England, who owned large estates on some of which were very valuable coalfields, who said once that a man ought to be able to jog along quite comfortably on £40,000 a year, and yet was one of the men most responsible for the first Reform Bill (with which I may say, they were entirely familiar), was known as 'Radical Jack' and was so much of an extremist that he was sent out to Canada to get him out of the way. No, I ought not to have been quite so surprised, when at the very end of the lesson some of them whispered to one another and then one of them said, 'Please Sir, the next time you come will you tell us about something which we find very difficult?' I said I would do what I could and asked what it was. 'Please Sir, the Revolutions of 1848, and especially Germany, Austria and Hungary.'

What I hope to do is try to explain to you the significance of this remark, perhaps the most significant made to me in South Africa. I should explain first that African, or, as it is styled, Bantu, Education in South Africa was wholly reorganised by the Bantu Education Act of 1953 which placed it entirely under the control of the Central Government. The principles of the Act can be illustrated by the following short quotations from statements by South African political leaders. The first three are from speeches by Dr Verwoerd. 'When I have control of native education, I shall reform it so that the natives will be taught from childhood to realise that equality with Europeans is not for them', and, 'The school must equip the African to meet the demands which the economic life of South Africa will impose upon him; there is no place for the native in European society above the level of certain forms of labour', and, 'If the native in South Africa today, in any kind of school in existence, is being taught to expect that he will live his life under the policy of equal rights, he is making a big mistake'. The fourth was made by the Minister of Bantu Education in 1959. 'It is the basic principle of Bantu Education that our aim is to keep the Bantu child a Bantu child.'

I am now working in London at an institution known as the City University, until last year a College of Advanced Technology. Once a week, I lecture to eighty-five students of the Departments of Electricity and Electronics and of Chemistry. Not one of these students took History at A Level; very few of them at O Level; very few have studied any History at all for years. It is inconceivable if I had taken one of the classes in which the very great majority of these students were educated, that I should have been asked that question. How was it that I was asked it in an African school in South Africa in which it was intended that the Bantu child should be so educated that he remained a Bantu child?

Perhaps I should say here that this was in no way a unique experience. I might give two other examples. One day, I visited a High School at Lange, an African township of Cape Town. By that time I think a good many African Headmasters must have come to hear of me. At any rate, I found that I always had a great welcome from them and, when I asked if I might take the Matriculation Class in History, I was always allowed to do so. The African townships of Cape Town are gloomy places. It is the policy of the government to move all Africans out of the Western Cape Province. It cannot be done because the demand for their labour is too pressing, so when they are moved out, others move in. But it gives rise to a most depressing atmosphere of uncertainty. The school had 900 children, but there were only eight in its Matriculation History class. I was not expecting much. 'Ask me,' I said, 'any question you like on the European history we have been doing and let's see where it leads us.' 'Please, Sir,' the response came at once, 'can you explain to us *why* Mussolini set up a totalitarian dictatorship?'

Or there was the occasion when I visited a school deep in a native reserve in Zululand. It was a boarding school and a good many of the children came from towns some way off. I asked the class which character during the French Revolution they would most like to meet in real life. Napoleon was the universal favourite. I suggested that we should exclude him. There was a pause and then the unexpected proposal 'Montesquieu'. I explained that he had died over thirty years before the Revolution, but I thought I should not let the chance slip. For the rest of the time we discussed Montesquieu's theories of the influence of climate on government.

The situation began to seem to me more and more paradoxical. In the end I came to realise that this was exactly what it was. These astonishing encounters of mine in African schools were reflections of the essential South African contradiction and this I must try to explain.

Far and away the most important social phenomenon in South Africa is what is known as Job Reservation. This ensures, with legal support where necessary, that the skilled jobs are all reserved for the whites, the unskilled are left to the blacks. To the great majority of whites nothing matters as much as that. Social segregation, I some- times felt, was only a means of making Job Reservation more easily maintained. And the economic development of South Africa is mak- ing Job Reservation more and more difficult to maintain. The utter absurdities that arise are a sign of this. In Johannesburg, if you have your house painted, you may get an African workman to carry it out, provided that the top two coats are applied by a white workman. Quite simply, there are not enough whites to go round. Industrial development, in South Africa as everywhere else, means that the proportion of skilled workers goes up and of unskilled goes down.

This has produced a quite remarkable parental demand for Sec- ondary Education, since this is necessary for their children if they are to hold skilled posts. The government resist this pressure, but anyone who gets to know the schools can see how they are being forced to retreat. It is even more important, perhaps, that more are staying on at school to take the Matriculation examination. The number is still pitifully small – last year there were about 1200 African children in the top form of the Secondary Schools in the whole country out of nearly 2 million African children at school. But it is growing.

It may be the aim of Bantu Education to ensure that the Bantu child remains a Bantu child, but it cannot ensure that he becomes a Bantu Matriculation candidate. Obviously, there is no Bantu Physics or Trigonometry. Equally clearly there is no Bantu English Literature. And there is not enough Bantu History or Bantu Geography. In despair, the Bantu Education Department arranges that most African schools take the same Matriculation as that taken in the independent English schools. This may seem very extraordinary and, to tell the truth I never quite understood it. As I came to know the Department better, I came to realise that it would be quite beyond it to moderate a Matriculation of its own. I never dared to ask them why they made use of this 'white' examination, as I was afraid that I might, by doing so, encourage them to organise their own one. That would have been quite appalling for the schools. But the results of using this 'white' examination at the summit of Bantu Education are very strange. My heart bleeds now at the thought of the African children whom I taught having to answer questions in the Matriculation Examination. Last month, of one of their set books, Trollope's *Barchester Towers*, I am prepared to argue that this is the least Bantu book ever written. Nor shall I ever forget going into an African school and finding the children in the top class learning by heart the names of the coalfields of Scotland.

The South African dilemma is this. The economic development of the country is forcing the government to allow the emergence of a politically conscious educated class of Africans. These will in the end make it impossible for white South Africa to maintain its social policy. All their history, their traditions, their present social structure and, above all, their deep, unexpressed fears urge them to uphold this policy. There are those who appreciate this dilemma. A member of the Prime Minister's Economic Advisory Council said to me last year that not a single member of it believed in Apartheid. I asked him if any were prepared to say so and he replied that that was another matter.

But to return to the remark that so startled me, 'Please, Sir, the Revolutions of 1848 and especially Germany, Austria and Hungary.' Those children had been brought up against one of the great revolutionary movements in history in the nineteenth century. I came to the conclusion that the economic development of South Africa made it inevitable that more African children – still only a few, of course – would come up against that revolutionary movement, or, to give another example, would find themselves faced with a question like this one in their Matriculation paper, 'Explain how social injustice and the despotism of Kings led to the French Revolution'. Going and teaching in these schools was like visiting the source of a great river, only the river will be flowing through the future.*

The request made to me was significant in other ways of course. It brought me face to face with the immense problems created all over Africa by the sudden and violent impact of Western European Education (I say Western European rather than English because we must never forget France, as we are so liable to do), its impact on the African mind. A school in Johannesburg or even in Cape Town is not in any way typical of Africa, of course, and hardly even of South Africa. Of the Africans in South Africa, only about one third live in what are usually called 'urban areas', a third in European farms, as labourers and a third in the native reserves. It is very easy for the visitor to South Africa to forget the Africans living in these reserves – for the very good reason that it is illegal for him to enter them, except along a main road from which he may not diverge. However, my wife and I were fortunate enough to be able on one occasion to masquerade as students in the Department of Anthropology and join a party of them in a visit to a reserve in the extreme north of the Transvaal, the territory of the Vendas, I suppose the most primitive tribe in the country.

There one might witness the Domba ceremony, part of the year-long initiation training for the girls of the tribe. It was almost unbelievably romantic. We were on a ledge near a village looking over an immense valley. It was a full moon and a brilliantly clear night. Round and round a fire, to the beating of drums, moved a circle of girls, naked except for a thin loin cloth, one behind the other, one hand holding the elbow of the girl in front, the other arm moving in an endless ripple. It was the Domba snake dance and the rippling was the movement of the snake's skin. In front of them were two young ladies of about twenty – tremendous, strapping girls, the leaders of the initiation training, nature's gym mistresses, I felt – and in front of them, leading the file, a young man who twisted his hands and his body in astonishing contortions, the head of the snake. As they shuffled round and round, the girls sang little songs. At one moment, I asked the chief, near whom I was standing, if he could translate the one they were then singing. 'Certainly,' he said, 'it goes like this. "It's very very late and I want to go to bed, but I've got to go on. It's very late and I want to go to bed, but I've got to go on."' I felt confirmed in my view that these initiation ceremonies were not intended only to

---

* During a tour of East Africa Robert asked rhetorically what the French Revolution could possibly mean to twentieth-century Africans. There was an instant cry of 'Everything'.

prepare the girls for the sexual experiences of marriage, but also to prepare them for a life of hoeing.

The dances in the end stopped and, for a moment, the students and we two stood alone on the ledge. All anthropologists become to some degree identified with the object of their research, like psychologists with their patients, but I am not an anthropologist. Raising my voice more than I ought to have done, I exclaimed, 'It's all very well, but, you know, it really won't do.' I was never allowed to forget that remark by the students of the University of the Witwatersrand. But, I felt, surely in due course one might hope that these girls would have a rather more interesting, varied and useful education than this.

The next day we went to stay at a hospital run by the Dutch Reformed Church, and there I thought my point of view, which the students found quaintly philistine, received some support. There they had instituted what was quite openly a rival to the Domba and had offered it to parents. It was a year's course in the hospital for girls, working as orderlies, helping with old people, and being taught mothercraft and homecraft. It had been running two years and, I was told, it was already showing itself a success. The first batch of girls who had left there were proving to be unusually marriageable. It was, I thought, the most interesting educational experiment I had seen in South Africa.

But it all seemed to be a long way from the Revolution of 1848. And then three days later I was given reason to wonder about this. We were visiting a chief and he asked us if we would care to come and see a Domba practice in a field at the back of his kraal. Now it was one thing to see the snake dance round a fire in the light of a full moon, but another to watch it under the afternoon sun with an old man swearing at the girls if they made mistakes in the singing or dancing. It was rather like going out to watch a house football practice. We walked back to the chief's kraal and he said to me, 'Tell me, have you ever met Mr Harold Macmillan?' 'Yes,' I said, 'I have.' 'So have I,' he said. 'A very remarkable man, I thought.' As we went on, an old lady came up and insisted on walking with my wife, holding her hand. 'Mrs Birley,' the chief said, 'you really mustn't let her bother you. I'm afraid she is a psychiatric case.' The wind of change, I thought, is indeed blowing through this country. Perhaps the Revolution of 1848 is not so very far from the Vendaland after all.

But what strains and stresses will be endured in the process, and what a responsibility rests on the European in Africa. It was easy to feel that the hospital had the right solution. The Bantu child they were creating was a very different kind of child, but still a Bantu child. But it only needed a return to Johannesburg, to the three-quarters of a million Africans living there in Soweto, the South Western Townships, to realise that one could not ignore the modern industry which Europe has brought to Africa. Soweto, in the end will conquer the Vendaland; the Vendaland will not conquer Soweto.

One might go further. Would the mothercraft which the hospital at Tshilindzini taught to the girls have been possible without modern medicine? No one who has seen children of a year old brought to a hospital suffering from acute malnutrition, nothing but skin and bones and, as one doctor put it to me in Zululand, 'having already lost the will to live', is likely to underrate the importance of 'mothercraft'. And can a country have the benefits of modern medicine without an education which introduces them to the Revolution of 1848? But we must not forget what Africa is now going through. My wife used to work in one of the poorest African Townships of Johannnesburg and she sometimes took sick children to an African doctor there, a very able young man, a graduate, I may add, of my own University from the days before the government forced racial segregation on it. One little girl, whom she was afraid might be epileptic, was responding very well to treatment when her family suddenly decided to turn instead to the local witch-doctor. Soon after, I was talking with this doctor and I asked him if there was any branch of study which he had never engaged in at school or university, but which he now regretted having missed. Certainly, he replied – Anthropology. He went on to explain how his education had cut him off from the people among whom he lived, and he referred to the family of the little girl. 'It was my fault,' he said, 'I ought to have been able to prevent it.' We are used to colonial administrators realising that they need some anthropology in order to understand the people whom they govern. But what a situation in a society when one part of it has the same need in order to understand another part.

This may be an extreme case and the young doctor is no doubt an exceptionally sensitive person, but no one who has been in Africa can regard it as irrelevant. I remember once a young African in Uganda, absurdly high in the Educational Service for his age, but making to all accounts a great success of it, telling me what it had been like to come from a primitive and polygamous home and go as a boarder to a strictly monogamous Church School, and, above all, what it has been like to go back home during the holidays. I asked if he complained. 'Complain?', he said, 'of course not. I'm very happily married, and it would be disastrous if either my wife or I thought I might take a second wife. All I ask is that you should have some sympathy for us, the first generation of educated Africans.'

> Our customs are dug up,
> And put aside, like the grass
> On which the dancer trod,
> And foreign crops implanted;
> And we pass by, eyes on the ground,
> Submitting to the foreign as ours.

There is, however, one product of European civilisation which need cause us no qualms, which is a quite unmixed blessing to Africa. When I felt uncertain and sometimes unhappy at seeing the clash of cultures, European and African, in South Africa, I used to comfort myself by thinking of this particular English contribution. It was Shakespeare. One of his plays is always one of the set books in the Matriculation Examination. Is Shakespeare's *A Midsummer Night's Dream*, or *Coriolanus*, any more Bantu than *Barchester Towers*? Perhaps not. He makes the question seem meaningless. So, incidentally, does Sophocles, as a performance of the *Antigone* by Africans in an African Township of Port Elizabeth showed clearly enough.

Shakespeare kept on cropping up, as it were, during my time in South Africa. There was the occasion, for instance, in an African School in Johannesburg when I saw a girl of sixteen reading *A Midsummer Night's Dream*. I asked her if she liked it. 'Oh,' she said, 'it makes me laugh till I cry.' I asked her if she had read anything else by Shakespeare. 'Yes,' she said, *'Julius Caesar.'* 'And what do you think of that?' 'Oh, that made me cry without laughing.' There was an unforgettable morning I spent with the students at the University in Basutoland, reading and discussing *Richard II*. I had to put up what defence I could for the King; all but one of them supported Boling-broke. He was a rebel. There was the special performance of *A Midsummer Night's Dream* at a theatre in Johannesburg for African schoolchildren on Shakespeare's birthday. With very great difficulty I persuaded the management to allow me to be present, which was quite illegal. I had to wait until the lights went down and, as the curtain rose, I crept into the theatre on all fours and crouched near the back row. Never has any performance of a Shakespeare play been more appreciated by the audience. There was an occasion when my wife and I were reading *Richard II* in our flat with three young Africans. We came to the scene, just after the death of John of Gaunt, when the Earl of Northumberland, Lord Willoughby and Lord Ross are left together on the stage and bewail the desperate state of the Kingdom. The two Lords become aware that Northumberland has some secret information which might give them some hope for the future. They press him to reveal it and he refuses.

> Be confident to speak, Northumberland:
> We three are but thyself, and speaking so,
> Thy words are but as thoughts; therefore be bold.

And at last Northumberland gives way and tells them that Bolingbroke may land at any moment. As we read, I became aware of a quite extraordinary sense of tension. I was not surprised: the most corrupting effect of living in a police state is the constant fear of informers among you. But it was more than that. Our little group did not meet again. By next week Northumberland had escaped across the border and was in Francistown in Bechuanaland. No doubt he was thinking, 'I wonder if the other two know that I am going.' And, quite probably they were thinking, 'We know he is going; we wonder if he knows that we know.'

The moment when I felt proudest of Shakespeare and what he could mean to a people so unlike his own countrymen was in the course of an incident as ridiculous, engaging and embarrassing as any I have ever experienced. If I had to choose one moment during my time in South Africa to treasure it would be this one. I was driving five young Africans – and there was only just room for them in my car – down to the station in Johannesburg, after a meeting when I had spoken to a group of young Africans about East Africa. It was at the very peak of the rush hour as shops and offices were closing in the city. Quite suddenly, on our way, there broke out a most violent argument for and against Christianity. 'Dr Verwoerd,' said one of its opponents, 'says his are the chosen people. I can tell you what the chosen people did. I've read it in the Bible. They invaded a country, killed most of the people there and made the rest slaves.' A little later, working himself up into an apparent state of the wildest excitement, though I could see that the argument was really a most friendly one, he stammered out, 'I-I-I-I-I-I'd rather be a Communist than a Christian.' To a member of the Nationalist Party, who believes that all liberals are Communists and all agnostics are, this would have been a puzzling remark. We reached the station. Villiers Street, which runs past it, was full from end to end with traffic. To stop for a moment brought down on one a storm of protest from the horns of the cars behind. We stopped at the 'non-white entrance' and I told them to get out quickly. Already the horns were beginning. They got out – and then suddenly they were all in again. 'Sir, Sir,' they said, 'will you give us a lecture on Shakespeare's tragedies?' 'Yes, yes, yes,' I said, 'but do get out.' 'But when, Sir?' 'Oh, I'll let you know, but do get out.' By this time, the horns of a quarter of a mile of cars were shrieking behind me. 'Sir, shall we come to your flat or go to the University?' 'For goodness sake, get out of the car. I don't know. I'll let you know.' At last they left me. All hell was let loose behind me. My car sprang forward and desperately I took the first turn to the left, hoping that I might thus throw off my pursuers. I dashed up Wanderers Street in a panic and hied for home.

THE CITY
UNIVERSITY –
GRESHAM
PROFESSOR

From 1967–71 Robert was Head of the Department of Social Science at The
City University, and from 1968–82 Gresham Professor of Rhetoric in the
City of London. In the first post he was able to nourish an interest in History
and ideas among groups of students whose principal studies were in the fields
of engineering and science. In the second he had the opportunity to lecture on
any subject he chose, a freedom which he relished and exploited to the full.
The titles of his Gresham Lectures contain many familiar themes: 'Resist-
ance to Tyranny', 'the Historical Background to the Irish Problem', 'Three
Divided Cities: Rome, Berlin and Jerusalem', etc. They also show a
continued delight in quaint explorations: 'Three Unusual Radicals',
'Three Remarkable Visitors to England', 'Jack the Treacle Eater'. Many
Gresham Lectures were delivered from notes and jottings. Occasionally
fuller versions were written out for publication in the City University
Journal, Quest.

CALLING THEM BY THEIR NAMES: THE COUNTRIES OF EUROPE

*The following lecture, re-christened 'Calling Them By Their Names',
was first given in December 1972 at the time of Britain's entry into the
EEC and later published in the* Cornhill Magazine, *in 1973. Although
at first reading it may seem fragmented, the emphasis on the tribal origins
of Europe and the similarity, inferred rather than stated, between
Ancient Europe and Modern Africa give a unifying theme. It is as
though we had gone into a theatre and the proscenium curtain showed a
map of the rigidly staked out frontiers of Europe. Then, as various lights
go on behind the gauze, we see something of the movements, shadowy
and shifting, of tribes and peoples usually on the edge of civilisation
rather than at the heart, fleeing, exploring, fighting, settling. The
paradoxes of etymology are eagerly seized upon. The penultimate
flourish, surely a surprise to most readers, is fired off like the highest
rocket on the fourth of June: a fourth-century tale that could have come
straight from the modern tabloid press, 'BORN AGAIN CHRISTIAN HIDES
FROM LEGAL WIFE'. It shows the unique solution that one Roman citizen
applied to the problem of domestic service.*

NAMES ARE A not infrequent subject of study. It is not difficult to
discover, if one knows where to look, what is meant if one is called
John or Robert or Algernon, Phyllis or Theresa, or what is the
meaning of the name of one's village or the county where it is to be
found. But the names of those larger units which we call 'countries'
usually seem to be taken for granted. Now that we are 'going into
Europe', as the saying goes, we might consider these names. We shall
find that this sometimes leads us into some strange nooks and alleys of
history.

We had better begin by considering the case of our own country. The earliest known name for the island on which we live was Albion. A late Roman poet of the fourth century AD, Festus Rufus Avienus, made use of the Sailing Directions of a sea-captain from Marseilles, written in the sixth century BC, in which after talking of the Sacred Island of the Hibernians, or Ireland, he refers casually to another one which lies stretched out by its side, the isle of the Albiones. (It may be rather embarrassing to Englishmen to realise that their country is first referred to as an unimportant appendage of Ireland.) The meaning of Albion is clear enough, the White Land. (The Latin word, *albus*, turns up often enough in place names, Alba Longa, the mother city of Rome, the Alps, the River Elbe and, as we shall see, Albania.) The reference, of course, is to the white cliffs of Dover. These, however, were foreigners' names for the island and its people. They called themselves Priten, or, as the Romans had it, Prettanoi. The meaning is again obvious. The clue is to be found in the Welsh word, *pryd*, a picture. They were adorned with pictures or tattooed.

Why then did they come to be called, and then call themselves, Britons and their island Britain? The reason is certainly to be found in the works of Julius Caesar. Although after his time we still find some writers speaking of Prettanoi, the spelling with the initial B became the usual one after his day. Various explanations have been given for the change. One is that Julius Caesar simply made a mistake, perhaps mishearing the word. Another is that there was at the time a Belgic tribe near Boulogne who were really called the Britanni and Caesar simply took it for granted that the people on the opposite side of the Channel had the same name. At any rate we may be grateful to him for his mistake. Rule Pritannia would sound comparatively feeble.

England seems obvious enough. In its earliest form, in the late ninth century, it was Englaland, the land of the Angles. It is not quite as straight-forward as it seems, however. The Venerable Bede tells us that they came from Angel, the angle or corner, in Schleswig between the Schlei and the Flensburg fiord. This is very possible, though they may have originated from some other angle. It has been suggested, however, that their name is derived from a word meaning a spear. Another theory is that it is a translation. The tribe occupied East Anglia, which had been the land of the Iceni, Boadicea's people, and no doubt the two became merged. The land between the Thames and the Wash forms a kind of promontory or angle and the Britons may have taken their name from a Celtic word, *icen*, meaning a corner or angle. It is not uncommon to get your name from where you are.

What is very strange is that England is called England, whatever the origin of the name of the Angles. For our country was not unified by the Angles, but by the Saxons. No one speaks of the Angles today; it is common enough to refer to us as Saxons. After all, the Irish call us Sassenachs. For some time there was no general term for the Anglo-Saxon land and at the end of the seventh century, Wihtred, King of Kent, had to call the Archbishop of Canterbury, the chief Bishop of Britain, 'Bretone heahbiscop'. But a new word was coming in and his contemporary, Ine, King of the West Saxons, uses in his Laws the term Engliscmon, or Englishman. The fact that we think of our country as England and ourselves as Englishmen, but never as Angles, while we may call ourselves Saxons, should show that the trails we shall have to follow in this study are liable to be rather confused.

Scotland was in no sense a different country until the Romans conquered the southern half of the island only, though naturally it was inhabited by different tribes. The first name for Scotland was Caledonia, to be found in Tacitus, and he probably invented it from one of the tribes, the Caledonii. Scotia and Scotland, at first, were terms always used to designate Ireland, where the tribe of Scots were living. Shortly before the year AD 500 the Scots from Ireland began to invade the western part of what we call Scotland, but as late as the very end of the ninth century King Alfred used the name Scotland for Ireland. In 933, however, we find it used in the Anglo-Saxon Chronicle for the northern half of the larger island, as it is today.

During the Dark Ages modern Scotland was divided into four parts, the Kingdom of the Picts, the Kingdom of the Scots who, as we have seen, came from Ireland, Strathclyde in the South-West and Lothian, the Lowlands, which were much influenced by the English. In 843 Kenneth MacAlpin, King of the Scots, finally crushed the Picts and he created a new kingdom. But he did not call this Scotland, but Alba. This was a survival of the old name Albion, which we have seen to have been the first used for the whole island. It had a competitor, however, as the Anglo-Saxon Chronicle shows. By 1050 all what we now know as Scotland was united, except the northern regions still held by the Norsemen, and by that time it was generally known as Scotland. The word Alba (or Alban) did not disappear altogether. In 1398 Robert, Earl of Fife, the second son of Robert II, was created Duke of Albany, in Latin Albania. Alban remained the name for Scotland in Welsh and Alba in Gaelic. The latter is the word for Scotland used by the Scottish Nationalists today. One wonders if they are all aware that they call their country after the white cliffs of Dover. However, they may comfort themselves with a recent suggestion that Albion is derived from the Celtic root, albio, meaning just 'the land', which is perhaps rather tame, unless one accentuates the word 'the'. (The whole of Scotland was recovered from the Norsemen by the middle of the thirteenth century. The Norse rule in north Scotland accounts for one of the most bizarre facts in the study of British place-names. The word, South, comes into the names of three districts in Britain: Surrey, the *Suther-ge*, or southern district, and Sussex, the South Saxons, where the compass is thought of as being in the centre of England, and Sutherland, which was the most southerly part of the Norwegian kingdom. Cape Wrath and Beachy Head are thus united.)

When we come to consider Wales we find ourselves in very deep waters. The Germans had a general word for the Celts, *Walha*, which was taken from a Celtic tribe, the Volcae, some of whom were to be found in south Gaul, others near the Rhine. Gradually the name came to be used for all Latin-speaking peoples, not only the Celts of Gaul. The word, therefore, turns up all over the place. We find it in the Walloons, the French speakers of Belgium, in the Vlachs, dotted about in the Balkans, in Wallachia, the southern province of Romania. In Icelandic writings of the thirteenth century the name of France is Valland (or Welshland). To this day the Polish name for Italy is Vlochy and for Italian, Wloch. The Anglo-Saxons brought the word with them. The British, as Latin-speaking Celts, became the *Wealas*. As is common among Teutonic peoples, the name of the country came directly from the people in it, without any necessity to add the word 'land'. (In the same way Sussex, for example, is Suth Seaxe, the South Saxons, and in Germany Baiern and Schwaben are used for what we call Bavaria or Swabia. To come nearer home again Cornwall is a tribal name, the Cornwealas, the Welsh who were called the Cornovii, from the Celtic word meaning a horn or, in this case, a promontory. The Cornishmen called their country Kernow.)

The Welsh, as we call them, do not, of course, themselves use the word Wales. Their country is Cymru, they are the Cymry. Even here there is a difficulty. In the Middle Ages the Welsh referred to themselves as Brython or Britons. It has been suggested that the name Cymry has a different origin. In the Middle Ages, *Cymro* (now a Welshman) was used in legal enactments to mean someone with a definite legal status, to be distinguished from a landless man or a slave. But it must have been used earlier as a tribal name among the Celts of south-west Scotland, for when part of the kingdom of Strathclyde was annexed to England by William Rufus it came to be known as Cumberland and as early as 945 it was called Cumbraland or the land of the Cumbras or Cymry.

Ireland is called in the Celtic tongue Eriu, in the genitive Erin. Julius

Caesar called it Hibernia. This was a corrupted Latin form of Ivernia, itself a corruption of the Greek Ierne, taken from the Old Celtic Iverio, hence Eziu and the modern Eire. In Celtic languages the initial letter 'p' had a way of disappearing. Probably the name was originally *Piverio*, the root 'pi' meaning 'fat'. Eire is the fertile country.

It is time that we crossed the Channel. The word Franci was used by the Romans as early as the third century AD to denote a confederation of tribes near the east bank of the Rhine. By the beginning of the sixth century they had conquered the northern part of Gaul and Burgundy. They still held a considerable part of northern Germany. The word, Franks, was often used quite generally for the people of North-Western Europe, usually divided into the Eastern and Western Franks. The Emperors of the Holy Roman Empire in the tenth century used to style themselves also Kings of the Eastern Franks. Gradually the Western Franks came to call their own country Francia, though as late as AD 1353 a Bishop of Bamberg complained that the French king called himself King of France, instead of King of Western France, as he should have done. (The names of Frankfurt-am-Main and Franconia – in German Franken, after its people – remind us of the eastern extent of early mediaeval Francia.) The term, Franci, came, in all probability, from the word for a kind of spear, for which they were famous, though it is not surprising that French philologists from an early age have seen a connection with 'franche', meaning free.

There is no name of a country in Europe as obscure as that of Spain (España). It is first mentioned by the Greek geographer, Hecateus, in about 500 BC as Iberia, clearly named from the River Ebro. (The Greeks knew very little about it. Aristotle thought that the River Guadalquivir rose in the Pyrenees.) The Greek name survives, of course, in the common term for Spain and Portugal, the Iberian peninsula. The Carthaginians, after having occupied coastal districts for generations, took possession of a large part of the peninsula about 230 BC. Thirty years later it had been conquered by Rome. The Romans made no use of the Greek name and at once called it Hispania. No reason is given for this and historians generally leave the new name unaccounted for. But there are some possible explanations. The Carthaginians were a Phoenician people and a Phoenician word, *span*, means 'hidden' or 'distant'. Spain was hardly very distant from Italy, though the Greeks sometimes called Spain Hesperia, the land of the setting sun. The Basques, living in the north-west and along the Pyrenees, with a language which, it has been well said, 'projects from a remote pre-Indo-European past with all the fascination which zoologists find in a coelacanth', had a word, *España*, meaning 'boundary' or 'limit'. But it seems very improbable that at that time the Romans would borrow the name from the Basques and there is no evidence that the Carthaginians had done so. There is another explanation which may seem very bizarre. The Phoenician word for a rabbit is *pahan*. But what could this have had to do with Spain? There must have been some connection. In the year AD 122 the Emperor Hadrian visited Spain. His visit was commemorated by special coins. On the one side is the bust of the Emperor, on the other a female figure representing Hispania is seated contemplating a rabbit. In some way the rabbit must have been a Spanish symbol.

In contrast to Spain Portugal is a simple name to explain. After the capture of Toledo from the Moors in 1085 Alfonso II of Castile married two of his daughters to two noblemen from Burgundy who had helped him, giving each of them a fief in north-west Spain, divided from each other by the River Mincio. The county to the south went to one Henry. It included the mouth of the River Douro, with its port named by the Romans Portus Cale, now Oporto. In 1143 it became an independent kingdom and was called after its most important town (Lisbon was not taken until four years later) Portucalia or Portucale, hence Portugal.

In Italy (Italia) before the days of Roman supremacy there were several distinct languages. Of those in the south the most important is known as Oscan. In this language the 'toe' of Italy, its south-west promontory, was known as Vitelliu, or the land of calves. (We may think of the Latin Vitellus for a small calf, the old French veil and the modern French veau, and our own veal.) Italia seems to have been the Greek rendering of this. There is no evidence of its use before the fifth century BC, but by the third century it was being used for all the land south of the River Rubicon. In 91 BC came the Social War, the last effort of the Italian towns and tribes to secure their independence from Roman domination. They chose the small town of Corfinium as their capital and renamed it Italia. They struck their own coins. One shows a bull goring the Roman wolf and with it the word VITELLIU in Oscan letters. The other has troops being driven in under a standard with the word ITALIA.

Let us now turn to the north. No place name was ever simpler than that of Iceland (Island). It means what it says, the Land of Ice. But Greenland is a strange contrast. When first discovered about 900 by one Gunnbiorn he named it, reasonably enough, the White Sheet. About eighty years later a remarkable Icelandic adventurer, Eric the Red, landed there and decided to found a colony. To attract settlers he called it Greenland.

Norway (Norge) was styled in early times Northmannland or Northweg – North way. In mediaeval Latin it was Norvegia, hence the French Norvege. The Norwegians themselves were naturally not concerned about the way in which it led other people. For them it was Nor-rige, the north country (we may compare the German word reich), and hence Norge.

Sweden (Sverige) derives its name from a tribe in central Sweden known in Roman times as the Suiones. The country was then occupied by several tribes, this one being in the Upland, north of Stockholm. It gradually became dominant. The name came from *suin*, meaning land just dry or covered with shallow water. Jordanes, a Goth who wrote a history of his people in the sixth century, called them the Suethidi, from which came the name, Sweden. Another variant of the name, to be found for example in Beowulf, was Svear, and, as in the case of Norway, we get Svea rike, the Swedish country, and hence Sverige.

The Danes were first mentioned as a people who had come from Scandinavia by the Byzantine historian, Procopius, in about AD 550, as the Danoi. The first appearance of their present name is in a translation of the geographer Orosius by King Alfred in about 895 in the form Denamearc. Dene meant a valley and mearc a region. (Mearc or mark in most Teutonic languages means a border region.) It appears that the name of the country may not have been derived from that of the people, but have been given it by foreigners, though this seems very improbable, since the native name is Danmark. Perhaps Alfred misinterpreted it, though no one can have known more about Danes than he did.

The Netherlands (Nederlanden), which we usually call Holland, have a strange history. In the Middle Ages the country consisted of a large number of entirely separate districts. In the fifteenth century these began to be brought together by the genius of Philip, Duke of Burgundy. The land was then usually known simply as *le pays de par deca*, 'the country on this side', perhaps the vaguest place-name ever invented. In the sixteenth century, now consisting of seventeen provinces, it came under the rule of Spain. The northern provinces rose in revolt and gained their independence, being styled officially the United Provinces. The southern remained under Spain until 1713 when they passed to Austria. The name, Nederlanden (in English Netherlands) only came into use as a popular term in the sixteenth century. In 1814 for a short period of sixteen years the northern and southern provinces were once more united. A new name was needed and the state was called the Kingdom of the Netherlands.

When it was divided again in 1830 the northern part retained this name.

Of the seventeen provinces the richest and most powerful was Holland, and in this country it came to be used for the land as a whole. In the ninth century some land north of the River Meuse, called Kennemerland, was granted to a Viking chieftain. In 1015 one of his descendants, Dirk III, seized from the Bishop of Utrecht some swampy lands amid the channels of the estuary of the Meuse. These were covered with bush, called *holt*, and the land was called Holtland, hence Holland. Dirk built a fort at the mouth of the river called Dordrecht to collect the tolls of merchants, and in consequence this part became the most important region of the land, which in time adopted the name of this district. The reason why we – and no one else – called the people of this country Dutchmen and their language Dutch must await a consideration of the various names of Germany.

Belgium (La Royaume de la Belgique or Belgie) gained its name from the Celtic tribe of the Belgae, the one the Romans respected more than any other. They called north-eastern Gaul as far as the Rhine Gallia Belgica. The name went on being used throughout the Middle Ages in a very confusing way and it is often difficult to tell just what it meant. In the sixteenth and seventeenth centuries in its Latin form it was often used for the Netherlands. Thus what we in England called the Dutch East India Company, which had nothing whatever to do with the Southern Provinces, now making up Belgium, was known officially as the Belgica Societas Indiae Orientalis. In 1790 these Southern Provinces rose in revolt against Austria and formed the Etats-Belgiques Unies. Within a few years they were conquered by France. In 1814, as we have seen, they were united with the northern provinces. When in 1830 they rebelled against the King of the Netherlands and became an independent state, they called it the Royaume de la Belgique.

Switzerland, with three official languages, has three names; Schweiz, Suisse and Svizzera. In the Middle Ages it was a conglomeration of towns and small country districts. In the thirteenth century the Habsburg rulers of Austria tried to gain control of the northern part. Three peasant communities, known as the Waldstaetten or Forest Cantons, Uri, Unterwalden and Schwyz, came together and formed in 1291 an Alliance or Confederation of Forest Cantons, which was soon joined by the city of Zurich. In 1315 the Habsburgs attacked and were defeated at Morgarten, on the borders of Schwyz. Other towns, especially Lucerne and Berne, joined them. In continuous struggles with the Habsburgs and the Emperors of the Holy Roman

Empire the Confederation became more united, remaining firmly on the foundation of the three Forest Cantons. From about the middle of the fourteenth century we find the name of one of them, Schwyz, beginning to be applied to the whole Confederation.

But Switzerland, as a land of three official languages – and one more, Romansch, styled not official but national – finds it necessary at times to have a name common to all, as, for instance, on its postage stamps. For this purpose it uses the name, Helvetia, from the Helvetii, the Celtic tribe to be found in the Alps in Roman times.

With Germany (Deutschland) we are faced with a new problem. There are so many different views about what it should be called. The Germans themselves use the name Deutschland, the French l'Allemagne, and ourselves Germany. The Italians get the best of both worlds, Germania for Germany and Tedesco for German. Julius Caesar always spoke of the various tribes beyond the Rhine as Germani, and Tacitus, writing a century and a half later, spoke of the country as Germania. Tacitus' book cannot have influenced people in the Middle Ages as it was not known then, but Germania and the Germani appear continually in later Roman writers. Did not Juvenal ask who was likely to be surprised at the sight of a German with blue eyes and yellow hair, twisting his greasy locks into a horn? But it was no doubt educated men who implanted the word Germany in England.

For a short time between about 1150 and 1250, when Germany was under the sway of the great Hohenstaufen Emperors who came from Suabia, the Germans themselves frequently used the word Allemania, as the Allemani were the tribe which had occupied this part of the country. They were the neighbours and the chief opponents of the Franks, and the French have in consequence adopted their name for their modern neighbours, L'Allemagne.

The origin of Deutschland is quite different from any we have considered already. We must not forget the extent to which Europe in the Middle Ages was bilingual; there was the Latin language and the Vernacular, the language of the people. The word for the people was *theod* and from this was derived the word *theodisc* for their language. This became *diutisc* and eventually *deutsch* – and the country took its name from this, Deutschland. (Oddly enough the word, *theodisc*, seems to have been used first in England in the second half of the eighth century and it may have been exported to Germany by Anglo-Saxon missionaries.) Latin speakers and writers then had to make something of the word *diutisc* or *deutsch*. In translation they used the word Teutonicus, taking the word from the Teutones, a tribe from the modern Denmark who moved south in the second century BC, wandered about especially in southern Gaul and defeated the Romans and thoroughly frightened them in 113 BC, but were then completely defeated by Marius, and disappear from history. There is no reason to suppose that they or their name survived. Teutonicus was a scholar's word, but as a proper translation for Deutsch it has played an important part outside Germany. We speak of the organisation of knights which conquered Prussia as the Teutonic Order. In Germany they were *Die deutsche Ordnung*. We may see how the word Teutonicus was evolved from *theod* if we consider the word used for the German 'nation' at the University of Bologna in 1265, *Theotonici*. (And then, one must add, to show how difficult it has been to find the right name for this particular country and its people, that we find only eight years later a statute of the University referring to the privileges to be granted to the 'nobiles de Alamania'.)

In the Middle Ages *diutisc* or *deutsch* was used for both the German languages, High and Low German. In the Netherlands it became *duutsch*, hence our word Dutch for the language and people of Holland. We are alone in this strange practice.

At the end of the eighth century a large part of Central Europe was under the control of the Avars, a nomadic tribe from the steppes. In 811 they were conquered by the Emperor Charlemagne and he created, south of Bavaria, a new province or Mark in Ostland, 'frontier district in the East land'. In 976 it seems to have become definitely established as Ostmark. Twenty years later we have the first reference to Osterrich. We have met the word *rich* or *rik*, meaning a state, in Norway and Sweden. It developed into Reich, hence Österreich, the modern name of the country. The English version, Austria, is no doubt an attempt to make this respectable by latinising it. If so, it was not a good shot, for *auster* meant the south wind and *australis* southern (hence Australia), while Ost means east.

Czechoslovakia (Ceskoslovenka Republika) is, of course, a modern name. It was created in 1919 out of three districts, Bohemia and Moravia, peopled by Czechs, and Slovakia by Slovaks. In Julius Caesar's time Bohemia was inhabited by a Teutonic tribe, the Boii. The name comes from *Boi-heim*, the home of the Boii. By the time of Tacitus the Boii had already been driven out by the Marcomanni, but the name persisted. Then came the Slavs. Moravia was named after the river Morava. The Cechs were one of several Slav tribes who occupied the two countries and, as we have seen with the Swedes, they eventually absorbed the rest. The national legendary history tells us of a tribal hero, named Cech, who led them into the land of Bohemia from the east. There is as much reason to accept this derivation as Geoffrey of Monmouth's explanation of Britain as coming from Brute, the son of Aeneas, who came to this island and found it 'uninhabited save for a few giants'. The Slovaks were another Slav tribe who were completely subdued by the Hungarians. Somehow they preserved their national identity through centuries of oppression.

The main problem with Hungary is to explain why we should call the country, styled Magyaroszag by its own people, by so very different a name. The Magyars or Hungarians were a Finno–Ugrian tribe living in the Urals. (Some of them are still there, the Ostigaks now east of the Urals on the middle Ob, and the Voguls near Perm.) In the middle of the fifth century they were swept to the south and west by the Bulgars and they were then for some time under Bulgar control. It is at this time that one begins to hear of a confederation of their tribes called the *Onogurs* or Nine Arrows, from which the name of Hungary derives. The Byzantine Emperor Constantine Porphyro-genitus in the tenth century called them Turks, and undoubtedly they had acquired from their Bulgar overlords many Turkish characteristics and words in their language. He also referred to one of their tribes as the *Megere*, and it was no doubt this tribe which gave their name, as Magyar, to the rest. In 830 they moved to the right bank of the River Don and were driven out by a most warlike tribe, the Pechenegs, to the mouth of the Danube. Harassed by the Pechenegs and the Bulgars they crossed the Carpathians in 895. In a short time they had not only created a strong state but for the next sixty years they terrified Europe with raids as far as Rheims and Laon, until they were defeated by the Emperor Otto the Great at the Battle of the Lechfeld near Augsburg. They then became converted to Christianity and settled down to found the state which exists, a strange anomaly in Europe, to this day. But why were they called Hungarians (in German, Ungar) and not Magyars? We may discount, perhaps, the view of the German writer of the tenth century that they were called Ungarn because they had a hunger for human flesh. A possible reason is that the name reminded people of the Huns, the terrible portent of four hundred years before, with whom they were often compared.

Another people of the same stock are those living in Finland (Suomi). In the first centuries of our era Finno–Ugrians lived over a large part of what is now central, eastern and northern Russia. Tacitus referred to the Fenni as living beyond the Germani, and as being utter savages, who 'have solved the problem of human existence by having no requirements at all'. Ptolemy mentions the Fennoi. Between the years 1000 and 1200 came the slow Slav penetration and the Finns were

pressed into the north west. It is significant that the names of many
Russian rivers have a Finnish origin. (River names are usually older
than town names. Thus, in England, the Thames, Trent, Ouse, Stour,
Avon and Severn are all Celtic names.) In the thirteenth century the
Finns came under the Swedes and remained so until 1809 when they
were conquered by Russia. The nineteenth century saw the rise of
Finnish nationalism, and in 1918 Finland gained its independence. But
that is not their own name for their country, but the Swedish one.
They call their country Suomi and themselves Suomilaiset. The word
comes from *Suo*, meaning a marsh.

Poland (Polska) only became the name of the country gradually
during the Middle Ages, and the rulers of various princedoms, such as
Greater Poland, Lesser Poland and Mazovia, fought with one another
and, when they strove for supremacy over the others, claimed 'the
throne of Cracow', not of Poland. Once more we find the name of one
tribe eventually being adopted by others. The name comes from the
Poliani or plain dwellers, the plains between the Oder and the Vistula,
and this from the word *pole*, meaning a field. Poland in Russian is
Ljach from *ljada*, a fallow field.

Yugoslavia (Jugoslavija) simply means the country of the Southern
Slavs. It was created in 1919 by joining the independent Slav king-
doms of Serbia and Montenegro with the Slav territories of the Croats
and Slovenes in the Austro-Hungarian Empire. We may perhaps note
that Serbia gained its independence from the Byzantine Empire about
1200 and lost it to the Turks after the disastrous battle of Kossovo in
1389. They regained it during the nineteenth century. From 1331 to
1355 Serbia was ruled by Stephen Dushan, one of the great kings of the
mediaeval Europe. His official title was, 'King of Serbia, Dioclea, the
land of Hum, the Zeta, Albania and the Maritime Region, partner in
no small part of the Empire of Bulgaria and almost all the Empire of
Romania'. We shall meet some of these names again.

The country we now call Bulgaria (Bulgariya) was occupied
towards the end of the sixth century by Slavs. About the year 480 a
Hunnish tribe called the Bulgars migrated from the Volga to the
shores of the Black Sea, and in the seventh century they crossed the
Danube and settled in the lands to the south of the river. Quite soon,
and one feels quite inexorably, they were absorbed by the Slav peoples
already there, taking from them their language and customs and
giving them only their name.

The Romans under the Emperor Trajan crossed the Danube and
conquered the land called Dacia, approximately the modern Hungary,
in 105. In 271 they found it necessary to evacuate it. We have seen that

eventually in 895 it was occupied by the Magyars. The country which we now call Rumania was practically depopulated after raids by the Tartars during the thirteenth century. Just before the end of the century there was a migration of people still speaking a Latin language from the modern Transylvania, which was under the Magyars, over the Carpathians into the lands between those mountains and the Danube. By 1330 they had formed an independent state, called Wallachia, because, as we have seen, they spoke a Latin tongue. Shortly after, in 1349, there was another migration from northern Transylvania into lands north of Wallachia. The state founded here was called Moldavia after the River Moldau. Twelve years later the Turks entered Europe, and by the end of the century the two principalities were part of the Turkish Empire though they were allowed a certain degree of independence. After the Crimean War of 1854 to 1856 the Great Powers of Europe would not allow them to unite to form one state. They were to have separate elected rulers and assemblies. The two countered this by electing the same man. In 1866 the Powers gave way and Moldavia and Wallachia were united to form Rumania (Romania). In 1878 it became fully independent.

But why Rumania? The obvious explanation is that theirs was a Latin language, but it was more complicated than that. We may remember that Stephen Dushan of Serbia had claimed to be 'partner in almost all the Empire of Romania'. He was thinking of the Byzantine Empire. When the Roman Empire was divided – the date usually given is 476 – the name Romania was preserved in the eastern half. When in 1095 Pope Urban II at Clermont called on the feudal lords of the West to join the First Crusade, the Bishop of Rome told them that they must rescue Romania. The provinces of Ravenna and Forli in north-east Italy were until recently known as Romagna. It was not called this because of its connection with Rome, but the exact op-posite. Until 753 it remained part of the Byzantine Empire. At the other end of that Empire Asia Minor was commonly called Rum. The majority of the inhabitants of Rumania are Orthodox Christians. In fact, the oppression from which they fled to Wallachia was one by Roman Catholics, not by pagans. The name, Romania, looks back both to the Classical Roman Empire in its great days and to the Empire of Constantinople.

Turkey (Turkiye) is named after the Turks of Central Asia. Some of them, known as the Seljuk Turks, nearly brought down the Byzantine Empire in the eleventh century. After the year 1200 Turkish tribes gradually infiltrated into Asia Minor which became a chaos of tribal struggles. In 1281 Osman became the ruler of one of these tribes near

Nicaea. He succeeded in unifying the Turks, and in 1353 under his grandson they entered Europe. A century later they took Constantinople. In Europe Osman was known as Othman and so the great state his successors were to build up was known as the Ottoman Empire. The Turks called themselves the Osmanlis.

Albania (Shkyiperia) should be distinguished from the country of the same name in the days of the Roman Empire near the Caspian Sea. Ptolemy the geographer, writing about AD 130, referred to the Albani and Albanopolis, the mountainous region north-east of Durazzo. Presumably the Romans called the country this because of the snow on the mountains. It was called Albanon in the fourth century and then the name is completely lost for some seven hundred years. But it had only gone underground. In the Alexiad, the life of her father, the Emperor Alexius Comnenus (1081–1118), written by Anna Comnena, she refers to people near the Dalmatian coast as 'the so-called Albanians'. We have seen that Stephen Dushan of Serbia styled himself King of Albania. After his death in 1355 it dissolved into tribal units though one of the leading clan chieftains usually called himself Prince of Albania. In 1414 the Turkish conquest began. The people put up a great resistance under their leader Skanderbeg, who styled himself Chief of the League of the Albanian people. Albania, however, became Turkish, and in 1878 at the Congress of Berlin Bismarck stated that 'there is no Albanian nationality'. The Albanians replied by forming the Albanian League for the Defence of the Rights of the Albanian Nationality. In 1913 Albania became an independent state, though the main reason for this was the determination of Italy and Austria that Serbia should not gain an outlet to the sea. The Albanians, however, call themselves by the name of a leading tribe, the Shkypetii or Sons of the Eagle. They claim that it was the name used by Pyrrhus for his soldiers from Epirus when he invaded Italy in 280 BC, but the evidence for this is not forthcoming. There is some reason to think that recently they are less satisfied with the name, Shkyiperia, for their country and that Albania may be coming back into fashion.

Greece has always been Hellas and it is absurd that it should be called anything else. The explanation is a simple one. A Greek colony was formed at Cumae, near the modern Naples, in about 750 BC. The Romans called the Greeks there Graii, probably because they came from Graia, a place of no importance whatever in Western Greece. From this came Graecia and then Graeci. Future historians will no doubt regard some of the names we have provided for African states as equally ridiculous.

When we turn to Russia (Rassiya) we come up against not only difficulty but danger. The conventional view is that the name came from the Viking traders who formed in the ninth century the principality of Kiev. The Arabs called them Rus, the Byzantines Rhos. The name, it is suggested, is essentially Finnish, for the Finns called them the Ruotsi. There are several explanations of this word. It may be the Finnish version of the Swedish Rothsmen, or sea-farers, or it may come from Roslagen, north-east of Stockholm, their point of departure. But all this is regarded by modern Soviet historians as nonsense. The word is wholly Slav and neither Swedes nor Finns had anything to do with it. To put forward the conventional view would certainly endanger one's position as a member of the Soviet Academy of Sciences. We had better leave it there.

The countries of Europe have an extraordinary variety, ranging in size from Russia in Europe of about 8,000,000 square miles to the Vatican City of 109 acres, a little larger than St James's Park. We ought not to overlook the smallest states of Europe. The names of two of these are quite simple. Gibraltar was originally Gebel-Tariq or Mount Tariq, named after the Moslem leader who crossed the straits there in 711, which began the Moorish conquest of Spain. The Phoenicians erected on the rock where Monaco now stands a temple to their god, Melkarth, which the Greeks called Heracles Monoikos, the Temple of Heracles. The Romans called the port between the headland and the modern town of Monte Carlo, Portus Herculi Monoeci.

Cyprus and Malta are more difficult. It is usual to regard Cyprus as the island where copper (in Latin *cyprium*) was mined, but the derivation is more probably the other way round. Possibly the island was named after the Kupros, a tree from the blossom of which a fashionable fragrant oil was produced. It grew on the island, but again one cannot be sure which came first. Malta was known to the Greeks as Melite, to the Romans as Melita. Already in the Antonine Itinerary, a list of roads of the Roman Empire compiled early in the third century AD, it is called Malta. The Arabs, after their conquest of North Africa, called it Malitah. The name was probably given to it by the Carthaginians, a word derived from or the same as the Semitic *Melitah*, meaning a refuge.

Striking inland we come to the little state of Andorra, rather larger than the Isle of Wight, to some extent controlled by the French Republic, as the successor of the Counts of Foix, and the Bishop of Seo da Urgel, an unusual combination. The local story accounting for its name is that Louis the Pious, the son of Charlemagne, defeated the Saracens there in about 830 and then said that he was reminded of

Mount Tabor and the Valley of Endor. He called it Endor, hence
Andorra. More probably the name comes from the Moorish word,
Al-darra, meaning a thickly wooded place.

The Grand Duchy of Luxemburg, which has gained so enormously
in prestige since the founding of the European Community – it is
about the size of the County of Durham – has a long history as a
separate country going back to the early Middle Ages. In 1814 it came
under the personal rule of William I, King of the Netherlands, though
it remained independent. It did not follow the example of Belgium in
the 1830s, but in 1890 King William III was succeeded by his daughter,
Queen Wilhelmina. But Luxemburg came under the Salic Law and no
woman could succeed to the Duchy. Adolphus of Nassau-Weilberg
became Duke and the connection with Holland was severed. Luxemburg in the Middle Ages was called Lutzelburg, a small fortress, the
archaic German word *lütt* meaning small.

There can be no independent state in Europe more charming than
the little Principality of Liechtenstein, about half the size of Rutland,
lying between Austria and Switzerland. Originally it consisted of two
distinct districts, Vaduz and Schellenberg. These were united under
one lord in 1419. In 1613 they were sold to the Count of Hohenems,
and his family held it through the seventeenth century, falling more
and more hopelessly into debt. Eventually the Emperor Leopold told
the Count that the two estates must be sold to pay his debts. They
were bought by Johann Adam, Count of Liechtenstein, Schellenberg
in 1699 and Vaduz in 1712. Next year the Emperor Charles VI created
them into the Principality of Liechtenstein, to be held directly of the
Emperor. When in 1806 the Emperor Francis II brought the Holy
Roman Empire to an end Liechtenstein became independent. None
of the Counts visited it until some hundred and twenty years after it
was acquired. They gained their title from a castle near Vienna.
Liechtenstein, therefore, has the distinction of being named after a
place not to be found in it at all, but some three hundred and fifty miles
away.

There remain two independent states in Italy, in themselves
stranger than any others and the history of their names is quite as
remarkable. In 1870 the Papal State in central Italy, which had existed
for many centuries, came to an end when the Italian troops occupied
Rome. The Pope became 'the prisoner of the Vatican', the hill on the
right bank of the Tiber. By the Lateran Treaty with Italy in 1929 its
complete independence was recognised and it is the smallest sovereign
state in the world. It was not one of the Seven Hills on which Rome
was founded, standing a little apart from them. The rites of Cybele, a

fertility cult from Asia were practised there and the phrase was used in them *ex vaticinatione archigalli* – 'according to the inspired out-pourings of the high priest'. The hill in consequence became known as the Mons Vaticanus. There a church was built over the tomb of St Peter.

Further north in Italy, high up on the north side of the Apennines, is the little town of San Marino. When all the various independent states and towns of Italy, except the Papal State, voted in 1859 to become part of the Kingdom of Italy, it stood out. The size of its population is about that of Abingdon. A modern guide-book will tell you that the Saint after whom it was named was a Christian who fled from the neighbouring town of Rimini to escape the persecution of the Emperor Diocletian soon after AD 300. His story, as told in the Bollandist Acts of the Saints after his body had been discovered in the town in 1586, is more elaborate. ★

Marinus (or Marino), we are told, came from Dalmatia and lived in the fourth century. He was a stonemason, and along with a friend, also a Christian, named Leo, he spent three years quarrying stone for the rebuilding of the walls of the town of Ariminum, now Rimini, on the summit of the neighbouring Monte Titano. At the end of this time Leo went off by himself to another mountain where he built a cell and became a hermit. (A church in the town is dedicated to him.) Marinus returned to Ariminum and worked for twelve years on an aqueduct, gaining a great reputation as an excellent workman and a pious man. At this point something wholly unexpected intervened. A peasant woman from Dalmatia appeared in Ariminum and said that Marinus, for whom she had been searching for years, was her husband. At the sight of her Marinus fled up to the quarries where he had worked on Monte Titano. But the woman followed him and found him in a cave which he had hewed out of the stone. Before she could enter he hurriedly blocked the entrance with stones. After six days he ventured out and found that the woman had abandoned the chase and left. To be doubly sure he climbed further up the mountain and there retired to a cave on the face of a cliff, where, like his friend, he became a hermit. In his spare time he tamed a bear to fetch and carry for him. He was subsequently ordained a deacon by the Bishop of Ariminum.

We have seen cases where a country gained its name from outside itself. We might take one last example, Europe. We can forget about Europa, carried off by a bull. Long ago Herodotus pointed out that she

---

★ The Bollandist *Acta Sanctorum* is a work compiled since the seventeenth century, involving the use of original or newly discovered source material.

was an Asian lady and had nothing to do with Europe. The early Greeks used the word for the mainland of Greece, north of the Peloponnesus. But the word came soon to be applied to the whole continent, and it came originally from the Assyrians. *Ereb* in their language meant 'darkness', in contrast to the rising sun. And with this final incongruity – in our eyes at least – we may conclude this strange study in nomenclature.

THE BRITISH EMPIRE AND COMMONWEALTH: A VIEW FROM AD 2373

From internal evidence it is not difficult to deduce that this Lecture was given in August 1973 at The City University, though it is based on the Chichele Lectures given at All Souls College, Oxford in 1967. The idea of examining The British Empire from the standpoint of researchers of the future involves no attempt to prophesy – as a survey of Imperial History it could easily be given a contemporary date. But the device enables some thoughts on the dangers of History to be repeated: the difficulties of eradicating myths from popular text-book writing, the immense diversities of time and place that have to be remembered. This is emphasised, if we remind ourselves of the impossibility of comprehending totally a phenomenon such as the Empire of Rome and its influences. The recommendations for caution about generalisations and the surprising nature of some of the examples of Imperial rule given may well have been inspired by arguments and seminars with students, for The City University has over the years had many Commonwealth and Overseas students. It can be assumed, no doubt, that by now no one is surprised that a pageant of illustration, which begins at the City of God, ends at Speakers' Corner.

'WHAT ARE EMPIRES,' wrote St Augustine, 'but "magna latrocinia★"?' – the large-scale and organised achievements of predatory man or, as it will probably be expressed in AD 2373, 'Institutions of Economic Imperialism'. 'The Roman Empire,' he said, 'was one of the worst; it surrendered pride of place only to the Assyrian.' The Roman Empire, we may remember, had been created by a people of whom their great poet, Virgil, had claimed that the father of Man and the Gods had said

★ "great dens of robbers".

that he could place no bounds to their rule – 'I have given them Empire without end'.

For another judgement we may turn to Dante. In his eyes Rome was the power which, in obedience to the divine will, had given Europe unity – not uniformity, which was the last thing Dante wanted – a unity based on an ideal of Justice. That was why in the *Paradiso* the sign formed by the Saints in the circle of Jupiter in their heavenly dome to symbolise the divine Justice was an Eagle, 'the ensign', he wrote 'which gained the Romans reverence from all the world'.

To complete the picture I should add that Saint Augustine once wrote a letter to a friend praising the old-fashioned virtues of the Roman Republic, and Dante admitted that as a young man he had thought that the Romans had gained their Empire merely by force of arms and so had no moral right to their conquests. And I might add that a lesser figure, John of Salisbury, accepted both views at the same time. The attitude of the medieval world towards the Roman Empire was in fact an ambivalent one and if we attempt to speculate on what the world of the seventh decade of the twenty-fourth century will think of the British Empire, we must expect to find the same phenomenon.

The examples I have taken have come from writers living in the Western half of the Roman world, that half where Latin became a common language and Roman culture reigned supreme. But a more complete study of such judgements should include some from the eastern half, where Greek remained the common language and Roman culture was faced with competitors which were too strong for it. One would expect such judgements to be different. In the same way, we must not expect the judgements on the British Empire to be the same in, let us say, India and Zambia. Allowing for differences due to local circumstances and what might be called different administrative patterns, the nature of British rule was on the whole similar in the various parts of the Empire. But the differences in those whom they ruled were immense. India was a country with a culture – or should we rather say two cultures, the Hindu and the Moslem – of great antiquity when the British arrived. These cultures were deeply embedded in the lives of the people, they had received the most sophisticated formulations in works of theology, philosophy and literature. I should not hold that four hundred years from now the two centuries of British rule in India – and a shorter time in much of the country – will seem to be a mere passing incident in its long history. I think it will seem more important than that. But what will come out of that period of rule will be some kind of assimilation of European ideas and principles by a dominant culture, the Hindu or the Moslem.

The culture of Africa south of the Sahara, on the other hand, was at any rate quite unformulated (there are exceptions, I should say, in some parts of West Africa, and I have White South Africa on one side as a separate problem). African culture four hundred years from now will not be the same as Western European culture is now, but I believe it will be more like a Western Culture which has assimilated an African one.

To return to my parallel with the Roman Empire, neither Dante nor any other medieval writer who looked back on that Empire referred to what was the greatest contribution it made to the Europe of the Middle Ages. That was Christianity, far and away the strongest link between the Roman past and the Europe of Dante's day. It was simply taken for granted. The saints and martyrs of Imperial Rome were no alien figures. Will the African four hundred years from now regard David Livingstone in the same way that the Venerable Bede regarded St Alban? Of course it was not all quite as simple as that. Assimilations of Rome by its barbarian successors took place, in the days when the Roman Empire came to an end, of which we are now hardly conscious. We have only to think of the exceedingly strange fact that the English took their days of the week from Teutonic Mythology (with one exception – Saturday) but their names of the months from Rome. (We probably do not feel it particularly odd that here today we are commemorating the God Odin, at a time of year dedicated to the first Roman Emperor.) Will similar assimilations be made? I once read a Zulu hymn which was, I thought, strange and beautiful. It begins with a reference to the lightning bird of Zulu folk lore. You will see how it develops. There is a reference to 'Ekuphakemeni', a religious centre near Durban, a name sometimes used for Heaven – and one thinks of Mount Zion or the Heavenly Jerusalem:

> O Mountain Eagle
> Lift thy mighty wing
> We need thy shelter
> Thou rock of our fathers.
>
> We have no fortress
> Other than thee
> In which to find shelter
> We thy wayward creatures.

We stand before thee
O, beautiful hen.
Thou dost not love
Jerusalem alone.

O love us and hatch us
Wondrous Hen!
We dwell in thy Kingdom
Our hen of heaven.

O Lord, bring it forth
This Ekuphakemeni
Just as a hen
Loveth her chickens.

O Jerusalem, Jerusalem!
How great was thy longing
To gather thy children
Under thy wing.

But they would not
Thus art thou left desolate.

As I read it, it seemed delightful but absurd. And then I remembered
the opening verse of one of the greatest Christian hymns ever written:

Dies Irae, Dies Illa
Solvet saeclum in favilla
Teste David cum Sibylla.

David and the Sibyl as two Christian witnesses. Were the hen that
would gather her chickens under her wing and the lightning bird a
stranger combination?

The historian of the year AD 2373 will, I have no doubt, look back on
the extraordinary influence in Africa of the Bible. In his research he
may come across a passage in a Report of an African Commission set
up in Kenya in February 1964, two months after it gained its independence. It was studying the future educational problems of the country
and it made this comparison between Christianity and Islam. 'Christianity, a religion of Hebraic-Hellenistic origins, became universalist
in its application to life; while Islam developed as a religion set in
an Arabic social and religious framework. Whereas, therefore,
Christianity whose founder spoke Aramaic and whose earliest extant
documents were in Greek, is presented to the world in countless

vernaculars, Islam, as a religion, is indissolubly linked with the Arabic language, the Muslim Law and the prophetic tradition (hadith).' He will very probably note that by AD 1973 portions of the Bible had been translated into 395 different languages in Africa south of the Sahara, the whole New Testament into 181 languages, the whole Bible into 74. Perhaps he will refer to the kind of contrast which I saw once in a primary school on the roof of a mosque in Port Louis, the chief town of Mauritius. The children, like very many of the people of the island, were of Indian origin. These were, of course, Moslems. At home they spoke Creole. At the school they were being taught – it was a staggering picture – English, French, Urdu and quite, inevitably – Arabic.

Our future historian, however, will certainly have some very critical remarks to make about the early days of Christianity in Africa. He will point out that it was introduced into this continent and preached there by a remarkable number of different Christian churches, often very hostile to one another. One day, ten years ago, I was asked out to dinner at his Club in Nairobi by a member of the Kenya Government. (He was not a very influential minister and he is no longer in the Cabinet.) Suddenly in the middle of the meal he asked me, 'Tell me, do you believe in the Second Coming?' 'Well,' I said. 'If you mean Christ descending to the sound of trumpets into the local cemetery for the Last Judgement, I cannot say I do. That does not mean to say that I believe that I can get away with all the sins I have committed.' 'Yes,' he said, 'I think I feel much the same. But it is very awkward for me, because you see, I am a Seventh Day Adventist, and it is not only that, I really must go to the meetings of my party (he meant KANU – The Kenya African National Union) and they are always held on a Saturday – and I ought not to go to them on that day.' Poor man, I thought, the Seventh Day and Advent both at risk. Later in our conversation, I asked him if he would tell me why he was a Seventh Day Adventist. 'But of course I am,' he said, 'I was born at Eldoret.' I understood what he meant: he had been brought up near a Seventh Day Adventist Mission with a school which he had gone to quite inevitably. How utterly casual we were in the way we scattered these different churches around. Of course, one must not imagine that the coming of Christianity to Western Europe created no problems. The first person from this country who may be regarded as a European figure was the heretic, Pelagius, who caused such trouble to St Augustine with his doctrine of Free Will. I remember once addressing a Synod of the Evangelical Church in Munster in 1947 and telling them that they must realise that nearly all Englishmen were by nature

Pelagian while all German Protestants were followers of St Augustine. And the great division created by the heresy of Arius was a direct contribution to the world of the Teutonic invaders from the Roman Empire.

While I believe that Africa in AD 2373 will be largely Christian, I do not imagine that the accounts given then of the Christian Churches during the days of the British Empire will make altogether pleasant reading if I could peruse them now. I do not think that Christianity will do for the world which was the British Empire what it did for the world which had been under Rome. I think the true counterpart to Christianity in the Roman Empire will be Technology. Just as the people of the Roman Empire could receive Christianity without any feeling of subservience in doing so, the twentieth-century inhabitant of India or Malaysia or Africa or the West Indies when he learns the secrets of Technology feels himself on an equality with the European. One of the results of this has been that London has become for them not only the seat of a government from which they freed themselves and of which they feel and will still go on feeling – though not I should say until AD 2373 – a traditional suspicion. It is also the seat of a University with amazing magnetic powers.

But what of the 'Magna Latrocinia'? Can one really suggest that Technology may prove to be a bridge between the two cultures without facing the question of Economic Imperialism? I feel sure of one thing, one book which will be part of the standard diet of History Students in the Universities of India and Africa in the twenty-fourth century will be J. A. Hobson's *Imperialism: A Study* which was published in 1902. This will not be just because it had a considerable influence on Lenin, when he wrote his *Imperialism, the Highest Form of Capitalism* and so brought Marx up to date, but because of the standing it will have gained as a recognised classical account of a most important historical phenomenon and, perhaps also because of its effect on the attitude of many British towards their own Empire. Hobson believed that the colonies had been conquered to provide markets for British manufactures and fields for investment of surplus capital, as well as in order to provide raw materials for British industries. Hobson's book is very far from being a work of scholarship. If he had added a bibliography it would have been a very meagre one. It is not particularly original. But it was a most disturbing work when it appeared and I think one can say that from that moment one can trace a gradual lack of confidence in British Imperial destiny.

It is not difficult to demolish much of what he says in his interpretation of Imperialism in economic terms. He says at one point, 'In most parts of the world a purely or distinctively commercial motive and conduct have furnished the nucleus out of which Imperialism has grown', and he takes as examples Sierra Leone, Uganda and Rhodesia. I should not be at all surprised if these examples turn up regularly in the text books in use in schools in AD 2373. Possibly some scholars may refer to a work by Ronald Robinson and John Gallagher which came out in 1960 [*Africa and the Victorians*]. It showed that this was far too simple a diagnosis. The Foreign Office refused to take Sierra Leone seriously and in spite of the strong pressure of the Chambers of Commerce of London and Liverpool, allowed the French to acquire territory which prevented any expansion of the British Colony inland. Uganda was acquired eventually, not because the government thought it ought to protect British traders, but for strategic reasons to protect the Upper Nile basin from the French, a move in the rivalry with France over Egypt. And the British government at last reluctantly agreed to take responsibility for Rhodesia in order to prevent it from coming entirely under the influence of the Transvaal Republic if not into its actual possession.

Hobson did not perhaps go quite as far as to promulgate what D. K. Fieldhouse in his book *The Colonial Empires* has referred to as 'the most commonly held and dangerous myth connected with modern empires'. This, he says, 'is that they were great machines deliberately constructed by Europe to exploit dependent peoples by extracting economic and fiscal profits from them.' But it is certainly not a very large step from Hobson's position to Mr Fieldhouse's 'dangerous myth'. I should think it surprising if it too does not play a considerable part in the text books of the twenty-fourth century. Nothing is more difficult for text-book history to accept than the unplanned, the casual and the uncoordinated.

Every school boy will know of the horrors of the Slave Trade. I am afraid that a myth about it which is beginning to see the light, may come to be accepted, that the Abolition of the Slave Trade and then of Slavery was due to purely economic causes since it no longer paid, and not in any way to the activities of the Abolitionists. William Wilberforce, at best, will be relegated to a footnote. But India will not be so interested in the Slave Trade as Africa or the West Indies. I cannot say whether Boswell's *Life of Johnson* will be read four hundred years from now, but, I strongly suspect that one quotation will be quite well known in India. Writing of the year 1779, Boswell says, 'On Sunday, Oct 10th, we dined together at Mr Strahan's. The conversation having turned on the prevailing practice of going to the East Indies in search of wealth.' Forgotten pamphlets which were produced in large numbers in 1813 will be dug up again. In that year the Charter of the East India Company was renewed, but it lost its monopoly of the Indian Trade. We shall find quoted a statement from *Considerations on Colonial Policy with relation to the renewal of the East India Company's Charter*: 'The most obvious advantages which spring from Colonisation are derived from interchange of such commodities as furnish employment to the population of the parent state.'

A favourite passage will be one from W. Lester's 'The Happy Era of One Hundred Millions of the Human Race, or The Merchant, Manufacturer and Englishman's Recognised Right to an unlimited Trade with India'.

> The vast peninsula of India has for centuries been harassed by wars and devastation, rendering property very insecure; but if it becomes open to free trade, under one mild, liberal and effective government that could protect the property, laws, lives and liberties of the subjects, what a sudden change might we not anticipate? We should not only see the palaces of the Rajah and the homes of the Vakeels, Shrofs and Zamindars furnished and decorated with the produce of English arts and manufacturers, but the Ryots who form so large a part of the Indian Population may, like the British farmers, have a taste for foreign produce as soon as they can acquire property enough to procure it; and this is only to be acquired to that extent under a free and liberal government, where property is held sacred. Under these circumstances a trade might suddenly grow up beyond the Cape of Good Hope to take off all the surplus manufactures that Britain can produce.

We seem to be getting very near the 'great machines', although there was nothing quite so well co-ordinated as Hobson and Lenin following him imagined. But there was very strong economic pressure and it was beginning to be directed by a lobby. Mr W. Lester and his Free Trade friends won their point; the East India Company lost its monopoly and the happy era of one hundred millions of the human race was inaugurated. Between 1813 and 1840 there was a spectacular development in the Lancashire cotton industry. In the latter year a Select Committee of the House of Commons heard evidence from Sir Charles Trevelyan who had been Secretary of the Government in the Political Department in India and later in the Revenue Department.

> The peculiar kind of silky cotton formerly grown in Bengal, from which the fine Dacca Muslins used to be made, is hardly ever seen; the population of the town of Dacca has fallen from 150,000 to 30,000 or 40,000 and the jungle and malaria are fast encroaching upon the town. The only cotton

manufactures which stand their ground in India are of very coarse kinds and the English Cotton manufactures are generally consumed by all above the very poorest throughout India. Dacca which was the Manchester of India has fallen off from a very flourishing town to a very poor and small one; the distress there has been very great indeed.

The history book will continue after dealing with what is now called the Indian Mutiny, but will not be so then, and reach the year 1874. Lord Northbrook was Viceroy and he had in mind to raise Indian tariffs to protect Indian manufacturers. 'I am very happy also on the progress of Indian Manufactures ultimately', he wrote in February 1874 to a friend, and added, 'Whisper it not in Manchester'. But Manchester had its ear to the ground. The British Government insisted on a gradual reduction of the tariffs levied on British cotton goods and this was followed by a despatch instructing Northbrook to look into the possibility of abolishing the cotton duties altogether. The Viceroy expostulated. 'The duty of the government of India is to govern India for the best interests of the people of India and not for the interests of the Manchester Manufacturers.' But the Secretary of State had his way. Northbrook resigned and under his successor the duties were abolished. This will be far from the end of the story of the pressure exerted by Manchester cotton interests on Secretaries of State for India related in the history text book of the future.

But the story, especially in Africa, will make difficult material for the text-book writer. What will have to be appreciated as more important than such sophisticated pressures is the steady though usually quite uncoordinated pressure of commercial interests. They were not engaged, except occasionally, in attempting to convince the Foreign Office of the need to adopt a positive policy, but in actually going to the country to trade and then facing the home country with some awkward questions, the answer to which might have to be occupation. At least it must be admitted that if the traders had not gone to these places, the Foreign Office would not have had to bother about them. One of the best descriptions I know of what economic imperialism really meant – the persistent pressure of economic interests in colonial territory often through very unimportant individuals – should perhaps be quoted. It comes in a little brown book *My Command in South Africa* by Sir Arthur Conynghame, but it was quoted by Edward Blyden in an essay written in 1886 in *African Colonisation*. Blyden will not be forgotten in 2373. He was a West Indian negro who emigrated to Liberia, represented that country in London and died in 1912. He has been called the Father of African

Nationalism. It was he who first pressed the Africans not simply to emulate other races, but to demonstrate the contribution of their own Continent to humanity. I may add that in his articles and addresses he was given to quoting very aptly from Virgil, Horace and Dante. This too is not without significance. However, to return to Sir Arthur Conynghame. The passage runs as follows.

> The facility with which these untamed savages (Kaffirs) can obtain any amount of villainous drink is one of the most fruitful sources of danger. Some of the chiefs being aware of the evil, forbid canteens in their localities and have repeatedly requested that the same prohibition should be extended among adjoining (British) districts. The answer of authority has always been that the natives should place a moral restraint on themselves and not imbibe more than is beneficial, and that trade cannot be impeded simply because it may engender evil consequences among the natives.

Edward Blyden's comment is perfect. It leaves nothing to be said: 'What a "simply"!'

And now what about the Eagle? Clearly it cannot be claimed that the British Empire brought Unity. In Africa it produced national units which had never been dreamt about before, twelve of them for 90 million people in 1973. It was pointed out in yesterday's *Times* that the West Indies are going to go much further. At the next Commonwealth Conference there will be twelve Prime Ministers representing three million people. In India it failed to bring Hindus and Moslems together. For that matter it may be held that the unity of the Roman Empire too hardly lasted after it had gone. But I believe that the historian of the year 2373 may well speak with appreciation of the establishment in the British Empire of the Rule of Law. The Indian Penal Code for which Thomas Babington Macaulay was largely responsible, though it was not completed until 1861, twenty years after he left India, was certainly one of the greatest achievements in the history of any Empire. We should note that it was not a mere transference, with some minor changes, of English Law to India. What matters most is that it is evidence of the way that British rule in India provided the country with the ideal of the Rule of Law. Indians have pointed out – and may well do so four hundred years from now – that the adoption in the Indian Constitution after Independence of a Bill of Rights was contrary to British tradition. When the Government of India Act of 1935 set up the last and short-lived Constitution for British India there were demands in India for the incorporation in it of a Bill of Rights. The British Government rejected this proposal on the grounds that freedom was best preserved not by constitutional enactments but by traditions and unwritten conventions. We may feel that it was a most obtuse decision. But it may well be appreciated four hundred years from now that the Bill of Rights in the Indian Constitution of 1950 was the greatest tribute paid by independent India to her former rulers, because it enshrined the principle of the Rule of Law, which was Britain's most important gift to India.

When Dante described the Roman Eagle in the *Paradiso* as the representative of the Law, Order and Unity which Rome had given to the world, he was not at all concerned with what had happened between the days of the Empire and his own times. It may be that Roman Law had never been quite forgotten; we may remember the book of Roman Law which was studied by Saint Aldhelm in Anglo-Saxon England. But to all intents and purposes it had to be rediscovered. Between the Roman Empire and Ulpian, and Justinian on one side and Dante on the other, came the Dark Ages. In the same way, if we try to imagine what the peoples of the lands which were the British Empire will think of that Empire four hundred years from now, we must not imagine that there will have been an unbroken process from one to the other. If the British idea of Law means something in India then, it may have had to be rediscovered. In fact the attitude of mind fifty or a hundred years from now may not be of any lasting significance. That may be a period of reaction from what will still be considered a colonial era. It may be a period of instability before a hard-won stability is gained.

I suppose that of all the British Governor-Generals and Viceroys of India the one who has done most to strike the historical imagination is Warren Hastings. Perhaps in the age to which we are looking forward more attention will be paid than is usually done now to his encouragement of Indian officials and his fostering of the study of both Indian and Sanskrit. His successor, Lord Cornwallis, is little remembered except perhaps for losing the Battle of Yorktown in 1781. Unlike his predecessor, he had no interest whatever in Indian literature and culture, and very little use for Indian officials. But in an astonishingly short space of time he swept away the old traditions of the East India Company: that is, for officials as much as anyone else, 'the prevailing practice of going to the East Indies in quest of wealth'. Perhaps his most important step was to persuade the Company to pay its servants generous fixed salaries. He laid the foundations of a civil service, though it was not until entry to this came to depend on competitive examinations that it became the body which we call to mind when we think of the Indian Civil Service. He was well aware, when he went to

202 THE BRITISH EMPIRE AND COMMONWEALTH: AD 2373

India, what he would find. Within a few months he had suspended the entire Board of Trade of the Company; most of them he subsequently dismissed. One of the Regulations issued during his term of office must be regarded as amongst the greatest documents of British History. I believe that it will be remembered by the historians of India, four hundred years from now. I do not think that the tradition created by it, which lasted for a hundred and fifty years, can fail to have a lasting effect in India, whatever periods of difficulty and trouble that country may go through in the more immediate future.

> The collectors of revenue and their officers, and indeed all the officers of the Government shall be amenable to the courts for acts done in their official capacities, and Government itself, in cases in which it may be a party with its subjects in matters of property shall submit its rights to be tried in these courts under the existing laws and regulations.

Cornwallis of course was a complete Whig. (We should remind ourselves what were the real roots of 'Whiggism'. 'Sir', said Sir Adam Fergusson once to Dr Johnson, 'in the British Constitution it is surely of importance to keep up a spirit in the people, so as to preserve a balance against the crown.' 'Sir', answered Dr Johnson, 'I perceive you are a vile Whig.') It was an unusual point of view for an imperialist. It led inevitably to a belief that the British Empire was not destined, as Virgil had thought the Roman Empire was, to last forever. This was an almost conventional view among officials of the East India Company. It suffered a setback with the Indian Mutiny and it was never held by planters and those engaged in commerce as it was by those in administration. Then it began to hold the field again in the last years of the nineteenth century. Macaulay, whose contempt for Indian literature and traditions is extremely embarrassing to read about, once said that the greatest day in the history of the British rule in India would be the day when it ended.

Turning to Africa, our future historian may perhaps see the significance of the British Government white paper of July 1923. The white settlers of Kenya had been complaining of their difficulties in securing African labour and they had demanded greater political power. The white paper stated: 'Primarily Kenya is an African territory and His Majesty's Government think it necessary definitely to record their considered opinion that the interests of the African natives must be paramount, and that, if and when these interests and the interests of the immigrant races should conflict, the interests of the former should prevail.' (The white paper went on to state that the same principle held good in Uganda and Tanganyika.)

Of course the historian will go on to tell of the Mau-Mau revolt which began less than thirty years later. He will no doubt point out that the total number of white civilians killed during the four years' struggle, was almost exactly half the number of Africans killed in twenty minutes at Sharpeville in South Africa five years later. I wonder whether he will quote the statement made in 1955 about Kenya: 'Throughout our enquiry we were impressed by the recurring evidence that particular areas were carrying so large a population that agricultural production in them was being so retarded, that the natural resources in them were being destroyed and that families were unable to find access to new land'. Will he note that these words come from the report of a British Royal Commission?

I have said little of the various historical figures who will, one hopes, be mentioned by our historian. He will hardly be able to ignore Lord Lugard and his book of 1922, *The Dual Mandate in British Tropical Africa*. Dual Mandate – a double responsibility – to the native peoples, who were to be led towards self-government, and to the rest of the world who had the right to ensure that the natural resources of the colonies were fully developed. A clash between the two mandates was inevitable. Will he refer to the critical case of the United Africa Company which in 1924 requested permission to acquire large plantations in West Africa and was refused it? I think he may in order to be able to quote the superb remark of Lord Leverhulme, the head of the Company, 'The African native will be happier, produce the best and live under the larger conditions of prosperity, when his labour is directed and organised by his white brother who has all those million years' start ahead of him'. Our historian will relish that word, 'million'.

If we could read the histories written four hundred years from now we should find many statements like this one to discomfort us. We should also find long-standing myths, especially in school text-books which will no doubt continue to be, as now, a happy hunting ground for them. In a book by Nirad Chaudhuri, *The Autobiography of an Unknown Indian*, I read, 'There is no belief more interesting than that which is widely held in India about the pietra dura work in the Taj Mahal and other Moghul buildings. Most Indians believe that the original inlaid pieces were diamonds, rubies, emeralds, sapphires and similar precious stones, but that they were stolen by the English who substituted coloured glass for them.' I should not be altogether surprised to find this story in the text-book. But I do not think one can be sure. After all one can still see inside the Fort at Agra the tablet set up in the year 1880 by his friend, the Viceroy, which reads:

In grateful Commemoration of
services rendered to posterity by
The Honourable Sir John Strachey GCSI
To whom not forgetting the enlightened sympathy
and timely care of others
India is mainly indebted
For the rescued and preserved beauty of the Taj Mahal
And other famous monuments of the ancient art
And history of these provinces
Formerly administered by him.

I think it may still be there in AD 2373. In Delhi you can still find side by side Curzon Avenue and Tilak Avenue, one named after the most autocratic of the Viceroys of India, the other after his great opponent, the founder of modern Indian nationalism. I should say that this is a striking example of the way in which India has, as it were, absorbed the two centuries of British rule.

I think we may be confident that some genuine research into the period of British rule in different parts of the world will continue, so I leave with you this last picture, acknowledging that I owe it to a note in Dennis Austen's *Politics in Ghana: 1946–1960*. I see in my mind's eye a research student of Ghana examining for his D. Phil the papers of the Convention People's Party in his country during the ten years before it gained its independence in 1957. He comes across the report of the Constituency Conference held in December 1950 of this party, which was the political organisation responsible for gaining independence for its country. It was written, he notes, by the secretary of the Party, a Ghanaian, and as he reads this passage he is puzzled. After a note of the main meeting of the day it continues:

The football match scheduled to take place at the Gyomji Park between the famous Cape Coast Majesties XI and the Kumasi Evergreen XI successfully came off before spectators numbering well over two thousand strong. Krobo Edusei took the kick off. The scores were Cape Majesties 1, Kumasi Evergreen 4. The teeming crowd would not rest satisfied to let this Sunday pass off without hearing the 'London Hyde Park Wizard' Kwesi Lamptey, supported by Krobo Edusei, Alta Mensah, Councillor Jantuah, Archie Hayford, C. E. Donkor, dilating on speeches of significance. The lecture closed at about 9.30pm.

How was it, he says to himself, that one of the football teams had the astonishingly imperialist title of the Majesties XI? And what was meant by the Evergreen XI? But I hope his research will eventually enable him to appreciate the significance of the term 'The London Hyde Park Wizard' and he will note that in London Kwesi Lamptey along with other notable African leaders who won independence for their countries, such as Jomo Kenyatta, Julius Nyerere, Hastings Banda and Kwame Nkrumah, had actually experienced freedom of speech and freedom of association. If his country experiences these freedoms at the time he is conducting his study, he will, I hope, know where they came from.

MEETING A CRISIS:
PATRON SAINTS FOR
BIBLIOPHILES,
PRINTERS AND BOOKBINDERS*

AT A RECENT conference of librarians at Colleges of Education it was proposed that, since the word 'Library' was really too forbidding for use in schools, it should be replaced by the term 'Resources for learning area'. I understand that the suggestion has already been accepted at a number of progressive schools. Moreover, a recent Schools Council Working Paper, entitled *School Resource Centres*, while it allows that 'It will be evident . . . that *a school library* is an important part of a resource centre', goes on to say, 'A book is a resource', and then – 'To emphasise this point, the expression *school library resource centre*, adopted by the Library Association . . . seems to us a good one, and should be inferred even when, for the sake of brevity, we employ the contracted form'. All this is surely evidence of an attitude towards books with which bibliophiles are, to say the least, unfamiliar. Let us face the situation. Boswell's *Life of Johnson* has become a 'resource'.

What bibliophiles need is a patron saint and it may seem strange that they are still without one. Nor should printers be forgotten. The same Working Paper tells us that the word 'resource' covers 'books, periodicals, newspapers, press cuttings, pictures, diagrams, maps, charts, photocopies and microforms, worksheets, slides, filmstrips, film loops, films, records, audio-tapes, radio and television programmes, videotapes, slide-tape and filmstrip-record combinations, multi-media kits, programmed materials, models, specimens and

---

* First published in the *Book Collector*, 1974.

realia.'* 'Some people', we are told, 'would also include zoological and botanical living items.' Moreover, while '*A resource collection*' is 'a multiplicity of such items', a '*resource library*' is 'a resource collection organised and indexed for use, much as a book library is organised'. It looks as though, with all these competitors, printers should find a patron saint as well. And we may surely add bookbinders. An attempt is made here to show how these needs may be met, though it is appreciated that other suitable candidates for these posts may be put forward.

As the patron saint for bibliophiles we might consider Saint Cadoc. Born towards the end of the fifth century, the son of a Welsh prince, he is said to have died in 577. He was a man of great learning and a friend of Saint Gildas, whose book *De Excidio et Conquestu Britanniae* holds an unbeatable record as the most puzzling of all the sources for the history of this island. His chief work was the founding of the abbey of Llancarfan, near Cardiff, and some twenty churches in Wales are dedicated to him. Like many of the Welsh saints of his day, he was equally at home in Brittany. He is said to have ended his days – most surprisingly – as Bishop of Benevento, whither he was transported from Wales in a white cloud and where he was known as Sophias. He founded also a monastery on an island, still named after him, near Belz in Brittany and it was there that the incident took place which may seem to have earned him the role for which he is here recommended.

Saint Cadoc had a great love for Virgil and he used to make his pupils learn him by heart. One day he was walking by the sea with Saint Gildas, carrying his Virgil with him, when he told his friend that he could not endure the thought that the poet was perhaps in Hell. Saint Gildas was shocked and rebuked him sternly for even suggesting the possibility that he was not. At this point, a gust of wind caught the book and carried it into the sea. That night in his cell Saint Cadoc declared, 'I shall not eat a mouthful of bread nor drink a drop of water until I know truly what fate God has allotted to one who sang on earth as the angels sing in heaven'. He went to sleep and in a dream he heard a distant voice say, 'Pray for me, pray for me; never be weary of praying, for I shall yet sing eternally the mercy of the Lord'.

Reassured, he sat down to his breakfast next morning. A fisherman

* Realia: One suspects that the word came from Germany, e.g. Realschule, to the United States. Webster gives the meaning, 'Objects or activities used by a teacher to relate classroom teaching to real life; especially things (as costumes, tools, objects of worship) relating to the daily living of people studied in geography or language classes'. [R. B.'s footnote.]

brought him a salmon which had just been caught. In it Saint
Cadoc found the Virgil which the wind had snatched out of his
hands.

It is a charming story, but it will not stand scrutiny. It appeared first,
translated from the Breton into French, in a book published in 1861 *La
Légende celtique* by the Vicomte Hersart de la Villemarqué. The
Vicomte had made his name with a collection of Breton ballads *Les
Chants du Barzaz-Breiz*, which had appeared in 1839 and was crowned
by the Académie. But unfortunately anything from the pen of la
Villemarqué must be regarded with suspicion. Baring-Gould in the
first edition of his *Lives of the Saints*, in 1872, accepted the story readily.
It appears again in the next edition of 1897, in the first volume as Saint
Cadoc is commemorated on 24 January. But by the time he came to
the final volume, Volume XVI, published in the following year,
Baring-Gould had become suspicious. 'La Villemarqué is now somewhat discredited among scholars.' In 1908, when he published with
John Fisher his *Lives of the British Saints*, he was a great deal more
outspoken. 'But everything produced by this author is open to
suspicion, as he was a wholesale fabricator of legends and ballads.'
And, in fact, anyone who reads the paper read by Monsieur F. M.
Luzel at a congress held at Saint-Brieuc in 1872, entitled *De l'authenti-
cité des chants du Barzaz-Breiz*, is not likely to pay much attention to the
word of the Vicomte.

However, we have not yet finished with Saint Cadoc. For his life
was written in about the year 1100 by Lifras, who was himself a monk
of Llancarfan. In his *Vita Sancti Cadoc* is to be found a story which
deserves to be taken a great deal more seriously.

It happened that one day the saint was rowed by two of his disciples,
Barruc and Guales, in the Bristol Channel from Holm Island to
another island called Barry. When they arrived he asked his disciples
for his Enchiridion. They had to admit that they had forgotten the
book and that it had been left behind. He ordered them to go back at
once and fetch it, exclaiming angrily, 'Go ye, never to return'. The
two left at once and rowed back to Holm Island, where they retrieved
the book, and began to row back again. The man of God was by now
sitting on a hill on Barry Island, looking out to sea. A sudden storm
caused the boat to overturn and the two disciples were drowned. That
evening the saint, 'wishing to refresh with food his body wasted with
fastings', told his servants to get a fish for his supper. They went down
to the shore, but before embarking they found on the sand a salmon of
extraordinary size which they brought back with them. On cutting it
open, they found inside it the Enchiridion, unsoiled and uninjured.

'The man of God', we are told, 'giving thanks to God and receiving it eagerly, exclaimed that with God nothing was impossible'.

Saint Cadoc, then, seems a very suitable candidate for the post of patron saint of bibliophiles. But we must turn to the printers. And here the candidate seems obvious, Saint Enurchus.

He was an unusual saint. To begin with, this was not his real name: he started as Saint Evurtius. A deacon in Rome, he was miraculously transported to Orleans, where he became Bishop in the middle of the fourth century, and he is traditionally held to be responsible for the building of the first church there. His body experienced the translations almost inevitable for a Gallic saint of the early Middle Ages, but the *Acta Sanctorum* is quite definite about the conclusion. 'Istud certum est, sacrum corpus conservatum in propria abbatia fuisse, donec impio Calvinistarum furore seculo XVI in cineres fit redactum.'* Like many other saints also at different times he was commemorated on different days in the year, but was eventually established on 7 September. He became better known with the appearance of the Life, written in the eleventh century by an author with the splendidly incongruous name of Lucifer the Subdeacon.† This tells us of numerous miracles. For some reason he became popular in the Province of York and he found a place in the calendar of the York Breviary on 7 September.

With the Reformation he naturally disappeared from the scene in England and he was omitted in the calendars of the two Prayer Books of Edward VI and that of Elizabeth. And then he made a most unexpected reappearance. In 1604, on the accession of James I, a new Prayer Book was issued with certain revisions, few of them of any great importance. Among these changes was the addition of only one Black Letter saint, on 7 September. This was Saint Enurchus. The reason is clear: 7 September was Queen Elizabeth's birthday, which had been appropriately celebrated for forty-five years. It was hardly possible to make her a saint, but to ensure that the date was not forgotten another way of marking it was discovered.

---

* 'This much is certain – his holy body was preserved in his own abbey until the sixteenth century when it was reduced to ashes, thanks to the unholy fury of the Calvinists.'

† The name Lucifer raises some problems. The word, used for the King of Babylon by Isaiah (14:12), is translated thus in the Vulgate and the Authorised Version. ('Quomodo cecidisti de coelo lucifer.' 'How art thou fallen from heaven, O Lucifer, son of the morning.') It was then employed as a title for the Devil by Saint Jerome. But it is also to be found in the Vulgate in the Second Epistle of Peter (1:19) to translate Phosphoros, and here it refers to Christ. ('Et lucifer oriatur in cordibus vestris.' 'And the day-star arise in your hearts.') [R. B.'s own footnote.]

But why Enurchus? The explanation is that it was a misprint, though one made earlier than in 1604. It is to be found first in a somewhat mysterious book, printed by William Seres in 1564, *Preces Privatae, in Studiosorum Gratiam Collectae, et Regia authoritate approbate*. For an official production at that time it was remarkably Catholic. It was itself based on the *Orarium seu Libellus Precationum per Regiam maiestatem Latine aeditus*, also printed by Seres, of 1560. But the *Orarium*, while it restored a good many saints to the Calendar, left 7 September a blank. In the *Preces*, however, where almost every day has its saint, we find for that day *Enurchi epi*. It can hardly be doubted that it was from the *Preces* that the compilers of the 1604 Prayer Book dug up the saint they needed. And the Enurchus of the *Preces* can be explained. It was in all probability taken from an edition of the York Breviary printed in Paris in 1526 by François Regnault for Jean Gachet of York. In this we find the name printed as Euurcius. Seres was no doubt careless and to him may be attributed the invention of the new saint. Enurchus then may reasonably be taken as the patron saint of printers, since he owes his existence to one.

To find a patron saint for bookbinders seems to be rather more difficult, and it is necessary to fall back on Charlemagne. The difficulty about Charlemagne is that he was canonised by an anti-pope, Guido of Crema, styled Paschal III. However, he appears often enough in French and German Martyrologies and his splendid shrine and the reliquary in the form of his bust are to be found in the Cathedral Treasury at Aachen. In an air raid during the Second World War a bomb came through one of the wonderfully elegant windows of the Choir of the Cathedral there, went right through the building and out by another window. Exploding outside it destroyed the south-west corner of the Cloister, but the Cathedral was spared. The official British Report on *Works of Art in Germany* (*British Zone of Occupation*): *Losses and Survivals in the War* records: 'The town was heavily damaged by air raids and ground fighting and of all the important historical monuments only the Cathedral escaped comparatively lightly'. I myself knew Aachen in the days soon after the end of the war and I found that it was commonly believed that, when the bomb came opposite the pointing finger of the Emperor's statue in the Choir, it hurriedly escaped – horizontally.

Of Charlemagne we are told that out hunting one day he lost his way and took refuge for the night in the house of a poor priest, who did not recognise his guest. He made him as comfortable as he could, invited him to hear him say Mass next morning and gave him the best breakfast he could provide. The Emperor, touched by his kindness and his poverty, offered him a piece of gold. But the priest refused it. He asked him, however, if he killed a stag in that day's hunting to let him have the skin as his old Breviary badly needed a new cover. Charlemagne was sufficiently impressed to appoint the priest to the bishopric of Trier, which became vacant soon afterwards.

It must be admitted that the story is not very well attested. But Charlemagne was certainly interested in the binding of books. When he attempted to stop his bishops from hunting and hawking and found that this was impracticable, he compromised by allowing them to hunt provided that the skins of any beasts they killed were used for the binding of books.

The selection of a patron saint is no light matter. It is hoped that this note may stimulate discussion on what has surely become an urgent need. But whoever are chosen, Saint Cadoc, Saint Enurchus and Saint Charlemagne or others, they will need all the invocations they can get or *The Winter's Tale*, *Pride and Prejudice* and *The Inimitable Jeeves* will all become 'resources', along with multi-media kits, programmed materials and realia. And how long will it be before the Bodleian becomes a 'Resources for learning area'?

NATIONALISM TODAY

The Clayesmore Lecture was instituted in 1969 by the Governors of Clayesmore School, 'with a view to the School's making a contribution to the intellectual life of the County of Dorset'. They succeeded in persuading some notable speakers to participate: Lord Snow, Cardinal Heenan, Enoch Powell and Lord Caccia. Robert's was the fifth in the series and was given on 18 May 1973. The words of the Rector of Münster, that Nationalism was still going to prove 'one of the strongest forces in the world', certainly resound with even greater force today than they did in 1973. The combinations of Liberal and National ideals, and their intermixture and confusion, are as powerful in 1990 as they were in 1848, from Azerbaijan to the Baltic States, from the Ukraine through the Balkans to East and West Germany. The lecture focuses attention on several regions where History may have seemed relatively static in 1973, but which have recently erupted into affrays and violence. It also draws in examples from Africa, from the regions of West Europe and even the Isle of Man.

MY MIND GOES back nearly twenty-five years. I had just flown from Berlin during the Russian blockade of that city to discuss certain educational issues with the Rector of the University of Münster. In the course of our conversation I said that I supposed I ought to face the fact that for the rest of my life-time politics would be dominated by the struggle between the Soviet bloc and the West. He interrupted me. 'Don't forget Nationalism,' he said. 'It is very far from dead. It is still going to prove to be one of the strongest forces in the world.' I think the last twenty-five years have proved him to be right.

There is nothing new about National feelings, of course, or the sentiment of Patriotism. One has only to think of Shakespeare's lines,

This royal throne of Kings, this sceptred isle,
This earth of majesty, this seat of Mars,
This other Eden, demi-Paradise . . .
This blessed plot, this earth, this realm, this England.

Or we may take the great French historian of the reign of Louis XIV, Bossuet, 'Human society demands that one loves the land where one lives with others and looks on it as a mother and a common nurse . . . Men, in fact, feel themselves to be closely bound together when they long that the same earth which has carried them and nourished them when alive will receive them into its bosom when they are dead.' We may think of the Italian poets, with their deep love of Italy. Dante spoke of Italy as the noblest region of Europe. Petrarch, returning to Italy from France, stood at the summit of the pass of Mont Genevre and, seeing Italy stretched below him, wrote one of the most beautiful of all Latin poems, which ends,

Now I gaze on Italy, from pine-leaved Ginevra!
The clouds are behind me; the warm home-breezes caress me,
Rising from far below me to bid me welcome.
This is the land of my fathers, I gladly greet her.
Hail, O beautiful mother, creation's glory!

But it never crossed the mind of either Dante or Petrarch that Italy might be united to form a single independent state.

Nationalism as a strong political force came into existence with the French Revolution. As long as the sanction behind government was what we in this country used to call the Divine Right of Kings, it did not make any difference, to take one example, if Frenchmen in Brittany spoke Breton, in Alsace German or in the extreme south-west Basque. They would be equally loyal to the King. But once it was accepted, to quote the words of the Declaration of the Rights of Man and of the Citizen, that 'the principle of all sovereignty rests fundamentally in the nation: no individual can exercise authority which does not emanate expressly from it,' we find very different views. In the Convention of 1794 prominent politicians on more than one occasion advocated the extermination within the boundaries of France of non-French languages – 'barbarous jargons and rude dialects', they were called – Breton, German and Basque. But we must not forget Poland. Lord Acton held that it was the partition of Poland that 'awakened the theory of nationality in Europe, converting a dormant right into an aspiration, and a sentiment into a political claim . . . Thenceforward there was a nation demanding to be united in a State – a soul, as it were, wandering in search of a body to begin life again.'

Before considering what part this sentiment of Nationalism plays in the world today, I should utter one very obvious warning. We are dealing with a most complex subject, one which it is almost impossible to define. Let me take two examples of this complexity from my own experience. One day, when a boy (I had just left school) I was in Strasburg talking with some young people of a family I knew of about my own age. They told me of the splendid occasion over three years before when, on November 18th, 1918, the French troops had marched into the city, how it had been impossible to buy red or blue cloth, for everyone was making tricolours to hang from their windows. Then a few minutes later I was left alone with the eldest girl in the family. She turned to me and said, 'That was the day when I realised that, while the rest of my family were French, I was a German.' Or I think of a German from the Sudetenland in Czechoslovakia, the German-speaking district of the country which Hitler occupied in September, 1938, after the Munich agreement. He was a Social Democrat and had come as a refugee to England. I asked him once if he felt himself to be a Czech or a German. 'I certainly started as a German,' he answered. 'And then I read Palacky's *History of Bohemia*.' (This was one of the greatest historical works of the nineteenth century. Palacky was not only an historian; he was also a Czech nationalist political leader. It is a work of ten volumes.) 'When I began it I was a German; when I had finished it I knew myself to be a Czech.'

Nationalist movements in the nineteenth century were to be found largely in central and eastern Europe, though not, of course, exclusively. (Ireland is an obvious exception.) Clearly I cannot cover the whole field – from China to Peru, as it were – of Nationalism today. I shall deal with three aspects of it: nationalism as a force in three large states in Europe, France, Germany and Russia; the remarkable growth of small-scale nationalist movements in Western Europe; and then the phenomenon of African nationalism.

Nationalism in France presents us with a very peculiar problem. General de Gaulle, the dominating figure in French history since the War, based his whole policy on the restoration of French national pride, emphasising continually 'Le trésor de la souveraineté française.' Yet the General and other statesmen who supported him were the chief architects of the new concept of Europe which has found realisation in the establishment of the European Community. It seems completely paradoxical, to encourage at the same time a sense of

national pride, which inevitably does much to make a country seem to
be separate from other countries, and a sense of belonging to a larger
community. Three months ago before the General Election, the
French Premier, M. Pierre Messmer, whose policy, of course, is
derived from that of de Gaulle, was asked in a press interview, 'You
spoke recently of the independence of France as the primary objective
of the majority. How can this objective be reconciled with the creation
of a truly united Europe in 1980?' 'National independence,' he
answered, 'is not only reconcilable with the creation of a united
Europe; it is the indispensable condition if such a Europe is to exist.
The question is not only to create an economic community as prosperous as possible, it is to create a community of people free to choose
their own destiny.' This is at least a remarkable example of political
gymnastics. I myself should say that it is a great deal more than that.
But I think historians in the next century are going to have a hard task
analysing the foreign policy of France in our own time.

When we turn to Germany we find an entirely different picture.
Few developments since 1945 have been as surprising as the weakness
of Nationalism in Germany during this period. West Germany seems
to have concentrated on her own economic recovery. East Germany
seems to show no interest at all in re-unification – rather the reverse. I
cannot see in the criticisms by the CDU of the Ost-Politik of Willy
Brandt any signs of a fervent nationalist feeling. From the year 1871 to
1918 the statue representing Strasburg remained in the Place de la
Concorde in Paris with the statues of the other seven great cities of
France, but draped in black as a continuing reminder of its loss. I have
often asked Germans if they could imagine a statue of Königsberg,
that great Prussian city, the home of Kant, now a Russian town,
named Kaliningrad, draped in black in a prominent Platz in Bonn. I
have never found one who thought it possible. No doubt the main
reason for this extraordinary change of sentiment is a revulsion from
the hysterical nationalism of Nazi times which led to such appalling
disasters. A few years after the war a monument was erected at
Munich University to Hans and Sophie Scholl, the brother and sister
who, with a friend, founded and ran the student organisation, the
White Rose, which with almost unbelievable bravery resisted the
Nazis in 1943. They were, quite inevitably, eventually executed. On
the monument were inscribed the words, 'Dulce et decorum est pro
patria mori.' The students were indignant. It was not their country,
they said, they had died for.

When we turn to Russia we are once more in a world of political
gymnastics. From the earliest days of Communism there has been a

kind of see-saw motion; at one moment the rights of nations
to self-determination have been supported, at the next they have
been subordinated to the demands of the class struggle and the
internationalism of the Communist movement. The Communist
Manifesto of Marx and Engels had no use for the new nationalist
movements of those days. However, in 1903 the programme at the
Conference at which the Bolsheviks first appeared as a separate party
upheld 'The right of self-determination for all nations comprising the
state.' Eleven years later Lenin in his book, *The Right of Nations to
Self-determination*, upheld this right. But he went on to say, 'National
self-determination, including the right to secede should be distinguished from the decision to secede. Secession might or might not be
desirable.' What this came to was obvious enough in 1917 when the
Communist party gained control of Russia. In November Lenin
signed the Declaration saying that the Council of People's Commissars had decided to base its work on certain principles, one of which
was 'the right of the nations of Russia to free self-determination,
including the right to secede and form independent states.' A month
later the government of the Ukraine adopted a hostile attitude towards
the Communist movement in Moscow, opened negotiations with a
French military mission and supported Kaledin, a Cossack leader
opposed to the Soviet. Stalin, who had also signed the Declaration of
the People's Commissars, declared, 'To invoke the principle of self-
determination in order to support the revolt of Kaledin and the policy
of disarming Soviet armies . . . is to make a mockery of self-
determination and of the elementary principles of democracy.' 'The
right to secede' was certainly being distinguished from 'the decision to
secede.'

The problem of nationalism in the Soviet Union is bound to be an
awkward one. The population of the Union in 1970 was 242,000,000.
The Russians themselves make up only about half of these. It cannot
be imagined that the central government of the Union would for a
moment really allow, to quote the resolution of 1903, 'The right of
self-determination to all nations comprising the state'. They have
shown that they can be completely ruthless when dealing with
subordinate nations or tribes whose loyalty they suspect, as the
forcible deportation of a million such persons during the war years
showed. I think it may be allowed that the normal treatment of the
more than one hundred different nationalities of the Union (the figure
is an official Soviet one) is not particularly repressive. For instance, the
native language is generally used and taught in the schools, including
the secondary schools; Russian is always the second language. But

there are very narrow limits to which separate nationalisms are confined and this is very obvious now in the Ukraine. There certainly exists in Russia today a good deal of what might be called 'underground' opposition and criticism. It is to be found particularly among the intellectuals, but one of its manifestations is a revival of the Christian religion. It is, perhaps, particularly evident in the Ukraine. Last year *Pravda* had an issue largely devoted to an attack on religion, stated to be one of 'the most tenacious survivals of the past'. 'It is very important,' it was stated, 'to expose the link between religion and nationalist survivals.' I do not believe for a moment that the Soviet Union has finished with the problem of Nationalism.

We must consider, however, not only nationalism in the non-Russian parts of the Soviet Union, but in Russia itself. And here again we find what I have referred to as the see-saw motion. In 1918 Lunacharsky, the Commissar for Education, declared that 'a teaching of history directed towards the creation of national pride, patriotic feeling and the like, or which strives to find a pattern for imitation in the examples of the past, must be rejected.' Twenty-three years later Stalin was to declare, 'Let us be inspired by the valiant images of our ancestors, Alexander Nevsky, Dmitry of the Don, Kuzno Minin, Dmitry Pozharsky, Alexander Suvorov, and Mikhail Kutuzov.' After the war there was what has been called a brief deflationary period, but it did not last long. It is hardly surprising that the advice given in a Soviet report on education issued in 1964, dealing with the teaching in the last year at school, must be somewhat difficult to interpret. 'History and social study are important means of bringing the pupils up in a spirit of selfless love for, and devotion to, their socialist motherland, in a spirit of peace and friendship among the nations and in the spirit of proletarian internationalism.' The statement echoes one by Stalin thirty years earlier, 'Proletarian in content and national in form – such is the universal human culture towards which socialism is moving.' This too is walking on a tight-rope, but it is a different one from General de Gaulle's.

I turn now to deal with another aspect of the development of Nationalism during the last twenty-five years, the appearance, or in most cases the renaissance of nationalist feelings in groups within the established National States of Europe. It seems strange that, while nationalism of this kind awoke as a strong political force during the nineteenth century in central and eastern Europe, it seemed to be comparatively dormant in western Europe during that period – with two very important exceptions, Ireland and Catalan nationalism in Spain. To some extent we find the pattern of the earlier movements repeated, in particular the very great importance of the revival, often almost the creation, of a national language. Nationalist movements seem to need in order to come into being two persons, a grammarian and a poet. The grammarian turns a spoken language into a written one. The first Slovak grammar appeared in 1787. Then a Catholic priest, Jan Holty, translated Homer, Virgil, Horace and Theocritus into Slovak, an incongruous beginning. Ukrainian nationalism was very largely the creation of a grammarian, Kobaz (before him Ukrainian could not be called a literary language), and a poet, Taras Sheveshenko. Kobaz was arrested and sent into the army as a private soldier. The Tsar very wisely ordered that he should not be allowed to write. In about 1880 leave to print an Ukrainian grammar was refused on the ground that you could not have a grammar of a language which had been officially declared non-existent. But for all that Ukrainian is now certainly a living language. If we turn to Catalonia we find that, having supported the losing side in the war of the Spanish Succession, it lost most of its privileges as a largely autonomous province in 1715 and its six Universities were suppressed. In the 1830s it lost the remaining privileges and Catalan, a language with a great literary past, was no longer allowed to be used in the schools. And yet in the 1860s one can see the beginning of a revival of Catalan, which had come to be spoken only in the villages, as a literary language and the appearance of the first Catalan newspaper and a Catalan theatre. Since the end of the Spanish Civil War Catalonian independence has been firmly suppressed. Catalan was no longer used in schools or in public worship, though there have been recently some slight concessions. No one can suppose that Catalan national feelings have disappeared. To turn to the other end of the Pyrenees the Basques with their strange and ancient language, which, it has been said, 'has the same appeal to the philologist as the coelacanth to the biologist,' had until 1840 their own Parliament and laws. Backing the wrong side in the Carlist wars, they lost many of their privileges. Basque nationalism is now one of the most difficult problems the Spanish government has to deal with. But we must always expect anomalies when we consider nationalism. There are valleys in Navarre among the Pyrenees where Basque is the language of the people, but they are without any enthusiasm for Basque nationalism. Many of its most vehement supporters in the great industrial centre of Bilbao do not speak Basque at all. Nor should we forget that both Basque and Catalan are spoken north of the Pyrenees in France, but there are no nationalist movements there. Marshal Joffre, who commanded the French army at the beginning of the First World War, spoke Catalan.

If we turn to what I had better call here the United Kingdom, we find a different picture. I do not think that Gaelic plays a very important part in the phenomenon of Scottish Nationalism, but Welsh certainly does in the similar phenomenon in Wales. And yet, unlike what is to be found in Slovakia, Catalonia or, to take a very different example, Finland, the number of Welsh speakers in Wales is falling. In 1891, 54·4% of the people in Wales spoke Welsh; in 1921, 43·5%; in 1931, 36·8%; in 1961, 26%, and I believe that the last census will show a further decline. And yet there has been a most deliberate attempt in the schools of Wales to reverse this fall. (I might add that the number of Gaelic speakers in Scotland was rather over 95,000 in 1957 and fell to rather over 76,000 in 1961, or 1·3% of the population, of whom only 1079 spoke Gaelic only.) There are no official statistics of those who speak Breton. The number has been estimated as about six or seven hundred thousand or about 20% of the population. No Breton is taught in the schools, except occasionally out of the regular school hours. Breton is allowed on the radio ninety seconds twice a week and once a fortnight thirty minutes. Gaelic is allowed twenty-four hours a week of radio and during term time a twenty minute school programme. Welsh, of course, is very much better served, including thirteen hours a week on television.

It seems to me clear that this new development of what might be called Nationalism within the framework of established Nationalism is a phenomenon which cannot be disregarded or ignored, as General de Gaulle was determined to do in Brittany. I think it likely that Europe will see more nationalist movements of this kind. Two years ago I came across one for the first time. It is the movement supporting the independence of Occitanie or Southern France. I first met it in a book shop in the little town of Cordes, north of Albi. The proprietor was very interested in the movement and had a good many publications of the Centre Culturel Occitan on sale. I thought it a purely academic movement until I saw its symbols, slogans and messages painted up on the walls in that part of France. This was something very familiar, the hallmark of a popular movement. Behind it lie, as in Wales for instance, historical memories to be found of those of Langue d'Oc, and a language, Provençal, with a great literature, which had never quite disappeared in peasant dialects and was revived by scholars and poets, especially Frédéric Mistral. And there was something more. Here are the opening lines of one of the books about it, which I have translated into English. 'Our plan is to show how, since the earliest days of history, there has been an Occitanian nation, constantly oppressed, always reviving, how this nation gave birth to one of the most original of civilisations, how, although humbled and enslaved during three centuries of wars and repression, the nation has endured against wind and tide by means of a nationalism which the excesses of centralism have been able to conceal and stamp upon, but not to extinguish, and which, now more than ever, appears before us as alive and whose emancipation has become one of the problems of our time.'

I think these words may give us a clue which will help us to understand the rise of these nationalist movements in Western Europe during recent years. It is, I believe, one form, and a very potent one, of a widespread reaction against the overwhelming power of the modern monolithic state. To be able to find a more intimate loyalty is a great relief to many. Of course, there must be something quite genuine in the bond which creates this loyalty. It is found in a common language and a shared history. These movements, therefore, tend, at least in their early stages, to live in the past, like Afrikaner Nationalism in South Africa, which is always looking back at their Voortrekker ancestors. But this reverence for the past may be supplanted eventually. In the nineteenth century and well on into the twentieth these movements were usually conservative. It was not only that they so often looked back to the past; they were often deeply embedded in what one might call religious conservatism. The first Carlist rising in Spain, a fiercely reactionary movement, was in Catalonia; its two main aims were the restoration of the Inquisition and the suppression of Liberalism. Down to the 1920s the Catalan nationalist movement was predominantly conservative. The same was true of Basque nationalism. Now, of course, one finds these nationalisms being used as an expression of anarchism and syndicalism. Twenty years ago in Quebec one felt oneself to be living in pre-Revolutionary France. It is surely significant that kidnappers in Quebec now demand to be allowed to go to Cuba. The Welsh Language Society, which is the most vocal nationalist association in Wales – it is quite small, about 2000 members – is certainly moving further and further to the left. This does not always happen, of course. It has not with the Afrikaners, no doubt because they now control themselves in as monolithic a state as one could ask for. But in general I think this development is an expression of the same feeling, a desire to revolt against an omnipotent state. I should say that this is an important element in Ukrainian nationalism, to which I have already referred.

Perhaps the Manx should be taken as another example. There are certainly those in the Isle of Man who want to withdraw from a world represented by the United Kingdom or perhaps in due course the

European Community. At the beginning of this century over 4500 people there spoke Manx. In 1961 the number had dropped to 165. I do not know where it stands now. I can give another example of the same phenomenon which is even smaller in scale, though it can hardly be called nationalist. In 1920 the boundaries of greater Berlin were redrawn by the Prussian House of Representatives to include a number of neighbouring parishes and estates. One little village called Steinstücken was included, but was not joined up geographically with the City. (A study of English county boundaries fifty years ago would show a good many similar examples of isolation.) It has about 200 inhabitants. When the Allies occupied Berlin in 1945, being part of Berlin it lay in the American Sector, but it was entirely surrounded by what was then the Russian Zone of Occupation and is now the German Democratic Republic. It was connected with Berlin by a road about a thousand yards in length. Every week-day for twenty-eight years one bus has gone from the village to Berlin in the morning, carrying schoolchildren and workers, and has returned with them in the late afternoon. Three individuals have been allowed to use the road at other times, a doctor, a single fireman and the postman. Now an exchange of land has been effected and Steinstücken is fully absorbed in Berlin. And the inhabitants are not very pleased. They miss the cosiness, quiet and independence of their isolation, now that they are absorbed into a great and flourishing city.

But one must agree that not all modern nationalist movements are covered by the generalisations that I have just been making. Two of the most important today seem to fit into no obvious category. One is that of Flemish nationalism. This is firmly rooted in what one might call language consciousness, though it is certainly also an expression of a social discontent. The Flemings have felt that they did not get a real chance. One strange aspect of it is that for a long time its main support was to be found in two classes which are not often found in alliance, students and peasants. But the most difficult point about the Flemish national movement is that it has been so deeply divided as to its aims. The majority probably do not ask for more than a fair chance in Belgian industry and society. But there have always been some who have aimed at a separate Flemish national state. And, before the War, there were those who have aimed at creating a new state altogether, Dietschland, combining Flanders, Holland, Luxemburg and Friesland. And there are those who say that the French-speaking inhabitants of Belgium, the Walloons, are really of the same racial stock as the Flemings and should be included in the same state. However, anyone who visits Brussels must be aware of the successes which the

Flemish have won in securing equality for their language and, in general, social advancement. It is surely a sign of how strong nationalism still is that recently it has been found necessary to divide both the two great Universities of Louvain and Bruxelles (Leuven and Brussel) so that there are now four, two French and two Flemish.

Of all the nationalist movements in Europe today none is more violent or more likely to cause a revolution than the Croat national movement in Yugoslavia. We should remember that when the Austro-Hungarian Empire disappeared at the end of the First World War, the new states formed out of them were not unitary national states. The name of Czechoslovakia is evidence enough and it says nothing of the Sudeten Germans. The new constitution of Yugoslavia, the land of the Southern Slavs, drawn up after the First World War (it lasted for eight years) included a two-chamber Parliament, one being called the Council of Nationalities with representatives of eight separate areas. And here we come to the strangest of all the nationalist phenomena in Europe. If we forget for the moment, the people of Bosnia and of Macedonia, and the Albanians, Greeks and Magyars in the country, the three main districts of Yugoslavia are Slovenia, Croatia and Serbia. The great divide in national sentiment is between Croatia and Serbia. Slovenia speaks one kind of Slav language; Croatia and Serbia another, known as Serbo-Croat. (There are, of course, some differences of dialect.) But the Serbs use one kind of alphabet, the Cyrillic, the Croats another, the same as ours. And behind this lies the fundamental difference. The Serbs belong to the Orthodox Church, the Croats owe their spiritual allegiance to Rome. And behind that we find the epoch-making decision of the Emperor Diocletian in AD 285 to divide the Roman Empire, for the line between the Churches still approximates very closely to this line of seventeen hundred years ago.

We find ourselves continually plunging back into History. But when we turn to Africa there is, in most parts south of the Sahara, little or no history to plunge into. Let me say at once that I am not now concerned with what is often called African Nationalism. This was defined by Ndabaningi Sithole, the Rhodesian African leader, in this way.

The basic ingredients that go to make up the present African nationalism may be enumerated as the African's desire to participate fully in the central government of the country; his desire for economic justice that recognises fully the principle of 'equal pay for equal work' regardless of the colour of his skin; his desire to have full political rights in his own country; his dislike of being treated as a stranger in the land of his birth; his dislike of being treated as a means for a white man's end; and his dislike of the laws of the country that prescribe for him a permanent position of inferiority as a human being.

This is not an expression of national, but of racial feelings. It is often spoken of as Pan-Africanism. What one wants to know is what Mr Sithole meant by 'his own country' and 'the land of his birth'.

The original African political group was the tribe and for the vast majority of Africans it is still the group to which they feel they belong. A short time ago it was only a very small educated minority who felt a loyalty to Kenya or Nigeria or Ghana or Senegal or the other states which had been created by European powers during the last hundred years and were entirely artificial. The number who feel it is certainly growing. But it is the cause of the greatest political problem of Africa today, a problem of divided loyalties. It is not unknown in Europe: we might think of the Clans in Scotland. Tribal feeling is deeply ingrained in Africa; nationalism, in the sense I have given to the term, is something very new. I myself learnt a great deal about this very new force one evening which I spent at Makerere University in Uganda with two students who both came from Kenya. I asked them what they meant by Kenyan Nationalism. They were completely convincing; they spoke of it with enthusiasm. I asked them whether when they crossed the frontier into Tanzania they felt they were going into a different country. They said they did. I asked them if they knew how that frontier had been created. (It is the most artificial frontier in the world. It was drawn on a faulty map in the British Foreign Office in 1886 with a ruler to demarcate the spheres of British and German influence.) Yes, they said, they knew about the frontier. Now, this frontier goes right through the lands of the Masai tribe and one of these two students was a Masai. I asked him to try to forget Makerere University and think back to the days when he had been a boy living with his tribe. 'Now,' I said, 'will you tell me what you think of that frontier.' He answered, 'It's the most damnable frontier in the world.'

The problem was expressed very clearly in a remarkable statement by Julius Nyerere, President of what was then Tanganyika, now Tanzania, in an address to the Norwegian Students Association at Oslo in September, 1963. He pointed out that the independence movements in Africa had to be organised on a national basis, because they had to overcome the colonial political units. It was the tribe which was the traditional unit of loyalty, but it was inadequate as a basis of the freedom struggle. Colonialism having caused the organisation of political units, they had to start from there.

> Yet once the tribal unit has been rejected as not being sensible in Africa, then there can be no stopping short of Africa itself as the political grouping. For what else is there? Nations in any real sense of the word do not at present exist in Africa. The nation states which are now members of the United Nations are artificial units, carved arbitrarily on the body of Africa. Not one of us is bound together by one language or a heritage common to its people but not to those of a neighbouring nation. Each exists because its boundaries were historical and administrative conveniences of the colonial powers.

This may seem a completely convincing statement. These African states do seem quite meaningless. And yet they have somehow acquired meaning. And President Nyerere himself showed that Tanganyika had a real meaning, when speaking in the Assembly there only a year before he spoke in Oslo. The proposal that Tanganyika should be a Republic was being debated and the President was arguing very sensibly that it was quite impossible to devise a perfect Constitution and that the only real protection against tyranny was what he called 'the ethic of the nation'.

> When the nation does not have the ethic which will enable the government to say, 'We cannot do this, that is un-Tanganyikan' or the people to say, 'That we cannot tolerate, that is un-Tanganyikan', if the people do not have that kind of ethic it does not matter what kind of constitution you frame. They can always be victims of tyranny . . . What we must continue to do all the time is to build an ethic of this nation which makes the Head of the State, whoever he is, say, 'I have the power to do this under the constitution, but I cannot do it, it is un-Tanganyikan'.

There is no getting away from the word 'un-Tanganyikan'. I could think of no more convincing an expression of a genuine national feeling. Perhaps those who have tried to explain the mysterious force of nationalism have somewhat neglected the simple fact that an administrative unit almost automatically calls forth sentiments of loyalty, however artificial the unit may be. And once it has done this they may prove to be remarkably tenacious. I do not doubt myself that we are witnessing in Africa the birth of nations.

Nationalism is indeed a very difficult problem and it is certainly a living one. We shall experience the difficulties it creates as much in the twenty-first century as in the twentieth century. In conclusion I should like to refer to two of these difficulties. The first is what I may call the tyranny of Nationalism. In his great essay on *Nationality* in 1862 Lord Acton said, 'The greatest adversary to the rights of nationality is the modern theory of nationality.' (This is one of the wisest paradoxes I have ever read.) He continued,

> By making the state and the nation commensurate with each other in theory, it reduces practically to a subject condition all other nationalities that may be within the boundary. It cannot admit them to an equality with the ruling nation which constitutes the state, because the state would then cease to be national, which would be a contradiction of the principle of its existence. According, therefore, to the degree of humanity and civilisation in that dominant body which claims all the rights of the community, the inferior races are exterminated or reduced to servitude, or outlawed or put in a condition of dependence.

We might put alongside this some words written at almost exactly the same time from John Stuart Mill's *Representative Government*. We may remember that he is rightly regarded as the prototype of the Liberal.

> Nobody can suppose that it is not more beneficial to a Breton or a Basque of French Navarre, to be brought into the current of the ideas and feelings of a highly civilized and cultivated people – to be a member of the French Nationality, admitted on equal terms to all the privileges of French citizenship, sharing the advantages of French protection and the dignity and prestige of French power – than to sulk on his own rocks, the half savage relic of past times, revolving in his own little mental orbit without participation or interest in the general movement of the world. The same remark applies to the Welshman or the Scottish Highlander, as members of the British nation.

It seems to me that Mill's statement leads straight into Acton's. Once you despise some of the people in your community – 'to sulk on his own rocks, the half savage relic of past times, revolving in his own little mental orbit' – you proceed to regard them as 'inferior races' to be 'outlawed or put in a condition of dependence'.

It is here I think that we find the explanation of the problem of Ireland today. Religion is the main cause of division between Northern Ireland and the rest of the island, but there is nothing unique in this. We may recall Croatia and Serbia. We have the terribly difficult problem of a minority within a minority. I think the treatment of the Catholic minority in Northern Ireland over the past fifty years has been disgraceful. But I think it has been largely due to the basic fear of the Protestant people of Northern Ireland who have regarded the Catholics in Ulster as inevitable allies of those in the Republic who wish to destroy their independence. I do not suggest that more than a minority of the people in the Republic are not now ready to accept the separation of Northern Ireland as a regrettable necessity, though it is still part of the Constitution of Eire that the Republic consists of the whole island of Ireland. But a very vigorous minority are certainly not ready to accept it. To them it is obviously wrong. They regard it as clearly quite inadmissable that any part of Ireland should not be part of the Irish Republic. They cannot see that the people of Northern Ireland have any rights of Nationality at all. 'The greatest adversary of the rights of nationality,' Lord Acton said, 'is the modern theory of nationality.' It is more than a theory, of course, it is a passionate political faith. Ireland today illustrates well the truth of Acton's paradox.

An even clearer illustration can be taken from another part of Europe. The Magyars fought desperately for their own independence, but they had no sympathy whatever with the aspirations of other nations within their borders, such as the Slovaks or the Croats. Their greatest fighter for their own national independence, Kossuth, said once, 'Verily, verily I say unto you that the Slovak nation has never existed even in a dream,' and at another time, 'I cannot find Croatia on the map. I know no Croatian nationality.' And, as a result, when Hungary gained its independence in 1867, its Constitution contained the following perfectly astonishing clause, 'since all citizens of Hungary, both in virtue of the principles of the constitution and from a political point of view, form a single nation in the indivisible unitary Magyar nation, to which all citizens of the country belong irrespective of their nationality.' The Sinn Feiners and the members of the IRA have the same belief in an indivisible Irish nation, whatever about a quarter of the population may want.

My second difficulty confronts us with what seems to me an obvious duty. We must set our face against the creation of national stereotypes. From the very earliest days of nationalism men have created them. They intensify national antagonisms; they depersonalise human relations. I can quote an early example from the twelfth century when the English historian, William of Malmesbury, writing of the fervour created by the First Crusade, said, 'Now the Welshman abandoned his forest hunting, the Scot his familiarity with fleas, the Dane his constant drinking, the Norwegian his raw fish.' Or, to take a more recent example, I was talking one day with a Jamaican lady in

Birmingham. She told me she was very happy, especially as she now had her own little house. 'The only trouble,' she said, 'is our neighbours. They will play the wireless so loud and so late at night, and they throw their rubbish all over the place.' My heart sank: it is just the kind of thing people say about West Indians. 'And what sort of people are they?' I asked. 'Oh, Irish of course,' she answered. I may say that not long after I told that story at a meeting in Londonderry. It went down very well. I pointed out that the words that mattered were 'of course', and that the Jamaican lady had obviously learnt that stereotype from us, the English.

I do not think that there is any doubt that the Rector of Münster University was right. Nationalism is still proving to be one of the strongest forces in the world. And I suppose that, like all other great political causes, it can call out both the best and the worst in men.

THE MOST DANGEROUS
SUBJECT IN THE CURRICULUM

The Bowra Memorial Lecture was founded at Cheltenham College as a tribute to Sir Maurice Bowra, Old Cheltonian and the late Warden of Wadham College, Oxford. This was the second lecture in the series and was given in October 1974, when Robert was Gresham Professor of Rhetoric at the City University. The original title was 'The Dangers of Teaching History', but the present lecture draws upon a number of other similar addresses and lectures which he gave on the subject and I like to think this is the one which he would have preferred today, as discussions on the National Curriculum proceed and as both the strategy and tactics of teaching History are under scrutiny. I have omitted some dutiful respects paid to Sir Maurice Bowra's knowledge of poetry and his fame as the subject of Oxford anecdotes with which the lecture begins. Certain comments here on the Communist view of History have already been included in this volume.

I SUPPOSE A VERY large section of my audience this evening will be studying History. It is now quite a usual subject in English schools, although it is a comparatively recent addition to the curriculum. (Classical History has of course been respectable for several centuries.) But I do not think that it can be said that the English are a people to whom History means a great deal. The figure 1066 is of course at the back of our minds. To most of us the words 'Magna Carta' are familiar. Only one episode in our history is regularly commemorated – Guy Fawkes' Plot in 1605.

> Please to remember the fifth of November,
> Gunpowder, treason and plot,
> I know no reason
> Why gunpowder treason,
> Should ever be forgot.

But I wonder how many children who importune us for pennies before the annual bonfires have the least idea why they are doing it. On the whole our past history may be interesting to us, but it does not matter very much, and I think most of us would accept the words of T. S. Eliot, writing of the tragic years of the seventeenth century in this country.

> We cannot revive old factions
> We cannot restore old policies
> Or follow an antique drum.
> These men, and those who opposed them
> And those whom they opposed
> Accept the constitution of silence
> And are folded in a single party.

It is not like this in many countries of the world.

What taught me that History was a potentially most dangerous subject was my experience in Germany before and after the war. I remember once, not long after Hitler gained power, talking with a Professor at Berlin University. He told me that he had recently read with very great interest two articles in an English Journal, *Antiquity*, one of which had given the arguments for the view that Anglo-Saxon London had been a direct continuation of the Roman Londinium, the other the case that there was a complete gap between the two and that London had for a time ceased to exist. He sighed and said that it would be impossible to print two such articles in a German Journal. I expressed some surprise, but he explained that it was really out of the question to support the view that there was a direct connection between Roman and Teutonic Germany. Early history, he said, was particularly dangerous because it dealt with the origins of the *Volk*. I could understand this, for the whole Nazi philosophy depended on a racial myth. Then, he went on, as one moved through the centuries, it gradually became less dangerous, until one approached modern times when it became once more very dangerous indeed.

After the war I had to deal with the problem of the text-books used in German schools during the Nazi period. There was nothing for it, we had to start again from scratch with the History text-books. All were mainly concerned with the promulgation of the standard racial myth. All had to be destroyed and new ones written. Berlin, although it was divided into four sectors occupied by the troops of the four allied powers, was an administrative unit. But the German administration could do nothing without the approval of the inter-allied body, the Kommandatura. The educational organisation and provision in Berlin depended then on the Education Committee of the Kommandatura, and we had, all four of us, to agree on any decision before anything could happen.

In the end, often after interminable discussions, we reached agreement in the field of Education on every subject but one. We agreed in the end on a new school law for Berlin. We even agreed on the very difficult issue of religious instruction. But on one subject agreement was impossible. This was the teaching of History. As a result no History was taught in Berlin after the end of the war until the city was split by the Russians in November, 1948.

Now the reason for this was quite clear. The whole Communist attitude towards politics, social questions, literature and even technology depends on the acceptance of the Marxist view of History, the Marxist dialectic as it is called, the Class War, leading to the Dictatorship of the Proletariat. They could no more allow History to be taught in schools or Universities which was not based on this view, than a monastic school during the Middle Ages could have accepted Atheism as a foundation for the study of History. In 1923 Pokrovsky, one of the first and perhaps the greatest of Communist historians, had written, 'Marx is historical to the core. Marxism is historicism. We must be historians because we are Marxist. Materialism is primarily an historical outlook.' And the official Soviet manual on *The Fundamentals of Marxism-Leninism* in 1963 stated that Marx had discovered the laws of history which made it possible to foresee the general direction of historical development. But we could not agree to this being the only kind of History taught in the City and the Russians could not allow that any other kind should be taught. So no History was taught, and I found myself plunged into a world in which History was clearly a very dangerous subject.

The teaching of History in the world today raises some very difficult and uncomfortable issues. If I take History as studied and taught in Communist countries as an example to illustrate what I mean, we can look first at the accounts of German resistance to the Nazi regime current within the German Democratic Republic (East Germany) and the Federal German Republic (West Germany). They are so different that it seems difficult to believe that they have to do with the same period of history. The only official account in the East is a book of over 1200 pages in two volumes, published in 1970 by the Institute for Marxism-Leninism in Berlin, called *Deutsche Widerstandkämpfer*, (German Resistance Fighters). This gives the lives of 533 men and women who died in the Resistance movement, and as far as I have been able to check it, the account seems to be quite accurate. About 450 of them were Communists. In Western Germany – and in the western world generally – the great moment of the Resistance was the conspiracy of the Twentieth of July, 1944 which failed so tragically. In this book very few of those involved in this plot are included. It is referred to as the culmination of a monopolistic–capitalistic movement. Goerdeler, who would have been Chancellor if the plot had been successful, is mentioned five times casually as an imperialist lackey. General Beck, who would have been President, is never mentioned once. Now, the only comparable work from West Germany is two volumes with nearly one hundred lives of those who died in the Resistance, written by Frau Annadore Leber, the widow of Julius Leber, a most remarkable man, the Social Democrat leader who was executed by the Nazis. The two chief Communist Resistance organisations were 'Die Rote Kapelle' (The Red Orchestra) and the 'National Committee for Free Germany', which was controlled by German Communist refugees in Moscow, led by Walter Ulbricht who was to become Head of the German Democratic Republic. Frau Leber's book does not entirely ignore the Red Orchestra and this organisation has quite recently been the subject of a book in the West, an unpleasant book, simply concerned to denigrate it.

The pictures given by these two publications in the two German States are simply quite incompatible. Taking the four volumes together, we have the lives of 626 people who died in the Resistance. Only 34 persons appear in both books. Recently there has been an extraordinary development. The Red Orchestra is fully represented in the book published in 1970 by the Institute for Marxism-Leninism, which was an official communist work. In 1969 the Praesidium of the Supreme Soviet in Russia had made a posthumous award of the Order of the Supreme Soviet of the Red Banner to five of the leaders of this organization who were executed. For some years before, they had been neglected by those who wrote on the Resistance from the Communist point of view. Now they were quite respectable. In August 1971 several more rooms were opened in the Museum of German History in East Berlin, bringing the story down from 1933 to 1945, and I visited it myself shortly after. To my astonishment I found that The Red Orchestra had been demoted again. They were referred to only once in an inconspicuous corner of one of the rooms; in the catalogue they were omitted altogether. The light is now entirely focussed on the National Committee for Free Germany. I asked people I knew for an explanation. One was that the leaders of the Red Orchestra were too bourgeois. There may have been something in this. But I thought a more likely reason that I was given was that Herr Ulbricht did not like the spotlight being on any other organization than his own.

Perhaps I might give one other example from the Communist world to show how History has to be controlled in the service of politics. The people of Bessarabia, as we call it, that strip of territory between Rumania and Russia, are Rumanians. Bessarabia, with an extraordinary history, became part of the Ottoman Empire. It was taken by Russia from the Ottoman Empire. At the end of the First World War it was annexed by Rumania, which was forced to cede it to Russia again in June 1940. The Russians held it for a year and then, with the German invasion of their country, Rumania annexed it once again. The Soviet Union reannexed it in April 1944. The people, as I have said, are undoubtedly Rumanian, though the Russians call them Moldavians, and they speak the same language as the Rumanians, though the Russians insist on it being written and printed in a different script. In 1956 a Rumanian communist faced with the extremely difficult task of justifying in a history text-book the annexation by Russia of a country which all Rumanians feel should be theirs, said that 'Thanks to the influence of the more advanced Russian state [in 1812] the decline of feudalism was speeded up, along with the development of capitalism, a fact which, in spite of the backward character of Tsarist policy, represented a step forward.' I suppose only those who have some experience with the Marxist dialectic can appreciate what a very neat piece of work this was, but the main point was that he had to find an historical justification.*

* In another lecture on the dangers lurking in History teaching, a further Rumanian example, very relevant to the new situation in Europe in 1990, is given. 'The land which throughout most of Europe is known as Transylvania . . . was part of the Roman Empire, known as Dacia. A language evolved based on Latin, the language now spoken in Rumania. On the collapse of the Roman Empire it was conquered by the Goths, overrun by various barbarian invaders and eventually in the eleventh century conquered by Magyars. After many vicissitudes it became part of the Habsburg Empire and then part of Hungary. Then at the end of the First World War it became part of Rumania. In 1940 a large part of the country was transferred back to Hungary. Then at the end of the Second World War it all became part of Rumania once more. As it moved backwards and forwards in this way, so did its History change, and in particular the History taught in its schools. When it was under Hungarian Magyar rule its History was that, when the Magyars entered the country, they found it uninhabited except for a few small Slavonic tribes . . . However, when Transylvania has been part of Rumania, as it now is once more, the History taught in the schools has been quite different. What matters is the continuity of its Roman culture since the days when, as Dacia, it was part of the Roman Empire, and it continued to be mainly inhabited by Dacians. The story of the empty land is dismissed as a myth. It must have been difficult for children at school there from 1938 to 1946.'

It is perfectly possible of course to hold a political creed which allows no importance whatever to History. I should say that most of the leaders of the French Revolution rejected it. Their politics were based on political principles, the validity of which was quite independent of History. The preamble of the Declaration of the Rights of Man and of the Citizen, the basic document of the French Revolution, declared that 'ignorance or neglect of or contempt for the rights of man are the only causes of public misfortune or the corruption of governments.' No one who had any belief in the value of historical experience could have written that. Quite obviously the anarchists do not accept the significance of history. They demand a completely fresh start and history is for them irrelevant and misleading. For five remarkable days in April 1919, Bavaria came under the rule of the Anarchists, the leader being the great dramatist Ernst Toller. The Minister of Education was Gustav Landauer, best known for his works on Shakespeare. As might have been expected the University of Munich was thrown open to all without any entrance examinations and all set courses were abolished. But he found it necessary to include in the new arrangements one prohibition. No history was to be taught because it was a most dangerous subject. There is some significance I think in the fact that the two great revolutionary forces of the modern world are so divided on this issue, Communism basing its entire philosophy and its decisions in practical politics on the study of History; Anarchism rejecting that study completely.

I have spoken at some length about Communist History because it is such a dominating factor in so large a part of the world, which we sometimes forget because we are not very familiar with it in this country. It would be altogether wrong to suppose that what one might call tendentious history, to put it very mildly, is only to be found in Communist countries. I shall, therefore, now take examples from two others.

I take my first example from South Africa. Professor van Jaarsveld in his book, *The Afrikaner's Interpretation of South African History*, has dealt in a most interesting way with his subject, but he has concentrated mainly, but not exclusively, on the Afrikaner's use of History in building up a national self-consciousness as a means of resisting domination by the British. In recent years South African history has necessarily been focussed in a different direction, that of the relations between the Europeans and the Africans. The Great Trek of the 1830s, the central point of South African history, when the Boers left the Cape Colony and moved towards the north, used to be regarded almost entirely as an act of defiance against the English. Now it is seen rather in relationship to the African peoples of the country. Perhaps the fundamental fact in South Africa today is that there are rather over sixteen million Africans and just under four million Europeans, while 87 percent of the land belongs to the Whites and 13 percent to the Blacks. So History has been called in to justify this extraordinary anomaly. A few years ago the then Ambassador of South Africa to England gave an address at the Royal Commonwealth Society, when he expressed this justification as clearly and firmly as possible. He stated categorically that the Voortrekkers, as the Boers who left the Cape Colony on the abolition of slavery in 1830 were called, went for 600 miles across a completely empty veldt, and so had a perfect title to it, which the Africans had not. There was nothing original in what he said. It is a commonplace in Afrikaner history teaching.

It is quite impossible to substantiate this picture. At the time, owing to the Zulu invasion, the African tribes were moving about the country in a very unsettled condition, but the promulgators of this explanation, which is now expressed quite dogmatically, go much further than that. They claim to have moved into an empty and unclaimed land. I think it might be called the Myth of the Empty Veldt. There is no question that it now plays a very important role in South Africa.

Let me turn to Ireland and consider the point of view of the Protestants living in the north of the island. There is no question here, looking back to the seventeenth century, of:

> These men, and those who opposed them
> And those whom they opposed
> Accept the constitution of silence
> And are folded in a single party.

Macaulay in his *History of England*, told the splendid story of the defence of Londonderry by the Protestants for a hundred and five days in 1689, of the treachery of Governor Lundy who opened the gates for the Catholic enemy to come in and how the gates were closed just in time. The name of Governor Lundy, he said, 'is to this day, held in execration by the Protestants of the North of Ireland; and his effigy is still annually hung and burned by them with marks of abhorrence similar to those which in England are appropriated to Guy Fawkes.' As I have said, I doubt whether you will find 'marks of abhorrence' in England to-day. And, in fact, they were clearly disappearing in England in Macaulay's day. He published the volume which tells of the Siege of Londonderry in 1855. Four years later the Church of

England quietly dropped from the Book of Common Prayer the special services for January 30th, May 29th and November 5th, when they remembered the Execution of King Charles I, the Restoration of King Charles II, and the Gunpowder Plot. People were no longer interested in them. But there is no lack of interest in Londonderry today. Every year the effigy of Governor Lundy is still burned there with the most eloquent 'marks of abhorrence'; every year there is held with the beating of drums the March of the Apprentice Boys of the City to commemorate the apprentices in 1689 who shut the gates opened by the traitor.

The Protestants in Ulster are still in many ways living in the seventeenth century. They have still the feeling of a minority in serious danger. It is perhaps impossible to determine how far this making of past history a living, present-day reality, is an expression of present-day stresses or how far this attitude towards History preserves the stresses today. Perhaps it will help if we turn to the other part of the island.

A glance at the map will show that it is not unnatural that the people of the Irish Republic should feel that the whole island should form one state, though no doubt next week we shall be reminded by the Scottish National Party and Plaid Cymru that this does not necessarily apply to all islands. But this alone will not account for the passionate belief of members of the IRA for instance, that Ulster not being part of the Irish Republic is an appalling political crime. We have seen something of the force of this conviction during the past few days. Some members of the present government of the Irish Republic have come to feel that it would be advisable to delete from its constitution the clause in which this claim to the whole of Ireland is made. But the mere mention of such a possibility has met with such strong popular opposition, that it has been quickly abandoned. I do not think there can be any doubt about the reason for this. It is because, in the south, as in the north, History is a living, present day reality. The division of Ireland began with the Ulster Plantation in the reign of James I. Much the strongest opposition to the English subjugation of Ireland came in the north with the resistance of Hugh O'Neill, Earl of Tyrone, ending, when he sailed from Ireland with his ally the Earl of Tyrconnell in 1607, with what is known as the 'Flight of the Earls'. In December 1921, with the signing of the Anglo-Irish Treaty setting up the Irish Free State within the Commonwealth, the division of Ireland was accomplished. There were those in the south who were not prepared to accept this, and the Free State began its career with a civil war. Among those who refused was Eamon de Valera, though in 1927 he entered the Free State

Parliament and it was largely due to him that in 1949 Eire became an independent Republic. In an article in an Irish newspaper in March 1926 he wrote these words and I think they do much to explain why the Irish in the Republic will not accept the division:

> It is hard to be calm when one remembers that it is our fairest province that is being cut off. The Ulster that the Irishman of every province loves best next to his own. The Ulster of Cuchulain, the Ulster of the Red Branch Knights. The Ulster of the O'Neills and the O'Donnells. The Ulster of Ben Burb and the Yellow Ford. The Ulster in whose sacred sod rest the bones of Patrick, Columcille and Brian of the Tributes.*

One cannot help feeling that the one thing needed in Ireland – the whole island – is that they should completely forget their past history and step into the twentieth century. I think these examples will be enough to show that History can be a most dangerous subject, and as a relief I should like to give you a description of a history teacher calculated to help us to regain our confidence in the teaching of the subject. It is, you may feel, a very heart-warming account.

> Few teachers realise that the aim of history lessons should not consist in the memorising and the rattling forth of historical facts and data: that it does not matter whether a boy knows when this or that battle was fought, when a certain military leader was born, or when some monarch (in most cases a very mediocre one) was crowned with the crown of his ancestors. Good God, these things do not matter.
> To 'learn' history means to search for and find the forces which cause these effects which we later face as historical events.

---

* In another lecture, 'The Use Politicians make of History', Robert amplified this reference: 'Let us consider this statement. Cuchulain and the Red Branch Knights are purely legendary. (One might compare this with someone speaking of the Germany of Siegfried and the Rhine Maidens.) The O'Neills and the O'Donnells were families which led the resistance to the colonisation of Ulster in the early seventeenth century. Ben Burb was a victory over the English in a rising in 1642, and the Yellow Ford a victory over the English in 1598. Patrick brought Christianity to Ireland in the fifth century; Columcille, or Columba as the English call him, was the greatest of the Irish missionaries in the sixth century; Brian of the Tributes, usually called Brian Boru, finally defeated the Vikings in 1014.

'On the face of it, it is quite absurd. There is nothing referred to later than three hundred years before and most of it is much earlier. But we must remember what had happened to Ireland. Her early history was splendid and to be looked back on with pride. Then came an heroic resistance ending in utter defeat and humiliation. It is not really surprising that when national hopes rose again the Irish looked back on their distant past. What came later was something to be put right. And in the past Ulster was truly part of Ireland, the home of heroic Irishmen.'

Here too the art of reading, like that of learning, is to remember the important, to forget the unimportant.

It was perhaps decisive for my entire future life that I was fortunate enough to have a history teacher who was one of the few who understood how essential it was to make this the dominating factor in his lessons and examinations. The old gentleman, whose manner was as kind as it was firm, not only knew how to keep us spellbound, but actually carried us away with the splendour of his eloquence. I am still a little moved when I remember the grey-haired man whose fiery description made us forget the present and who evoked plain historical facts out of the fog of the centuries and turned them into living reality. Often we would sit there enraptured in enthusiasm and there were even times when we were on the verge of tears.

Our happiness was the greater in as much as the teacher not only knew how to throw light on the past by utilising the present, but also how to draw conclusions from the past and apply them to the present. More than anyone else he showed understanding for all the daily problems which held us breathless at the time. He was the teacher who made history my favourite subject.

It comes as something of a shock to realise that this quotation is from Hitler's *Mein Kampf*. I have omitted two sentences from it. 'He used our youthful national fanaticism as a means of education by repeatedly appealing to our sense of national honour, and through this alone he was able to manage us rascals more easily than would have been possible by any other means.' And – 'Who could possibly study German history with such a teacher and not become an enemy of the State (he referred to the Austrian Empire) which, through its ruling dynasty, so disastrously influenced the state of the nation?' (And by 'nation' Hitler meant here the German people.) Later in the book Hitler had this to say about the teaching of History:–

A change will have to be made especially in the present method of teaching history . . . The result of our present teaching of history is in ninety-nine cases out of a hundred a miserable one. A few dates, birth figures and names usually remain, while a great clear line is completely missing . . . Particularly in history lessons a shortening of the material has to be carried out. The main value lies in recognising the great lines of development. The more the lessons are restricted to this, the more it is to be hoped that benefit will arise out of this for the individual later on, which, summed up, is beneficial to the community. For one does not learn history in order to know what has been, but one learns history in order to make it a teacher for the future and for the continued existence of one's own nationality . . . This is the *end* and the history lessons are only a means to it.

When one thinks of the thousands who suffered and often died in the concentration camps of the Nazis, of the millions of Jews who died in the gas chambers, of the millions killed in the last War, I think Doctor Ludwig Poeltsch of the Linz Realschule becomes one of the most sinister figures in the history of education.

Is there anything to be done about it? Let me turn now to two suggestions for dealing with the problem of the dangers in teaching History. The first is that the teaching of History should be both morally and politically neutral. The duty of a teacher is simply to analyse and record, and to help his pupils to do so. His duty as a citizen is, of course, to make moral and political judgements and to act accordingly – as a citizen. This attitude towards History seems to me to be completely unreal. One cannot divide life in this way into water-tight compartments. Those whom he is teaching will not make this nice distinction. Supposing he remains strictly neutral when talking about, let us say, the partition of Poland or the trial of Warren Hastings, or the origins of the Franco-Prussian War. He will then inevitably lead his pupils to believe that he himself thinks that no moral issues are involved in international politics or in the relationship between an imperial power and a subject race.

I have no doubt whatever what was the most important lesson I ever sat through in my life. I was a boy of fourteen and the somewhat elementary history we were doing was the history of England in the eighteenth century. We came in having read a chapter on the history of Ireland from the reign of King William III to the Act of Union in 1801. The lesson began and we were witnesses of a magnificent performance. The master, an elderly and highly respected figure, simply tore the book to shreds, striding up and down the room as he did so. He showed us how the book had omitted or sometimes glossed over all the monstrous injustices of English rule in Ireland during that period, and above all, he attacked the book for its complacency. The effect on myself was profound and lasting. It taught me once and for all never to accept the doctrine 'My country right or wong'. It meant also, that I never again took a text-book seriously. There is something rather sinister about history text-books. Just because they confine themselves to simple facts there seems to be a general belief that text-books must tell the truth.★

★ An illustration of this problem was given in another of Robert's many addresses on the subject. Always a stern opponent of conventional cheating in examinations this quotation displays again his pleasure at the idea of subversion in a good cause. 'A revealing conversation came in 1962 from a young teacher in Johannesburg, who said how much he detested the official South African text books he had to use. "I know

I feel very differently about my second suggestion. It is that it is the inescapable duty of the teacher of History to say what he believes to be true and to inspire his pupils to adopt this principle. 'Let her and Falsehood grapple; whoever knew Truth put to the worse in a free and open encounter?' If I had to choose one sentence to express the highest ideal in our secular society, it would be this one from Milton's *Areopagitica*. Only, of course, it is not true. It neglects altogether too many factors – the prejudices, the vested interests, the sloth of Man. Still, that does not mean that it is not an ideal worth fighting for, or, when it is accepted, worth defending.

But we ought to remember its consequences, and sometimes its political consequences. If one is going to see that Truth is victorious in the encounter, one must be prepared at times to let down one's own side.

Let me take a simple example from a period of history distant and little studied, a very melancholy one, the period of utter degradation through which the Papacy passed in the first half of the tenth century. Sergius III, an Italian bishop, was Pope from 904 to 911. According to the contemporary evidence he was the lover of Marozia, one of the ladies of a family who then dominated Rome. In fact a later Pope, John XI, was, we are told, his son.

It is a safe rule always to discount any scandal to be found in tenth century writers. But the evidence for this is stronger than one might think – strong enough to make the best students' text-book on the period, the *Shorter Cambridge Mediaeval History*, state unequivocally as a fact that Pope John XI was their son. I do not refer to this merely to tell an unpleasant story about the Papacy, but to draw attention to an historian, Monsignor Duchesne, author of a great work on this period and editor of that most important source of medieval history, the *Liber*

---

perfectly well," he said, "that Van Riebeck's one idea when he landed at the Cape in 1652 was to get back to Holland as soon as he could, and that he was continually pestering the government at home with requests that he might be recalled . . . But I have to tell the boys that he was founder of this country eagerly and proudly looking forward to its great future." To this I made what I realise was the infuriatingly naive remark, "But why don't you tell them the truth?" "If I did," he replied, "they would fail in the Matriculation Examination." This rather baffled me, but I went on: "You know, it is sometimes possible to get a form of boys to feel that they and the master are in league to outwit the wicked examiners. Why not try that technique? Tell them the truth, but tell them to answer the Matriculation papers from the book. Then go on to point out to them that it would be up to them, when they grew up, to see that South Africa had a Government which would not place you and them in such a monstrous dilemma." "Yes," he said, "I suppose you are right. But I can tell you what would happen if I did. Before long I should find myself transferred to some school in a small town in the Northern Transvaal and no-one would ever hear of me again."'

Pontificalis. He cannot have liked telling of this unfortunate fact, but he stated his conviction that it was true. The view he expressed, as one might expect, was attacked with some violence, especially by an Italian historian, Fedele, and a conflict of articles in learned journals ensued. Only those with some experience in this field can realise how bitter articles in such journals often are. To my mind there is something admirable in the way Monsignor Duchesne stuck to his guns.

Few tasks are more difficult for an historian than to decide what to omit. It is the omissions which only too often show an historian's bias. If I may take an example from my own experience, there has been nothing in the history of my country I am more proud of than the work of a small number of men – at the start very small indeed – who brought about the abolition first of the slave trade and then of slavery in the British Empire. I cannot accept the view of Eric Williams and his followers, the view based on a Marxist theory of history, that the Abolitionists had very little to do with this and that it was due to the fact that slavery in the West Indies was ceasing to be profitable. It seems to me that all the facts are against them, but I do not see how one can point to the Abolitionists without referring also to the fact that as a nation we were at the same time so completely blind to the horrors of the Industrial Revolution, such as the employment of women and children in the coal mines. We ought not to forget some very uncomfortable words in *The Pickwick Papers*:

> Everyone whose genius has a topographical bent knows perfectly well that Muggleton is a corporate town, with a mayor, burgesses and freemen; and anyone who has consulted the addresses of the mayor to the freemen, or the freemen to the mayor, or both to the corporation, or all three to Parliament, will learn from thence what they ought to have known before, that Muggleton is an ancient and loyal borough, mingling a zealous advocacy of Christian principles with a devoted attachment to commerical rights, in demonstration whereof, the mayor, corporation and other inhabitants have presented at diverse times, no fewer than one thousand four hundred and twenty petitions against the continuance of negro slavery abroad, and an equal number against any interference with the factory system at home.

I hope I have been able to show you what a dangerous subject History can be, though I think in this country its dangers are little understood. It is a great weapon in the hands of mass movements and totalitarian regimes. Can it be a weapon in the armoury of a free society also? I believe it can. Freedom depends on the free and open encounter: democracy demands a critical, but informed public opinion. History can help in promoting it. I do not think we can understand our own times without some knowledge of the past. And this will become even more important in this country as we move – as I feel inevitably – into Europe. I think one can go further than that. History, it is true, does not repeat itself, but nor does life. Yet we expect to learn from our experiences in life and I believe we can learn also from the experiences of History.

It is probably clear to you by now that it is just because History is such a dangerous subject that I have so much enjoyed teaching it. I cannot feel that the neutral history of which I have spoken is any solution. In life one must be ready to make a stand and History deals with life. But the teacher of History should certainly not spend all his time making moral judgements. He should not be afraid of them, but most of his time should be spent in considering what really happened and which events in History seem to have special significance and why.

I see I must end with a confession. I remain faced with a most baffling problem. Why do I – and why have I for so long – found the study of History so exciting? I find no particular difficulty in understanding why Mathematics is an exciting subject, or Literature. It is my own subject which is so elusive.

I think I come nearest to the secret of the lure of History in a footnote in Gibbon's *Decline and Fall of the Roman Empire*. He is describing the preparations for the invasion of Africa by the Byzantine general, Belisarius. He referred to the contemporary Byzantine historian, Procopius, who had upheld the value of archers in the armies of his day against those who pointed out that Homer used the word 'archer' as a term of contempt. In a footnote Gibbon gives the relevant line from the *Iliad* and then he adds, 'How concise – how just – how beautiful is the whole picture! I see the attitude of the archer – I hear the twanging of the bow.'

We must never forget that Clio is a Muse. And so here is my confession. If at the end of a lesson I had succeeded in making my pupils feel unhappy about Frederick the Great's tremendous success in the partitioning of Poland, or in helping them to understand the significance, not only at the time when it happened but also for our own day, of the attempt by King Charles I to arrest the Five Members, or the Fall of the Bastille, I experienced a sense of satisfaction. But this was nothing to what I experienced if, at the end of the lesson, I felt that I had been successful in making them see and hear.

EPILOGUE

FOOTNOTES

I DO NOT KNOW who was the genius who invented the Footnote and it would be an interesting subject of enquiry to discover this. Somewhere, I suppose, there is to be found the first book which abandoned the marginal note and was printed with footnotes only. For it is certainly from the marginal note that the footnote derived. Marginal notes were common enough, of course, in mediaeval manuscripts and early printed books. When Osric puzzled Hamlet by speaking of 'most delicate carriages and of very liberal conceit', Horatio said, 'I knew you must be edified by the margent before you had done.' Usually the notes were written or printed in the side margins, but often these did not give enough room. They had to be placed also below and even above the text, and the text itself had to shrink to allow enough space for the notes. There is certainly something splendid in the appearance of a page of a Renaissance Classical text. In the middle of a great folio page, defended by the powerful rampart of the notes, may be found two or three lines from Virgil, say, or Horace, lines perhaps of unforgettable beauty. But there is an hour's solid reading before you can get on to the next line over the page. At least you know with which lines the commentator is dealing. It is more awkward when the text is allowed more of the page to itself. A single note will extend down the margin, right or left, for both are pressed into service, far beyond the word to which it refers. The next note will have to start far below. The reader's eye moves up and down, desperately trying to bring text and

notes into some sort of relationship. And so, at some time, somewhere, some printer thought it would be simpler to place all the notes
at the foot of the page. There are no doubt early examples of which I
am unaware, but I am fairly certain that this practice first became a
normal one in Holland in the first half of the seventeenth century and I
suspect that it was invented at Leyden. But whoever he was and
whenever and wherever he was, the inventor unwittingly started a
revolution, not only in printing but also in literature.

So far I have only referred to the notes written by one commentator
on the text of another writer. Of these I shall say no more. I am not
going to concern myself with the notes which tell you what Horace
meant when he spoke [*Odes* 2, 14] of 'ter amplum Geryonen' [one of
the monster guardians of Hell] or Shakespeare when he makes Hamlet
say that

> :the dram of eale
> Doth all the noble substance of a doubt,
> To his own scandal.

[An example of a much-disputed passage in Shakespeare.]

I am going to speak of footnotes in original works of Philosophy,
History, Criticism or even Belles-Lettres. For these also, we should
remember, had had their notes in the margins before the footnote
appeared. When the footnote came in, the writer of an original work
was given a scope for using this device that he had never had before.
He was given space for quite lengthy excursuses, for criticisms of his
authorities, for asides. These I think are very rare before the appearance of the footnote, even in the works of Sir Thomas Browne, for
instance, who if he had lived a hundred years later would surely have
been among the greatest of all footnoters. Here is a passage from the
conclusion of *The Garden of Cyrus*:

> But the Quincunx of Heaven runs low, and 'tis time to close the five ports
> of knowledge; We are unwilling to spin out our awaking thoughts into the
> phantasmes of sleep, which often continueth praecogitations; making
> Cables of Cobwebs and Wildernesses of handsome Groves. Besides
> Hippocrates hath spoke so little and the Oneirocriticall Masters have left
> such frigid Interpretations from plants, that there is little encouragement to
> dream of Paradise itself. Nor will the sweetest delight of gardens afford
> much comfort in sleep; wherein the dullness of that sense shakes hands
> with delectable odours; and though in the bed of Cleopatra can hardly with
> any delight raise up the ghost of a rose.

All Sir Thomas Browne can allow himself is a note on Quincunx of
Heaven – 'Hyades, near the horizon about midnight at that time';

on Hippocrates – 'De Insomniis'; on the Oneirocriticall Masters – 'Artemidorus and Apomazer'; and on the bed of Cleopatra the succinct remark – 'strewed with roses'.

The first and last of these are getting nearer what I consider to be the footnote proper. Browne could use these marvellous phrases, so successful because they are so mysterious – 'the Quincunx of Heaven' and 'the bed of Cleopatra' – and he could explain them in a note without disturbing the rhythm of his prose or tearing aside the veil of allusion. To take another example, in the *Religio Medici*, he says 'I hold that the Devil doth really possess some men, the spirit of Melancholy others, the spirit of Delusion others; that, as the Devil is concealed and denied by some so God and good angels are pretended by others; whereof the late detection of the Maid of Germany hath left a pregnant example.' The Maid of Germany is delectable. Half her success is due to the fact that you have not the least idea who she was and what she did – and yet you must know if the passage is to make any sense at all. The note in the margin saves the situation; you can read the passage without it and then slip a glance across to find the explanation – 'that lived without meat upon the smell of a Rose'.

Browne, I have suggested, would have revelled in footnotes. And yet it was perhaps as well that he did not have them to play with. Here is an example from his *Vulgar Errors* which will show the danger. The Chapter is 'of sundry Tenets concerning Vegetables or Plants, which examined prove either false or dubious'. Dealing with 'the Rose of Jericho that Flourishes every year just about Christmas Eve', he refers to the 'Thorn at Glassenbury' and concludes, 'thus much in general we may observe, that strange effects are naturally taken for miracles by weaker heads and artificially improved to that apprehension by the wiser. Certainly many precocious trees and such as spring in the winter may be found in most parts of Europe, and divers also in England.' At this point there is a marginal note, 'Such a Thorn there is at Parham Park in Suffolk and elsewhere'. Now that is not a reference or an explanation. It is an example, strictly relevant to his argument. He left it out because he could not conveniently fit it in, but he still needed it. The marginal note solved the problem for him, but perhaps it did so too easily.

Hazlitt, to move on over a hundred years to an age when the footnote was a commonplace, makes use of footnotes in a way which seems to me illegitimate. I cannot see that the footnote has any place in Belles-Lettres unless it is a spoof footnote of the kind Swift added to the fifth edition of *The Tale of a Tub*, which purported to have been added by one W. Wotton. Take, for instance, Hazlitt's Essay which

appeared in *The Examiner* on May 26th 1816, 'On Gusto'. Gusto in art
Hazlitt defined as 'power or passion defining any object'. In the essay
he refers to Rubens, who, he says, 'has a great deal of gusto in his
Fauns and Satyrs and in all that expresses motion, but in nothing else' –
incidentally a fantastically erroneous observation – and to Rembrandt,
who he says, 'has it in everything'. Turning to Raphael, he says that
his 'gusto was only in expression; he had no idea of the character of
anything but the human form. The dryness and poverty of his style in
other respects is a phenomenon in the art. His trees are like sprigs of
grass stuck in a book of botanical specimens. Was it that Raphael never
had time to go beyond the walls of Rome? That he was always in the
streets, at church, or in the bath? He was not one of the Society of
Arcadians.' He then goes on to deal with Claude's landscapes, which,
he says, 'perfect as they are, want gusto'. But at the end of the passage
on Raphael there is a reference to this footnote:

> Raphael not only could not paint a landscape; he could not paint people in a
> landscape. He could not have painted the heads or the figures or even the
> dresses of the St Peter Martyr. His figures always have an indoor look that
> is a set, determined, voluntary, dramatic character arising from their
> own passions or a watchfulness of those of others, and want that wild
> uncertainty of expression which is connected with the accidents of nature
> and the changes in the elements. He has nothing romantic about him.

I am not denying that this observation was worth making. Even if it
does not tell us much about Raphael – and myself I think there is
something in what he says – it tells us a great deal about Hazlitt. But
either it was relevant to the subject of the Essay or not. If it was it
should have been included in it; if not, it should have been omitted
altogether. And, if Hazlitt felt, as perhaps he did, that though relevant
it would, if included, have spoilt the proportions of the Essay, giving
too much to Raphael as compared with other artists, then, again, he
should have omitted it altogether. As it is, either you read the
footnote, in which case the proportion is in fact destroyed, or you do
not, in which case you miss something Hazlitt wants you to consider.
    Hazlitt transgresses rather frequently in this way, and often his
footnotes are about the best things in the Essay. An Essay is a difficult
Art form, in which proportion and relevance are essential characteristics. This kind of irrelevant and often anecdotal footnote is, I think,
more excusable in a longer work such as a Biography. Boswell
indulges occasionally in such footnotes. At one point in his *Life of
Johnson* he makes an immense dip into his store of what he calls
Johnsoniana, which he compares to 'Herculaneum or some old

Roman field, which when dug fully rewards the labour employed'. And so, my word, it does. I should like to be able to use a footnote myself to include some in this paper, utterly irrelevant as they would be to my subject. One of these is a story about Richardson, the novelist, which Boswell gives us as quite a long footnote:

A literary lady has favoured me with a characteristick anecdote of Richardson. One day at his country-house at Northend, where a large company was assembled at dinner, a gentleman who was just returned from Paris, willing to please Mr Richardson, mentioned to him a very flattering circumstance, – that he had seen his *Clarissa* lying on the King's brother's table. Richardson observing that part of the company were engaged in talking to each other, affected then not to attend to it. But by and by, when there was a general silence, and he thought that the flattery might be fully heard, he addressed himself to the gentleman, 'I think, Sir, you were saying something about, –' pausing in a high flutter of expectation. The gentleman, provoked at his inordinate vanity, resolved not to indulge it, and with an exquisitely sly air of indifference answered, 'A mere trifle, Sir, not worth repeating.' The mortification of Richardson was visible, and he did not speak ten words more the whole day. Dr Johnson was present, and appeared to enjoy it much.

Was this legitimate? On the whole, I think it may pass. It is a good story. It is fitted into a string of disconnected anecdotes. But, although Johnson was present on the occasion of the incident, it could not be actually classed among the Johnsoniana.

I am more doubtful, however, about the propriety of the long footnote about the Round Robin, one of the most famous in literature. Johnson had just composed a Latin Epitaph for Oliver Goldsmith. Several of his friends, dining with Joshua Reynolds, thought of various emendations and decided also that the Epitaph ought to be written in English. 'But the question was, who should have the courage to propose them to him?' In the end it was decided to send him a Round Robin, signed by all those who were present, except for Bennet Langton who refused, twelve persons in all. 'Sir Joshua', Boswell says, 'agreed to carry it to Dr Johnson, who received it with much good humour and desired Sir Joshua to tell the Gentlemen that he would alter the Epitaph in any manner they pleased as to the sense of it, but that he would never consent to disgrace the walls of Westminster Abbey with an English inscription.'

At the words 'Much good humour' there comes the footnote. It is very long and full of richness. It tells us that Johnson said, on seeing Dr Warton's signature, 'I wonder that Joe Warton, a scholar by profession, should be such a fool,' and on seeing Burke's, 'I should have thought Mund Burke would have had more sense.' It tells how Langton refused to sign. It gives another statement by Johnson at another time on the subject of inscriptions which ended with the words, 'Consider, Sir, how you should feel were you to find at Rotterdam an epitaph upon Erasmus in Dutch!' It gives us Boswell's personal opinion on the subject, which was that Epitaphs should be written in both languages. It criticizes Johnson for applying to Goldsmith the epithet, Physicus, tells us how Johnson, hearing that Goldsmith was intending to write on the subject, had said, 'if he can distinguish a cow from a horse, that, I believe, may be the extent of his knowledge of natural history,' and ends with Boswell's own criticism of Goldsmith for having relied too much on Buffon, and especially for having taken from him the observation that the cow sheds her horns every two years. 'I suppose', he concludes, 'he has confounded the cow with the deer.'

By the time we reach the horn-shedding cow we are a long way from the Round Robin. What is the poor reader to do? Is he to read all this and then go on in the middle of the sentence with the words 'and desired Sir Joshua to tell the gentlemen'? Is he to ignore any footnotes until he comes to a break in the narrative and then come back to them? Is he to start the sentence again when he has finished the footnote? All that Boswell says in this note could have been incorporated somewhere in the *Life*, except perhaps Goldsmith's cow. I admit, however, that I should be sorry to lose the cow. After all, Boswell's Johnson is a long and leisurely book. It can be read slowly and read often.

The problem of arrangement facing Boswell at this point is one constantly met with by historians and it is in works of History that the footnote plays its most important role. For the commonest footnotes, of course, are merely references. They perform an obvious duty – and for that matter could go quite as well in the margin; though to us that would probably look ugly. I do not think we need concern ourselves with them. But I shall now turn to consider the function of the footnote generally in historical books.

The mere giving of a reference may not be enough. The author may also wish to show what he thinks of the authority on which his statement is based. Thus, for instance, Macaulay in the Third Chapter of his *History* speaks of the rebuilding of the City after the Great Fire, and adds a note on his sources, ending 'There is an account of the works at St Paul's in Ward's *London Spy*.★ I am almost ashamed to

★ The unexpurgated editions of Ward's *London Spy* are usually placed in the 'Reserved', i.e. locked up, sections of the major Libraries.

quote such nauseous balderdash; but I have been forced to descend even lower, if possible, in search of materials.' I am not suggesting that this is at all a good note. It is, in fact, a very bad one. All that matters to us is to know whether Macaulay believed Ward to be reliable about the works at St Paul's. It is really immaterial to us that he was queasy about using his book.

I have suggested that footnotes are sometimes used to give additional details which cannot be fitted into the narrative without disturbing its balance. While I doubt the propriety of this device I do not feel it should be ruled out altogether. It is sometimes more satisfactory to give an illustrative example in a footnote. Take, for instance, this one again from Macaulay's Third Chapter. He is speaking of the education for women in England at the time and he says, 'Ladies highly born, highly bred and naturally quick-witted, were unable to write a line in their mother tongue without solecisms and faults of spelling such as a charity girl would now be ashamed to commit'. He adds the note: 'One instance will suffice. Queen Mary, the daughter of James, had excellent natural abilities, had been educated by a Bishop, was fond of history and poetry, and was regarded by very eminent men as a superior woman. There is, in the library at The Hague, a superb English Bible which was delivered to her when she was crowned in Westminster Abbey. In the title page are these words in her own hand, "This book was given to the King and I, at our coronation. Marie. R."' I think it may be agreed that to have introduced this example into the general description of England in 1685 would have entailed a loss of proportion and if Macaulay wanted to give an illustrative example the best place here was a footnote. Unfortunately, as you will have noticed, it is a very bad example. It is no evidence that women in the latter part of the seventeenth century were not educated. It is evidence that one woman at that time was educated and, though educated, she did not know her English grammar.

Sometimes an author may feel it necessary to give detailed consideration to the evidence on some particular point. If so, a long footnote may be necessary and, I should say, quite inevitable. Thus Macaulay was, I feel, justified in using a footnote for his study of the tangled problem of the evidence as to what exactly happened at the death of King Charles II. To have introduced this into the main body of the work would have spoiled one of the supreme pieces of narrative in English literature.

It is, I think, right for an historical writer to regard the flow of his narrative as of the utmost importance and I should be prepared to condone many footnotes, although they must to some extent interrupt this if you glance down and read them, when the alternative would be to damage it more by the inclusion of the point in the narrative itself. But the author should be considering all the time whether the footnote is really necessary. For an example of a thoroughly bad footnote I turn to Carlyle's *Frederick the Great*. He is describing a meeting between Frederick's father and Karl Philip, the Elector Palatine, in 1730. 'What Friedrich Wilhelm got to speak about with the old Kur-Pfalz, during their serene passages of hospitality at Mannheim, is not clear to me . . . They could talk freely about the old Turk Campaigns, Battle of Zenta, and Prince Eugene; very freely about the Heidelberg Tun.' To the words 'Battle of Zenta' he gives this footnote: '11th September 1697; Eugene's crowning feat; – breaking of the Grand Turk's back in this world; who had staggered about, less and less of a terror and outrage, more and more of a nuisance growing unbearable, ever since that day. See Hormayr (iii 97–101) for some description of this useful bit of Heroism.' Now, this seems to me quite indefensible. Apart from the nauseating style in which it is written, it is wholly irrelevant. Carlyle merely succeeds in making you forget for a moment the King of Prussia, who, at that point in the narrative, was holding the centre of the stage. You do not want to be reminded of the Turks when you should then be thinking of the relations between Frederick William and his son. Carlyle, in fact, as so often, was only showing off.

Here is another example. Dealing with the Alliance built up by William III against France in 1692, Macaulay says, 'The King of Sweden, who, as the Duke of Pomerania, was bound to send three thousand men for the defence of the Empire, sent, instead of them, his advice that the allies should make peace on the best terms which they could get.' To this he added the footnote: 'The Swedes came it is true, but not till the campaign was over.' I must admit to some doubts about the legitimacy of this footnote. Macaulay, it seems to me, is salving his conscience. The case made against the King of Sweden is made more striking by relegating a very relevant point in his favour to a footnote. I feel that the narrative would not have suffered if this sentence had been incorporated in the text.

The problem, however, is a real one and I shall attempt to show from an instance taken from a more recent work the part that footnotes have to play in a modern book of History. In Ronald Symes' *Roman Revolution* which deals with the end of the Republic, an excellent book which is not properly appreciated, there is a passage on the preliminaries to the Battle of Actium, in which occurs this sentence: 'Perhaps the picked army which Antonius mustered in

Epirus was composed in the main of survivors of his veteran legions.'
It is an entirely honest statement. The word 'perhaps' might be
thought to cover the author satisfactorily. But, in a work of scholarship such as this, the footnote is, I feel, inevitable. It is a somewhat
terrifying one.

> As Tarn argues (*Classical Quarterly* Volume XXVI (1932), pages 75
> following). It is clear, however, that provincial levies were heavily drawn
> upon. Brutus, for example, raised two legions of Macedonians (Appian,
> *Bellum Civile*, 3, 79, 294). As for Antonius, O. Cuntz (*Jahreshefte* XXV
> (1929), pages 70 following) deduced from the gentilicia of a number of
> soldiers of Eastern origin the fact that they were given the Roman franchise
> on enlistment by certain partisans of Antonius. Note also the inscription
> from Philae in Egypt, *Orientis Graeci Inscriptiones Selectae*, 196, dated 32 BC
> mentioning an eparchos (praefectus), Caius Julius Papius, and some
> centurions, among them a man called Demetrius. A neglected passage in
> Josephus (*Bellum Judicium* I, 324; compare *Archaeologica Judica* 14, 449)
> attests local recruiting in Syria in 38 BC.

It is nervousness about such footnotes, which seem to me perfectly
legitimate, which has led to the modern practice of placing the notes,
not at the foot of each page, but at the end of the book. I can see no
defence for this though it has a respectable antiquity. Robertson, one
of the best eighteenth-century historians, and even Gibbon in the first
edition of his first volume followed this pattern. But the latter soon
saw his mistake. In order to save the susceptibilities of the reader who
wants to ignore the footnotes, and, after all, he need not read them
unless he wants to, they are placed in a position which makes reading
the book a matter of extreme physical discomfort for those to whom
the notes are of interest. The result can be fantastic. I can appreciate the
problem which faced John Livingstone Lowes in his splendid book on
Coleridge, *The Road to Xanadu*. It is a work of 434 large pages. The
notes, which contain some of the best passages in the book, take up
152 pages of considerably smaller type. For all that, he found it
necessary to include some genuine footnotes, presumably because he
wanted to make sure you read them. But his fear that footnotes might
upset the reader was so strong that he kept these as short as possible,
thereby making necessary the extraordinary refinement of notes at the
end of the book on footnotes on the text.

What seems to me even more indefensible, however, is a more
recent practice, which can be found, for instance, in Professor
Tillyard's well-known *Elizabethan World Picture*. There the notes are
placed at the end of the book and also no reference to them is given in

the text. You never know, therefore, as you read the book, whether you are not missing a note, unless you keep a finger in the final pages and continually turn to them. And it may be quite essential that you do read the note. Thus Professor Tillyard says, I believe justly, 'In trying to picture how the ordinary contemporary of Shakespeare looked on history in the gross we do not need to give much heed to Machiavelli. His day had not yet come.' The remark, however, might easily be misunderstood and the author realised it. In a note, therefore, he says, 'I wish to make it plain that in this section I deal with the way the Elizabethans took Machiavelli's historical doctrines, not with the influence of Machiavellianism on the Elizabethan Drama, which I do not seek to minimise.' Unless you are prepared to suffer an aching finger, you are sure to miss this very necessary comment.

So far I may appear to have been somewhat critical of footnotes and, at the most, to have allowed that they are sometimes inevitable. But one great author has shown us that the footnote itself may be a legitimate art-form. It is to Gibbon, the master of footnotes, that I turn in conclusion. In *The Decline and Fall* the footnote attained its apotheosis.

The very great majority of Gibbon's footnotes are, of course, strictly part of the critical apparatus. They give in detail the sources of his narrative. But many go far beyond this. And it should be realised that Gibbon's style of writing made them almost essential. For he composed his work, as is well known, by paragraphs at a time, walking up and down until the whole passage was completed – and some are very long – before he wrote them down.

Before I consider the various categories into which they may be divided, I should start, perhaps, with his one really unfortunate footnote. Dealing with the first Arab invasion of Syria and the Byzantine reaction to it, he describes the battle of Aiznadin in which, he tells us, the Byzantine army was commanded by a general of the Emperor Heraclius named Werden. He adds this footnote: 'The name of Werden is unknown to Theophanus, and, though it might belong to an Armenian chief, has very little of a Greek aspect or sound. If the Byzantine historians have mangled the Oriental names the Arabs, in this instance, likewise have taken ample revenge on their enemies. In transposing the Greek character from right to left, might they not produce from the familiar appellation of Andrew, something like the anagram Werden?' Apart from the fact that Werden, as Bury pointed out, is obviously a form of the well known Armenian name Bardones what an extraordinary howler Gibbon has perpetrated. For how could the Arabs make an anagram from the modern English for Andrew, of the Greek name Andreas? I cannot help wondering sometimes whether Gibbon really meant this as a joke. Perhaps he is smiling now at my having fallen into the trap. I should like to think so, but I am afraid that I am doubtful.

I have said already that it is sometimes necessary for the historian to give a footnote to examine critically the evidence for a particular incident. Gibbon has a footnote on his rejection of the story of how Belisarius was blinded and had to beg his bread: 'Give a penny to Belisarius the general'. The note, though nothing like so long as Macaulay's on the death of Charles II, is a model.

The source of this idle fable may be derived from a miscellaneous work of the XII century, the *Chiliads* of John Tzetzes, a monk [he then gives the references and quotes the relevant passage]. This moral or romantic tale was imported into Italy with the language and manuscripts of Greece; repeated before the end of the XV century by Crinitus, Pontanus and Volaterranus; attacked by Alciat for the honour of the law; and defended by Baronius for the honour of the Church. Yet Tzetzes himself had read in other chronicles that Belisarius did not lose his sight and that he recovered his fame and fortunes.

Gibbon's use of footnotes to criticise his authorities is inimitable. The criticism had to be made succinctly and epigrammatically or it would exceed the proper limits of the footnote. He tells of the silk trade under the Romans with China, and adds the footnote, 'on the texture, colours, names and use of silk, half-silk and linen garments of antiquity, see the profound, diffuse and obscure researches of the great Salmasius [he then gives ten references and continues] who was ignorant of the most common trades of Dijon or Leyden.' He refers to the account of Peter III of Aragon by the Spanish historian, Mariana, and adds, 'The reader forgives the Jesuit's defects in favour of his style and often of his sense'. But the best of all, I think, is to be found at the beginning of his unexpected 'Digression on the Family of Courtenay', which comes at the end of his chapter on the Latin Empire of Constantinople. 'I have applied but not confined myself to *A Genealogical History of the Noble and Illustrious Family of Courtenay*, By Ezra Cleaveland, Tutor to Sir William Courtenay and Rector of Honiton; Exon. 1735 in folio. The first part is extracted from William of Tyre; the second from Bouchet's French History; and the third from various memorials, public, provincial and private of the Courtenays of Devonshire. The Rector of Honiton has more gratitude than industry and more industry than criticism.' Almost as devastating is the footnote at the end of the geographical survey of the Roman Empire under the

Antonines which concludes the first chapter, 'See Templeman's *Survey of the Globe*, but I distrust both the Doctor's learning and his maps'.

These examples may show what Gibbon was really trying to make of the footnote. Kept very short and epigrammatic, it could produce its effect by very contrast with the tremendous periods of his narrative. The footnote becomes an integral part of a work of art. 'The stream' we read, as the Emperor Julian approached the Tigris, 'was broad and rapid; the ascent steep and difficult; and the intrenchments, which had been formed on the ridge of the opposite bank, were lined with a numerous army of heavy cuirassiers, dexterous archers and huge elephants; who (according to the extravagant hyperbole of Libanius) could trample with the same ease, a field of corn or a legion of Romans.' 'Rien n'est beau que le vrai', comes the comment from the foot of the page, 'a maxim which should be inscribed on the desk of every rhetorician'.

It was only to be expected that Gibbon would find in the footnote, used in this way, the perfect means of planting his shafts of scepticism in the armour of the Christian historical tradition. 'A superstitious age', he writes, 'was prepared to reverence as the testimony of Heaven, the preternatural cures which were performed by the skill or virtue of the Catholic clergy; the baptismal fonts of Osset in Baetica, which were spontaneously replenished each year on the vigil of Easter; and the miraculous shrine of St Martin of Tours, which had already converted the Suevic prince and people of Gallicia.' The footnote coolly whispers its aside: 'This miracle was skilfully performed. An Arian King sealed the doors, and dug a deep trench around the church, without being able to intercept the Easter supply of baptismal water.' Or, best of all, when he tells us of the initiation of the Emperor Julian the Apostate into the Eleusinian mysteries. 'As these ceremonies were performed in the depth of caverns and in the silence of the night, and as the inviolable secret of the mysteries was preserved by the discretion of the initiated, I shall not presume to describe the horrid sounds and fiery apparitions which were presented to the senses or the imagination of the credulous aspirant, till the visions of comfort and knowledge broke upon him in a blaze of celestial light.' Here, surely, as Gibbon guys these pagan ceremonies, there is no attack on the early Christians. But listen to the footnote – and see how the effects of the comment could be gained only in a footnote: 'When Julian, in a momentary panic, made the sign of the Cross, the demons instantly disappeared (Gregory Nazianzien *Orationes* iii, p71). Gregory supposes that they were frightened, but the priests declared that they were indignant. The reader, according to the measure of his faith, will determine this profound question.'

But I have yet to refer to what seems to me is the most skilful of all Gibbon's footnotes. It seems to break all the rules – or rather they do, as there are two, one following the other, which should be taken together. They are, for one thing, apparently completely irrelevant. But let me give them to you as a final tribute to the Master of Footnotes.

He is telling of the feats of the Emperor Commodus in the amphitheatre. 'Whether he aimed at the head or the heart of the animal, the wound was alike certain and mortal. With arrows whose point was shaped in the form of a crescent, Commodus often interrupted the rapid career, and cut asunder the long bony neck of the ostrich.' The first footnote is slipped in here. 'The ostrich's neck is three feet long, and composed of seventeen vertebrae. See Buffon, *Histoire Naturelle*.' The splendid account continues. 'A panther was let loose; and the archer waited till he had leaped upon a trembling malefactor. In the same instant, the shaft flew, the beast dropped dead and the man remained unhurt . . . Neither the huge bulk of the elephant nor the scaly hide of the rhinoceros could defend them from his stroke. Aethiopia and India yielded their most extraordinary productions; and several animals were slain in the amphitheatre which had been seen only in the representations of art, or perhaps of fancy.' Again, our eyes fall to the foot of the page. 'Commodus killed a camelopardalis or giraffe, the tallest, the most gentle and the most useless of the larger quadrupeds. This singular animal, a native only of the interior parts of Africa, has not been seen in Europe since the revival of letters, and though Monsieur de Buffon has endeavoured to describe, he has not ventured to delineate the giraffe.' How could the author have shown us more skilfully the farce in Commodus' performance than by these apparently pointless pieces of Natural History?

But if these are Gibbon's most skilful footnotes in the book, there is another which I feel to be his most inspired. It is surely the most surprising footnote in the *History* and I do not know that it is possible fully to understand Gibbon without considering it. It shows us the poet to be found in the heart of Gibbon, perhaps in the heart of all really great prose writers. He is writing on the preparations for the great campaign of Belisarius to recover Africa and describing the Byzantine Army. He quotes from the contemporary historian Procopius at unusual length for him and refers to his panegyric on the Greek soldier in the time of Justinian. Procopius compared the splendid armoured and mounted archers of his own day with the naked youths of Homer who 'lurking behind a tombstone or the shield of a friend, drew the bow string to their breast and dismissed a feeble and lifeless arrow.' The wonderful passage in the fourth book of the *Iliad* where, prompted by Athene, Pandarus aims his shaft at Menelaus must at that moment have come into his mind. He gives the reference to these lines, and – utterly irrelevant you may say, but in fact what a brilliant comment on the true contrast between Greek and Byzantine, between Homer and Procopius – he adds this note on Homer's lines: 'How concise – how just – how beautiful is the whole picture! I see the attitudes of the archer – I hear the twanging of the bow.'

In Gibbon, indeed, the footnote, that necessary tool of scholarship, was raised into a work of art. Never again, I imagine, are we likely to be blessed with an author who will be able to use it as he did. Our only consolation must be that in the whole of the *Decline and Fall of the Roman Empire* there are over 9000 of them and that number, consulted as frequently as they deserve, should last the lifetime of most of us.

INDEX